Dr. Gina and Dr. Dathan open a groundbreaking of chivalry, manners, and decorum that our younger generation has never visited and, indeed, has never even heard described. The feminists have repeatedly manifested a particular animosity toward the word "lady." But this remarkable book puts male and female behaviors in proper focus, historically, biblically, and in contemporary relationships.

**—Phyllis Schlafly,** President, Eagle Forum

Drs. Loudon and Paterno have hit a home run! Filled with captivating stories, they take the reader through a journey of history, revealing long-forgotten truths. They warn of the dangers we face by abandoning the virtues and freedoms that took centuries to manifest, and challenge us to rediscover our noble heritage. I highly recommend this eye-opening book!

**—William J. Federer,** best-selling author
and nationally known speaker

As President and CEO of Concerned Women for America, I am confronted daily with the fallout of a culture that has forgotten its manners and morals. Dr. Gina Loudon and Dr. Dathan Paterno remind us of the consequences of our current path. More importantly, they evoke the memory of America's rich heritage of faith and freedom and the bearing these have on our national discourse and civility. Perhaps my hero William Wilberforce's 18th Century quest for the reformation of manners, coexisting with his noble efforts to abolish the slave trade, can reemerge with a renewed vibrancy with this important book. Count me in!

**—Penny Young Nance,** President and CEO,
Concerned Women for America

Gina Loudon and Dathan Paterno diagnose the political controversies of our age magnificently, rightfully perceiving them as symptoms of a much deeper malady. The unique and profoundly perceptive cures they prescribe are right on target. If the analyses in this book are heeded, our country will be on track to regain the position of preeminence that it once won not by force of arms, but by the power of ideas and the ladies and gentlemen who exemplify them.

—**Pamela Geller,** Author, *Stop the Islamization of America:*
*A Practical Guide to the Resistance*

America needs the message in this book if we are to win the culture war and reclaim a constitutional culture of "One nation, under God…" Drs. Loudon and Paterno lay out a compelling path to real victory via restored virtue and show us why hope lives for those who know Truth and proclaim it boldly.

—**Liz Santorum,** Spokeswoman for and
Daughter of Senator Rick Santorum

Every great war has heroes or heroines. Conservatives have had Sarah Palin and Rand Paul. Their forces now include Dr. Gina Loudon and Dr. Dathan Paterno, the perfect combination of brainy and bold, stirring and sensible. They aren't doctors for nothing. With surgical precision, *Ladies & Gentlemen* reveals the history, diagnosis, and treatment plan for our great nation. The prognosis is good—if we are courageous and wise enough to fill the prescription and take our medicine.

—**Steve Bannon,** Executive Chairman, Breitbart News

# Ladies & Gentlemen

## WHY THE SURVIVAL OF OUR REPUBLIC DEPENDS ON THE REVIVAL OF HONOR

RECLAIMING
THE TITLES
"LADY" AND
"GENTLEMAN"

## DR. GINA LOUDON
## DR. DATHAN PATERNO

GOD & COUNTRY PRESS

First Printing, June 2012

| | |
|---|---|
| Print Edition | ISBN 13: 978-0-89957-527-8 |
| EPUB Edition | ISBN 13: 978-1-61715-376-1 |
| Mobi Edition | ISBN 13: 978-1-61715-377-8 |
| E-PDF Edition | ISBN 13: 978-1-61715-378-5 |

Layout by Kristin Goble, PerfecType, Nashville, TN
Cover layout by Michael Largent, InView Graphics, Chattanooga, Tennessee

Printed in the United States of America
16 15 14 13 12 11 –B– 6 5 4 3 2 1

To our childrens' childrens' children...
freedom is worth the fight.

Fight on!


Dr. Dathan Paterno, "Daddy" to Micayla,
Eden and Kirk

and Dr. Gina Loudon, "Mama" to Lyda,
Lily Love, Jack "Tade," Samuel,

and Bo "Booce"

# Table of Contents

## Part Four: Reclaiming the Lady and the Gentleman

# Acknowledgments

A PROPER LIST OF acknowledgements would double the length of this book, but I (Dr. Loudon) must begin with my warrior agent, Diana Flegal. I must thank my brainstorming posse: Jennifer Bahr, Sarah Greek, DJ Ford, Rep. Kathy Conway, Letitia Wong, Sara Dickson, and "Aunt Roz." I acknowledge my designer, Nicole Challans Pettis of NBC Designs, and my associate producer, Angela Love. I am deeply indebted to my mentors, all of whom have led and continue to inspire me personally and professionally: Sarah Palin, Phyllis Schlafly, Lois Linton, Bev Ehlen, Mary Ueland; Laura Kostial, Jennifer Keifer, Kris Wightman, Niel Harris, Cynthia Saffa, Deb Ritter, Angie Delay, Caroline Mueller, and Zan Green. I am deeply appreciative for my first editor, Michael Walsh, as well as my first publisher, mentor, and co-troublemaker, Andrew Breitbart. I eagerly thank my listeners of the *Dr. Gina Show*—the smartest audience in radio—who inspire me every day. I express thanks to all my friends, as well as my enemies, from whom I have learned so much.

I thank my coauthor, Dr. Dathan Paterno—the champion of this book. Huge thanks goes to my *chupacabra* producer, Jason Browning, "MSH15," without whom I am mush. I would be remiss not to mention my matriarchs: Grandma Janice Cheek Gee and my mother,

Deitra Spencer. I love you, and ponies and noodles. I thank my beautiful daughters, Lyda and Lily, and my brave sons, Jack, Samuel, and "King Bo." Your presence makes my life complete. My deep gratitude goes to my soul mate, Sen. John Loudon, for continuing to be an exemplary gentleman and giving me room to dream big. Finally, I recognize my Lord and Savior, Jesus Christ; it is in His grace that I write.

First and foremost, I (Dr. Paterno) thank my family for tolerating both my absence and my droning on and on about virtue and manners; I promise I will recall all of your names as soon as possible. Second, I am deeply grateful to Dr. Gina. Her boundless energy and genuine passion are infectious and spurred me on to complete this project. I owe a deep debt of gratitude to her family as well; thank you for loaning her to this project. I also thank Jason Browning for cracking the whip and keeping this project grounded.

I also acknowledge Diana Flegal for her tireless efforts and faithfulness, the staff at AMG for their keen insights and for fast-tracking this project, Margaret Mullenix for a good deal of mundane legwork, John Mullenix for his amazing talent, Mike Kobler for reminding me about simplicity, and Burton Seitler PhD for his exemplary civility.

*Soli Deo Gloria.*

## Introduction

# Once Upon a Time . . .

ONCE UPON A TIME, in a quiet kingdom near the sea, there lived an aging king and his lifelong bride. The king and queen had lived in peace for decades, ruling over a country that was hardly known to others, in part because it was on the edge of the civilized world, but also because it had been without scandal or upheaval for as long as anyone could remember.

There was one thing lacking for the royal couple and their people: an heir. Although they had a daughter—a beautiful, wise, and talented girl who had grown to marrying age—there was no suitable man in the kingdom for her to marry.

None of the men in the kingdom were warriors, for the kingdom had always been so peaceable that it had no use for military men. There were no learned men, as the common folk valued simplicity more than education. Certainly there were good men, but none of them had done any valiant deeds or accomplished anything particularly noteworthy (this part of the world had long since been rid of dragons). Finally, because the king and queen were so isolated, they had few interactions with other rulers who might have had suitable princes available for marriage.

The king was concerned for both his daughter and his people. He was certainly wise enough to recognize their need for a sovereign. But because he was advanced in age, he began to worry. It was only the queen's steadying faith that pulled him from despair and buoyed their belief that God would one day reveal a solution.

One day, during the kingdom's annual Christmas festival, the royal couple was treated to the music of a strange, unknown minstrel. The traveling musician was an expert on the lute, several flutes, and an almost infinite number of exotic drums; when he lifted his voice, his tone filled the great hall with angelic clarity. His songs were so magnificent that they seemed to possess a hypnotic quality. At the end of his final song, the king and queen were indeed mesmerized; every word and every note had sparked the king's imagination. No one dared invade the silence that followed.

Images and ideas flooded through his excited mind. Without pausing to consider what was coming out of his mouth, he exclaimed, "Kind sir, you were brought here by the Almighty; no man can make music like this without the hand of God residing in his being. Perhaps you can aid my heart, as you have my ears. Tell me, good gentleman, what kind of man should marry my daughter?"

Every ear in the great hall quivered; every eye was transfixed on the minstrel's steady lips and glimmering eyes. The minstrel studied the king's desperate expression. A pleasant grin dawned on his ruddy face. Sensing that the king might burst if he waited another moment to answer, he replied, "Why, Sire, you have already answered your own question."

While the king recollected and studied what he had just said, the queen began to smile. She nudged her anxious husband. "Your Highness, the good minstrel is right. The princess should marry a gentleman. It need not matter if he is a warrior or has made his fortune or has distinguished himself as a scholar. Your throne has not been honored by war or gold or argument; it has been honored these many years first and foremost by a gentleman."

The king's face flushed, and then he stood tall before his lords and ladies. His eyes darted to his only daughter, who, sitting next to him, had followed the entire drama with keen ears and anxious eyes. She could not wait to hear what her good father would pronounce.

"From this day," the king declared with booming voice, "We decree that the princess may be wed—MUST be wed—to a man whose character and virtue are sufficient to be worthy of the term 'gentleman.' This is to be his primary qualification. We will determine which qualities will make up this man. Furthermore, we will endeavor to assure that the princess will be a worthy lady for her true gentleman. From henceforth, all children will be raised with these paragons of virtue in mind."

## A Different Time, an Identical Need

Have no fear; this fairy tale certainly ends with the usual programmed ending: ". . . and they lived happily ever after." But such a happy ending requires that the prince and princess be a certain type of man and woman.

The king decreed that this type of man—the ideal that encapsulates all of what is noble and noteworthy about a man—should be named *gentleman*. And the princess—presuming she truly deserved this gallant prince—had the corresponding qualities of a *lady*.

In this story, the king had absolute authority to define the traits of the lady and the gentleman. He also had authority to demand that all his subjects—parents, teachers, church leaders, and artists—teach, support, glorify, and uphold these ideals. Finally, the good king and queen had plenty of incentive to model gentlemanly and ladylike virtues for their people, for the benefit of both present and future generations. They knew that the people would first look to their sovereign to lead them and show them how a gentleman and a lady behaved.

*Lady* and *gentleman* are somewhat familiar terms, for sure. We hear them from magicians and carnival emcees. Billboard advertising manipulates those words into a twisted description of strip clubs[1]. We sometimes view examples of them on quaint Hallmark films. Our

---

[1] If a gaggle of men gawking at women stripping describes a "gentleman's club," then a bunch of druggies experimenting with mushrooms constitutes a "study group."

children even study literary characters with these names (e.g., Lady Macbeth).

But rarely do we hear the terms used to teach or uphold virtues. When was the last time you heard a parent say to a child, "That was not very ladylike" or "Hold the door open like a gentleman, son"? When was the last time anyone heard a politician or actor referred to as a "true gentleman" or an actress's behavior mentioned as "ladylike"? How many television programs lift up virtuous young men and women while decrying their polar opposites?

Modern culture is more desperate than ever for a return to solid character with uniform, universal virtues. Our nation is starved for male and female models of virtue. Recall the Michael Jordan commercial with the tagline "Be like Mike." Right idea, wrong model. Sure, Michael Jordan inspired many to desire excellence, fame, and financial success. But he inspired few to behave with virtue (one could argue that he inspired the opposite).

Parents wander in a wilderness of disparate parenting techniques and philosophies, without adequate terms to refer to or ideals to emulate. Mothers lack commitment to behaving like ladies; our culture does not inspire them to exhibit ladylike virtues.

And why would they? Where are these virtues modeled and glorified? Certainly not in popular magazines or television shows. Certainly not on *YouTube*. Certainly not in their social circles, where peers could encourage, reward, and model female virtue with the dual goals of personal satisfaction and bequeathing their values and character to their daughters.

Fathers are performing no better in this regard. Normally the parent responsible for more direct instruction of values and virtues, fathers are by and large neglecting this solemn duty. Some fathers, of course, have indeed become more involved in their children's lives; they now bear some of the everyday burdens of driving, helping with homework, and sharing household chores. But they are quite often taking a backseat in the discipline of their children.[2] The inevitable consequence is that fathers are inadvertently training their children

---

[2] More accurately, they have retreated to (or been stuffed in) the trunk.

to perceive themselves as entitled, overly free autocrats. The results have been disastrous.

A generous perception of Hollywood would view them as complicit in the devolution of the American character. The unfiltered reality, however, is that they have been waging a directed assault on virtue. They seem to live under the crude assumption that moviegoers are not interested in heroes and heroines of virtue.[3] Clearly, the vast majority of popular films centers on amoral themes or glorifies characters whose virtues are deplorable at best.

The political climate is rife with dialogue about civility, but we lack leaders who not only model civility and other virtues but the moral platform with which to demand it. There are exceptions, to be sure—some of whom we will mention throughout this book—but the overall tone of politics serves as a poor model for both national and personal virtue.

## Imagine

Imagine if parents, teachers, politicians, media personalities, and artists utilized the same terms to describe virtuous behavior. Imagine if they agreed to uphold and emulate models of these virtues. Imagine if they utilized the same terms to describe these ideals and the men and women who lived them.

Imagine if parents spoke with each other about the virtues they wished to instill in their children. Imagine if they encouraged each other to model these virtues and speak about them explicitly in their homes. Imagine if they praised each other when they and their children exhibited these virtues, yet lovingly rebuked each other when they frequently and inevitably failed. Imagine if Dad and Mom referred to certain parents as gentlemen or ladies. Imagine their children internalizing the desire to think and behave like these paragons of virtue.

Imagine if teachers (at private and public schools) and parents agreed to explicitly encourage the same virtues; imagine if they even

---

[3] This is debatable; more on that in chapter nine.

used the same language. Imagine if the education of virtue were weaved into the schools' curricula.

Imagine if artists produced heroes whose behavior and heart made them role models for children to glorify and emulate. Imagine that these heroes were not only strong but good, kind, generous, and accountable to a higher authority. Imagine if they lived their virtues in private just as they did in public. Imagine children asking for stories about these characters and having birthday parties with themes about them.

Imagine politicians speaking to and about each other with gracious attitudes. Imagine them exhibiting true humility, admitting mistakes and ignorance. Imagine them speaking charitably about their political adversaries and chiding others from their own party who do not. Imagine them being wholly transparent about their worldview and the philosophical beliefs that inform their political positions. Imagine them with the courage to take positions that might anger a special-interest ally, even if it means evaporating financial support. Imagine that their political work reflected service of God and country far more than self.

Imagine cable television news personalities who exhibit hope, faith, and love. Imagine that the national viewership rewarded this with high ratings. Imagine that other personalities and networks followed. Imagine these personalities reinforcing each other's efforts by referring to each other as *gentleman* or *lady*.

This book imagines all these things. But it goes further. It believes that our culture can indeed make these things happen. We believe that individuals—parents, teachers, priests, pastors, cable television news personalities, politicians, actors, musicians, and authors—have the collective power to dramatically alter the personal, social, and political landscape. This is change we can believe in!

This book believes in fairy tales. This book believes that this nation was founded and made possible by the virtues and character traits found in the best, noblest fairy tales. This book recognizes that plenty of Americans believe in these virtues and long for their return. Most importantly, this book believes in a God who makes fairy tales come true.

## The Blueprint

*Ladies and Gentlemen* offers a blueprint for such a return. Just as every great building begins with a vision, this book offers our vision for a return of American virtue.

The first section explores the origins of the terms *lady* and *gentleman*. If we are to return to the terms and the values and virtues inherent in them, we had better know something about where the words and ideas came from and how they developed and were maintained. We promise it will not be a boring history lesson!

The second section examines how the ideals of the lady and gentleman have been severely damaged and how this has affected the soul of our society. Specifically, it is our belief that three cultural movements and their philosophies have deeply wounded our nation's psyche, in part by degrading the ideal man and woman: atheism, liberalism, and radical feminism.

We will describe how each philosophy and movement has wreaked its destruction—both inadvertently and by design.

After we have surveyed the damage, we will then offer our treatment plan. Beginning with a call to personal virtue, we will offer many fresh ideas on how individuals can alter the cultural landscape in their roles as parent, spouse, friend, teacher, pastor, voter, employer, employee, and neighbor.

For parents, we paint a portrait of the modern lady and gentleman, proving that women can be warriors without burning bras and men can be tough without smoking Marlboros on horseback. We offer parents several keys to raising their own children to be ladies and gentlemen. Recognizing how difficult it is to navigate the murky waters of today's culture, we incorporate biblical principles and an awareness of modern-day challenges into our advice.

Then we will explore the roles of those in the public arena, including artists, authors, actors, television news personalities, and filmmakers. Those who have the biggest microphone wield enormous influence; we will call them to task and encourage them to inspire the culture in a more courageous direction.

To conservative activists and personalities, we speak directly: Do not accept a society devoid of honor and dignity. Do not stand idly while our leaders slouch toward Gomorrah. Do not remain mute while the enemy mocks this nation's godly virtues, or you compromise the very values and virtues you claim to defend. Stand firm against diminishing standards simply to ingratiate ourselves to the masses, or we risk invalidating ourselves and become indistinguishable as ladies and gentlemen. The world is watching!

Finally, we will hold politicians accountable for their role in the demeaning of our culture. We will challenge them directly. We will also offer them a truce, if they will pledge to turn to a more virtuous course. Finally, we sound a warning: If they do not turn, we will commit to finding other leaders who will live out our values for us. We will not be satisfied with anything less.

We believe the prognosis is good; we have the American people, history, and God on our side.

## Imperfect Architects

This book began with an insult.

I (Dr. Paterno) had been thinking of writing a book about ladies and gentlemen for some time. I thought it would be best if it were co-written with a woman; it seemed wise to me that a female voice who could speak to the virtues of women would have a greater impact.

I racked my brain for a list of conservative women who could fit the bill. I needed someone intelligent who had an edge, was comfortable with media, could write well, and was a *bona fide* conservative. Ideally, she would share my Christian faith. It wouldn't hurt if she was also good-looking.

And then I came across an article by Dr. Loudon in which she refuted a gutless and ignorant *Vanity Fair* article that essentially comprised a series of insults. In the article, she fervently and precisely asserted and defended the truth. More impressively, she did so with grace.

I instantly knew that this was the lady with whom I wanted to coauthor this book. I couldn't think of a better combination of strength and femininity; here was a "mama grizzly" who could float like a butterfly and sting like a bee. I quickly got to work drafting her into my two-person army and was pleasantly surprised when she enlisted willingly.

Dr. Gina (as she is called on her radio talk show) has been involved in politics for many years. Her husband, John, was a conservative state legislator in Missouri for fourteen years; Gina herself ran for Congress in 2006. Together, the Loudons raise five beautiful children. I would be hard-pressed to find a family who more exemplifies ladylike and gentlemanly traits.

Dr. Gina is a *policologist*—a term she coined to mean the study of psychology and politics. Her expertise and thinking in this sphere is perfect for establishing the personal and political nature of the terms *lady* and *gentleman*.

Dr. Paterno has practiced as a licensed clinical psychologist since 2003 and been in the mental health field for over twenty years. He owns and is clinical director of Park Ridge Psychological Services— a private psychology practice that emphasizes holistic treatments and stresses the importance of raising children to be gentlemen and ladies. Dr. Paterno's parenting book, *Desperately Seeking Parents*, has helped hundreds of parents reclaim their families in ways that foster virtuous living and values. Most importantly, he and his wife are raising their own two ladies and a gentleman.

We are imperfect architects. Neither of us has perfect hearts, minds, or wills. We readily admit that while we hold high standards for others and ourselves, we do not always meet those standards. However, we do hold perfect ideals; we strive to attain them, model them for our children, and hope that they will inherit them. Hopefully, our humility will help us communicate to our readers the necessity for change and a realistic blueprint for success. ★

PART ONE

# The Genesis of the Lady and the Gentleman

BEFORE WE ARE ACCUSED of wanting to return to the "glory days" of sex roles, when "a man was a man and a woman was a woman," be assured that we are asserting no such thing. We do not believe that women should be chattel. We are not visualizing a return to a strict division of labor whereby men exclusively work outside the home and a woman's place is exclusively in the home. Neither of us is arranging marriages for our children.[1]

At the same time, we do not envision women glorying in the modern feminist ideal where she ". . . can bring home the bacon, fry it up in a pan, and never let you forget you're a man."[2] Something has gone terribly wrong with the concept of virtue for each gender. The concepts of the lady and the gentleman have been poisoned. Rather than rejecting the ideals altogether, we must understand the good and separate it from the bad.

In part one, we show that there are facets of traditional gender roles that not only reflected each gender's virtues, but fostered them. Later, we will argue that modern feminism has gone too far—and with fundamentally flawed presumptions—and that a surviving and thriving America must return to the ideals of virtue and honor that developed throughout history and were firmly entrenched until the latter century. Additionally, if our republic is to return to its rightful position as the "shining light on a hill," it must study and return to a common language of behavior, demeanor, and honor. The lady and the

---

[1] Unless the dowry is really, really big.

[2] One wonders what place a man has in a relationship with this kind of woman. We envision the lyric: "I bring home the bacon, fry it up in a pan, and you laze around all day? Go get a job like a man!"

3

gentleman must return, separating the essential, edifying, and glorify-ing wheat of both sexes from the ugly historical chaff.

For now, we explore the history and development of the wheat and the chaff. ★

## Chapter One

★★★

# From Eden to Gethsemane

*Finally, brothers and sisters, whatever is true, whatever is noble, whatever is right, whatever is pure, whatever is lovely, whatever is admirable—if anything is excellent or praiseworthy—think about such things.*

—PHILIPPIANS 4:8

*Virtue is more to a man than either water or fire. I have seen men die from treading on water and fire, but I have never seen a man die from treading the course of virtue.*

—CONFUCIUS

*The moral virtues, then, are produced in us neither by nature nor against nature. Nature, indeed, prepares in us the ground for their reception, but their complete formation is the product of habit.*

—ARISTOTLE

## Flintstone Virtues

Cave drawings recently discovered in the foothills of Barataria depict a series of scenes displaying heroic and virtuous behavior. In one of the drawings, estimated at more than fifteen thousand years old, a large man holds open a cave door, made out of animal skins, for a woman. In another, a cavewoman kisses her male counterpart as she hands him something like a sack lunch, presumably as he departs with his friends on a hunting expedition. Anthropologists were surprised to find attention paid to such gentile gender roles.

OK, the first paragraph is not really true. Barataria[1] doesn't exist, and no such cave drawings have been discovered—at least that we know of. Our point is that the concept of the lady and gentleman did not begin with Miss Manners or Queen Elizabeth. In a culture that esteems each successive generation as the brightest and most aware and that elevates Darwinian theory to Scripture-like status, it is easy to imagine that the concepts of the lady and gentleman are as new as laptops, and that virtue was born in the Renaissance.

Virtue and the idealization of virtues in man and woman have been circulating since recorded history. For millennia, the virtues have been upheld by both civilized and less sophisticated societies. The question is not whether virtues have been upheld and supported by the various cultures but which virtues have been defined and how societies elevated those character traits to the status of virtue.

## Biblical Virtue

The Bible remains the foundational document of Western society, providing the existential base for the founding documents of the United States, including the Mayflower Compact and the Declaration of Independence. It holds the narrative of man's salvation, as well as a great deal of information about the human condition, God's expectations for mankind, and many contrasting examples of people who did and did not meet those expectations. As such, the concepts

---

[1] Baritaria was a fictional island kingdom in *Don Quixote*.

of the lady and the gentleman originate in its pages. Similarly, the virtues taught in Scripture reflect a human understanding and inter-pretation of God's direct commands to His people. In a very serious way, virtue refers to the habits, beliefs, and attitudes one holds about oneself in relation to the world and its Creator.

The Ten Commandments are part of God's "virtue code." The first section deals with man's relationship to the Almighty—how man is to think, speak, and behave in relation to God. The latter command-ments focus on man's relationship to his fellow man. "Honor your mother and your father . . ." says the fourth commandment (Exodus 20:12). Here we see one of the first virtues—respect for one's elders and for the familial hierarchy that God created for His people. A lady or gentleman seeks to obey these commandments not only by avoid-ing sins like murder, theft, adultery, lying, and coveting but striving for the opposite: mercy, charity, faithfulness, honesty, and contentment.

The New Testament specifies this virtue code. Jesus summarizes and prioritizes God's commands in the gospel of Matthew: " 'Love the Lord your God with all your heart and all your soul and with all your mind.' This is the first and greatest commandment. And the second is like it: 'Love your neighbor as yourself.' All the Law and the Prophets hang on these two commandments." (Matthew 22:37–40) In Paul's letter to the Colossians, he offers a set of rules for holy living, implic-itly marking the virtues for which every Christian lady or gentleman should strive.

> Put to death, therefore, whatever belongs to your earthly nature: sexual immorality, impurity, lust, evil desires and greed, which is idolatry. . . . You must rid yourselves of all such things as these: anger, rage, malice, slander, and filthy language from your lips. Do not lie to each other, since you have taken off your old self with its practices and have put on the new self. (Colossians 3:5, 8–10)

Paul describes in Ephesians how a lady and gentleman should treat each other as spouses: "Wives, submit to your husbands as to the Lord. . . . Husbands, love your wives . . ." (Ephesians 5:22, 26). Several other epistles in the New Testament speak to the behavior of men and women—specifically how they are to evidence their faith by living out the virtues.

Without using the term "lady" or "gentleman," one can find archetypes of both in Scripture. Obviously, the central character of the gospel is also its chief gentleman: Christ Himself. He was and remains the perfect human. Modern biblical "scholarship" has attempted to reduce the potency of Scripture by portraying Jesus as merely a supremely gifted teacher—essentially a man whose mission was to teach people how to live virtuous lives. Such liberal interpretation of Scripture is fundamentally flawed. Even so, it is pointless to forget that although He was much more than a great teacher and example of virtue, he *was* the consummate gentleman and a man of exquisite, perfect virtue. Even putting aside the centrality of His redemptive work, modern man can learn a great deal from how Jesus lived.

## Jesus: Savior, King, and Gentleman

One of Christ's central virtues was *patience*. Jesus demonstrated substantial forbearance with His disciples, who many times proved themselves dimwitted, selfish, impetuous, and faithless. Jesus also possessed an inexhaustible well of *grace* and *mercy*, both for His disciples and for those who attacked and even killed Him. He said, "Father, forgive them; for they know not what they do" (Luke 23:34, KJV).

Particularly noble was how much attention Jesus devoted to women and how gentle He was with them—a fact that was nothing less than scandalous in His day. Who can forget Jesus's response to the "immoral" woman who crashed the Pharisee's dinner party at which Jesus was a guest? Not only did Jesus allow the woman to touch him[2] (with her mouth, no less), but He welcomed her and forgave her sins, which He acknowledged were many and serious (Luke 7:36–48).

However, Jesus the gentleman was not always meek, mild, or deferential—a lesson that should not go unnoticed. He demonstrated the full range of emotions, including anger; he was not afraid to express the latter. When His Father's house was being desecrated,

---

[2] About as politically incorrect as a politician mentioning Jesus.

He unleashed His *righteous anger*. When the Pharisees and others tried to trap Him into denying the legitimacy of Caesar's authority, He cleverly answered the question without incriminating Himself. Still, when the time came for Him to answer Pilate as to whether or not He was the Messiah, He did not back down. Finally, there is no modifier that can accurately describe the perfection of His *courage* in facing the wrath of His Father on the cross. In fact, all of His virtue coalesced on that day, proving Him the perfect gentleman.

## Additional Biblical Men and Women of Virtue

There are several additional biblical men and women—both in historical narrative and in parable—who exhibit virtue. Gratefully, we do not have to contend with such supremely virtuous men and women whom we simply cannot relate to. All the greats of the New and Old Testaments were deeply flawed. This should inspire all of us who strive to be virtuous but become frustrated with our deep imperfection.

David provides a perfect example of both the presence and lack of great virtue. David, the apple of God's eye, is a humble man in his youth. He is also righteous and faithful to his God. When he sees Goliath threatening and taunting the Israelites, David's righteous indignation spurs him into action. Disregarding his diminutive stature, he gathers courage not from his own skills but from God Himself: "The Lord who delivered me from the paw of the lion and paw of the bear will deliver me from the hand of this Philistine" (1 Samuel 17:37).

The same David who exhibits great virtue later exposes a pitiful lack of integrity when, as king, he lures Bathsheba to his home, essentially forces himself on her, then tries to heap sin upon sin by orchestrating the death of her husband.[3] After breaking just about every commandment possible, David is confronted by the prophet Nathan, where he is chastened and displays genuine, profound repentance. David goes on to demonstrate both the presence and absence of several virtues throughout his life.

---

[3] This sounds eerily like an episode of *Real Housewives*.

Abraham is another character who could easily make both the Gentleman's Hall of Fame and the Virtue Hall of Shame. Abraham reveals himself to be a man of great faith when he responds to God's command to leave his people and homeland to travel to an undisclosed land with an unknown future. Then he pleads to God for mercy on behalf of Sodom, appealing to His justice and graciousness. Equally impressive, he trusts God implicitly, even when He asks him to offer up his son Isaac—his only son—as a sacrifice. In all three cases, he looks like a true gentleman.

On the other side of the ledger, Abraham encourages his wife Sarai to lie to Pharaoh in Egypt and tell him that she is Abraham's sister. Essentially, he gives up Sarai for the Pharaoh to take into his harem in order to save his own skin. He also laughs faithlessly after God tells him that He will bless him and his wife with a child, despite their old age. Finally, he exhibits very poor moral leadership when Sarai suggests that he use a maidservant to produce children. Not exactly a traditionally protective husband, is he?

Sarai (who later goes by Sarah), for her part, doesn't represent ladies very well. Offering her servant to her husband for sex, for example, isn't exactly what one would consider the behavior of a dutiful wife. Also, because of her cooperation in Abraham's lies, "the Lord had closed up every womb in Abimelech's household" (Genesis 20:18).

In contrast, Esther offers an example of a woman of great virtue. As queen, she risked death for herself by breaking with courtly formality—entering the king's court without permission. At the prospect of being killed for her bravery, she famously responded, "If I perish, I perish" (Esther 4: 16). Even more poignant was her ability to use her physical beauty and attractiveness for noble rather than selfish purposes.

To be sure, Mary, the mother of Jesus, was a paragon of grace and faithfulness. Her humility before God is revealed in her song of praise: "My soul praises the Lord and my spirit rejoices in God my Savior, for he has been mindful of the humble state of his servant" (Luke 1:46–48). She and her betrothed evidenced a perfect surrender to God's mighty acts and ability to perform miracles. Joseph, for his part, displayed a tender demeanor and extraordinary mercy after discovering Mary's pregnancy.

## Babylonian Virtues

Several ancient societies lionized virtue in their mythologies. One of the earliest was the Babylonian Empire. Governed by Hammurabi in the eighteenth century BC, the Hammurabi Code was written in part to protect the weak and promote honor and virtue. Hammurabi's Code utilized an array of laws and consequences in order to support the virtues of hard work, fairness, and justice. It did not speak directly of virtuous behavior of men in contrast to women, but it did offer protections for men and women in terms of marriage, divorce, and childbearing. It is safe to say that Babylonian society did not look favorably upon men and women who committed adultery or a man who abandoned his wife or children.

## Virtue in Ancient Greece

The examination, development, and exposition of virtue gathered momentum in ancient Greece. Prior to the great trinity of Greek philosophers—Socrates, Plato, and Aristotle—Homer's *Iliad* and *Odysseus* profoundly weighed on Greek culture. Homer's mythology produced in the eighth century BC illustrated a code whereby virtue was attained by heroic exploits and individual accomplishment. These heroes had to contend with mercurial gods whose capricious meddling in their affairs was marked by prejudice and malice. Still, in the Homeric code, certain virtues are consistently upheld, such as aggressiveness, cleverness, endurance, and bravery.

Heroes and heroines as ideal forms of man and woman were common in ancient Western literature.[4] Male heroes in Greek mythology tended to utilize impressive, perfect, or even superhuman physical traits (such as Heracles). In one myth, Heracles (Hercules, in Roman mythology) chose virtue, based on honest labor, over pleasure. Women tended to rely more on their feminine wiles, such as intelligence or sexual allure, to accomplish their ends (such as the faithful

---

[4] Although, female virtue was far less represented, in contrast to the Bible's myriad examples of female virtue.

Penelope).[5] An interesting exception is the myth of the Amazons, the self-exiled warriors known mostly for their brutality and for eschewing sex with men (except for once a year, and that only to prevent their people from dying out).

The Roman orator Cicero credited Socrates as the first ethical philosopher. At the very least, he was the first Greek thinker to systematically approach ethical and moral issues and paint an outline of the virtuous person. He posed the question, "How should I live?" Socrates's conception of virtue (*arete*) focused less on heroic deeds or accomplishment and refers more to excellence or even perfection in comprehending one's purposes and using one's means to attain those purposes. Importantly, Socrates noted that attaining virtue merely for self-interest is not a noble pursuit.[6]

Plato and Aristotle expanded and further specified the notion of virtue. Plato viewed virtue as the pure exercise of thought, by which a human can have pure union with the divine. He labeled wisdom, courage, and temperance as the virtues stemming from the three elements of the soul. Aristotle defined virtue as the perfect meeting point of rationality and desire. He distinguished intellectual virtue—or practical intellect (wisdom)—from moral virtue, which equates in modern language to something like prudence, or the practice of avoiding extremes with moderation.

## Virtue in Rome—an Oxymoron?

Rome's most prolific commentator on virtue was Marcus Porcius Cato Uticensis. Also known as Cato the Younger, he was a military leader, orator, and politician who fiercely supported the republic of Rome against dictatorship.[7] His character traits and priorities provide a stark contrast to the historical reputation of Rome as a decadent, immoral, and virtueless society.

---

[5] One could argue that little has changed over the past two or three millennia.

[6] A notion that modern psychology seems to have ignored.

[7] It is no coincidence that the Cato Institute is a *conservative* think tank.

Interestingly, the Romans gave us the word *virtue*. It stems from the Latin word *virtus*, which provides the root *vir*, or *man*. This root word is the basis for several words related to masculine power, including "virility" and "virtual." It should be no surprise, then, that Roman concepts of virtue were synonymous with more masculine traits.

The Greco-Roman historian Plutarch, who himself wrote extensively on the virtues, wrote that Cato had a reputation for integrity and other virtues at an early age. This served him well during his military assignments, where strict discipline and fairness earned him the deep respect of his soldiers. As a senator, he was well known for his morally scrupulous campaigns and refusing to accept bribes,[8] which contrasted himself to most of his peers. While it sometimes resulted in political failure, his allies and foes alike held a deep respect for Cato. His reputation was one of a man driven by moral integrity, steadfastness, and justice.

Marcus Aurelius, Roman emperor during the second century, adhered to the philosophy of Stoicism. As such, he believed in four primary virtues: wisdom, justice, fortitude, and temperance. Not only did he believe in and legislate according to these virtues, he modeled them. F.W. Farrar, in *Seekers after God,* described Aurelius as a man with great integrity:

> He regarded himself as being, in fact, the servant of all. The registry of the citizens, the suppression of litigation, the elevation of public morals, the care of minors, the retrenchment of public expenses, the limitation of gladiatorial games and shows, the care of roads, the restoration of senatorial privileges, the appointment of none but worthy magistrates, even the regulation of street traffic, these and numberless other duties so completely absorbed his attention that, in spite of indifferent health, they often kept him at severe labor from early morning till long after midnight.

If only our senators and representatives exhibited such fortitude and commitment.

---

[8] There was no "Cato Cornhusker" scandal.

Toward the end of the Roman Empire, a collection of European peoples led by Attila the Hun led a massive army that constantly threatened the outer Roman provinces. In order to avoid a costly war, the Romans paid tribute to the great emperor. The Roman historian Jordanus wrote gushingly of Attila:

> He was haughty in his carriage, casting his eyes about him on all sides so that the proud man's power was to be seen in the very movements of his body. A lover of war, he was personally restrained in action, most impressive in counsel, gracious to supplicants, and generous to those whom he had once given his trust.

Although Jordanus did not have the term *gentleman* at his disposal—and Attila does not quite compare to the modern concept of a gentleman—his description shows how clearly the Romans valued confidence, restraint, wisdom, graciousness, and generosity as ideals of male virtue.

Regarding women, Rome is not well known for its friendliness to the "weaker sex." Women held a particularly low status, barely above slaves and children.[9] Still, there were female archetypes in both mythology and in Roman history. One such woman was Porcia, the younger daughter of the aforementioned Cato. As Romans admired women for their devotion to husband and children, Porcia was extolled for her devotion to her husband Brutus—one of the conspiring senators who assassinated Julius Caesar. When she overheard her husband considering a plot against Caesar, she attempted to persuade him to reveal the secret. Her method was to prove that she could keep a severe, painful secret by stabbing herself in the leg and enduring it without complaint. Legend says that when she exposed her significant wound and its purpose, she immediately and implicitly gained Brutus's trust.

Another such heroine is Cloelia. During a fifth-century-BC war in which Rome lost to Clusium, Roman hostages were taken by the

---

[9] One of the reasons Jesus's treatment of several women provides such a stark contrast.

victors. Cloelia was one such hostage. Somehow, she managed to escape her captors. The leader of the Clusium army demanded that she return. To his amazement, she miraculously did so. The army, shocked at her courage, relinquished half their prisoners in her honor.

## Introducing . . . the Gentleman and Lady!

The term *gentleman*, as identified in the *Oxford English Dictionary*, refers to a "chivalrous, courteous, or honourable man" or, alternately, "a man of good social position, especially one of wealth and leisure." Easily translated from the French *gentilz hom*, or "man of good birth," the term was originally limited to describing men of noble birth. It soon was broadened to refer to any man from a good family who displayed the aforementioned qualities. Similarly, the *Oxford English Dictionary* defines *lady* as "a woman of good social position" or "a courteous, decorous, or genteel woman." Its meaning has a curious history.

Just as word *woman* derives from *man*, the term *lady* gathered its original meaning in relation to another counterpart, *lord*. In Anglo-Saxon, the lord *hláfweard* meant "warden of the loaf," referring to the privilege of the man of the house to determine who in his house had earned his daily bread and who had not. This was soon condensed to *hláford*; the *f* was soon dropped, leaving something sounding similar to *lord*. *Lady* comes from the Anglo-Saxon *hlæfdige*, which literally means "loaf-kneader." The *f* sound dropped as it did with the male equivalent,[10] leaving something sounding remotely like *lady*. Interestingly, we have an early example of gender words denoting the complementary nature of the sexes, with the woman of the household kneading the bread and the man doling it out appropriately.

There is some genuine disagreement among scholars as to when the terms *gentleman* and *lady* first appear in literary form. While some historians place the first reference to a gentleman in the late thirteenth century, the first undisputed mention in literature is in

---

[10] Terrified of potential "F-bombs," the Anglo-Saxon Vocabulary Police determined to rid their language of all Fs. It's in a history book I once read (in public school, of course).

Geoffrey Chaucer's late fourteenth-century *Canterbury Tales*. In one of the tales, Chaucer draws the connection between a gentleman and his virtue:

> Loke who that is most vertuous alway
> Prive and apert, and most entendeth ay
> To do the gentil dedes that he can
> And take him for the gretest gentilman

Surprisingly, the term *lady* arrives even earlier, this time independent of a male counterpart. The mystical Lady of the Lake makes her appearance in the late twelfth century, in one of the earliest manifestations of the Arthurian legends. The Lady, a goddess-like creature, appears in *Conte de la Charrette* by Chretien de Troyes.

## The Context of Early Gentleman and Lady

It is important to understand the timing of these terms; they were not simply created *ex nihilo*. Much of Europe—England, in particular—enjoyed an age of expansion during the thirteenth century. Its population grew rapidly—a trend halted by the Black Death of the next century—as did the education and economic status of many citizens. Because there was a significant increase in wealth during the reigns of Henry III and Edward I, there were more resources to invest in war, which required a greater number of knights. It also allowed for more funds to funnel into monasteries, which were the seats of higher education in medieval Europe. Finally, there was more time for domestic matters, including pomp and ceremony.

During the long reign of Henry III, several works of literature became extremely popular with nobility and knightly classes that clearly influenced courtly behavior and the coming age of chivalry. The first was the *Roman de la Rose*, written in the 1230s by William de Lorris. The poems of this work glorify courtly love. Another example was the *History of William Marshal*, written two decades later. In this fictional biography, a virtuous knight, once landless and with few prospects, conducts himself with great chivalry and high values.

The reign of Edward I saw the merging of practical formality at court with the mythical ethos of King Arthur and all of its legends and connected tales. Edward publicized a supposed association with King Arthur in several royal ceremonies. In 1278, in the presence of Edward and his royal court, the bones of King Arthur and Queen Guinevere were removed from their supposed tombs in Glastonbury Abbey and then reburied. When he returned from his conquest of Wales, he claimed to have discovered the crown of King Arthur. He followed his victory with a week-long festival of tournaments, feasts, and ceremonies, involving many trappings of Arthurian legend, including a huge round table.

Royal pomp and circumstance had been a part of most European monarchies, but in large part, the reigns of Henry III and Edward I heralded the beginning of the age of chivalry, a time that would foster the ideals of the lady and the gentleman for centuries to come. ★

*Chapter Two*

★★★

# Court and Courtesy:
# The Chivalric Code

*Society expected each man to aspire constantly to Chivalric Behavior; in return, they gave him an honorable place in the union of men . . .*

—ARNO BORST, MEDIEVAL WORLDS

*The institution of chivalry forms one of the most remarkable features in the history of the Middle Ages.*

—HORATIO ALGER

*More than a code of manners in war and love, Chivalry was a moral system, governing the whole of noble life . . .*

—BARBARA W. TUCHMAN, A DISTANT MIRROR

# Transmission of Virtue

Understanding how the virtues and the ideals of ladylike and gentlemanly behavior developed and were historically transmitted to the masses requires answering a larger question: How were *any* ideas communicated to people in the Middle Ages? After all, there were no newspapers, comic strips, tabloids, or afterschool movie specials.[1] There was no Medieval Miss Manners advice column, Facebook, or Mister Rogers.[2] As far as our exhaustive research could discover, churches did not hold coffee cake socials where youth pastors held seminars teaching young men and women how to behave like godly gentlemen and ladies.

Until the late Middle Ages, communicating ideas to the general public was almost exclusively personal and was most often transmitted orally. Tales and myths were spread orally throughout Europe— especially Western Europe. The poetical and musical activity of the Middle Ages—often centered in monasteries but also in alehouses, public squares, and other public places—was transmitted via bards, minstrels, troubadours, and other professional musicians and reciters. Popular tales, including those with virtuous heroes and heroines, spread and grew throughout the various classes and peoples. Children and adults alike learned these tales, as well as which behaviors were admirable. They also began hearing the terms *virtue*, *lady*, and *gentleman* in this manner.

Writing did not become the primary method of teaching the virtues to more than the noble classes until the Renaissance period. In the ancient world, scrolls, or *volumens*, were the primary method of writing. Scrolls were phased out of most written communication with the invention of the paper book in the fourth century. However, most people do not realize that books were exceptionally rare prior to the High Middle Ages (eleventh–thirteenth centuries), in part because they were expensive to produce and because literacy was limited to nobility and other wealthy classes. Except for the very wealthy,

---

[1] The *Lifetime Channel* wasn't invented until the sixteenth century.
[2] Also sixteenth century.

most people simply would not have read any works of literature that expounded the concepts of the lady and the gentleman.

With the invention of the printing press in the fifteenth century, books became far less expensive, and therefore more readily available. This, along with other independent factors, encouraged an increase in literacy. In this way, the written word became the primary method of transmission of ideas.

The particular ideas that concern us are that of the virtues and the lady and gentleman who hold and practice them. The location for the explosion of ideas in this sphere was medieval Europe, where literature—including myth, verse, painting, rule book, tract, and history—became the focal point of the virtues and of the burgeoning ideas of the lady and the gentleman.

## King Arthur and Queen Guinevere

Arguably, the first popular and expansive contributions in Western literature to the idea of chivalry—including honorable behavior, nobility, and decorum that go with it—are found in the myths and legends of King Arthur, his Queen Guinevere, and the knights of the Round Table. One of the first appearances of the Arthurian legend was in a collection of lyrical verses written by Chretien de Troyes between 1170 and 1190. In one of his poems, an idealistic knight named Perceval is involved in a sort of finishing school for knights, where he is versed in the ideals of chivalry. He learns that self-sacrifice is the highest ideal, as well as the necessity to be clearheaded, morally pure, humble, compassionate to the less fortunate, and respectful to others. In one verse, the young Perceval is admonished to please the ladies by maintaining good hygiene, remaining courteous, and carrying himself with elegance.[3]

In another section of de Troyes's work, Sir Lancelot, the most heralded knight of Camelot, is tutored by the mystical Lady of the Lake.

---

[3] Someone should add this poem to the" Occupy" movement's "recommended reading" list.

21

In this passage, she catalogs the ideals of chivalry and describes how a genteel knight should behave:

> They were as big, strong, gallant and agile as they were loyal, noble and valiant, that is, they possessed spiritual and physical qualities. . . . They had to be attentive without villainy, pleasant without hypocrisy, compassionate to the suffering, generous and prepared to help the less fortunate, quick and ready to punish thieves and murderers, impartial judges, unaffected by both hate and love, without favouring the unjust or against the just. . . . Contrastingly, they should fear dishonor more than death.

Later manifestations added to the legend of King Arthur, ascribing various virtues—and/or evils—to a whole cast of men and women, including brave Gawain, fearless Kay, charming Aggravaine, cunning Mordred, pure Galahad, treasonous Morgan le Fay, and the unfaithful Lancelot and Guinevere. Some legends even include an inventory of activities appropriate for ladies, such as hawking, making tapestries, singing, dancing, and speaking French.

## A Gentleman's Constitution

One early document made a critical contribution to the chivalric code and to the knight's or gentlemen's lexicon during the Middle Ages: *The Song of Roland*. The French epic (or heroic poem) written in the late eleventh century chronicles some of the battles and deeds of Count Hrodland. In the midst of these chronicles, several knightly ideals are illustrated:

- Faithfulness
- Truthfulness
- Perseverance
- Taking up the cause of justice for all manner and class of people
- Aiding the poor and destitute
- Caring for the widowed
- Obedience to proper authority
- Respecting and preserving the honor of women

- Fearing God and maintaining His church
- Faithful service to the king
- Guarding the honor of fellow knights, even in battle
- Bravery (accepting challenges from any knight)

One of the more famous and influential books on chivalry was the *Libro de la Orden de Caballeria*, (in English: *The Book of the Order of Chivalry*) written by Spaniard Ramon Llull in the late thirteenth century. Translated across Europe and standard reading for much of the noble class, this book reads like a constitution for knights, with a list of customs and duties that a man must perform to be worthy of knighthood. Some of the principal virtues listed in the book include loyalty, strength, courage, manners, generosity, humility, hope, promptness, inward resolve, and moderation. Because of the explicit nature of this text and the growing reality that men of all classes desired to become knights and noblemen, Llull's work became something of a handbook for aspiring gentlemen.

Eustace Deschamps was a fourteenth-century French poet who spent most of his adult life in service of King Charles V and his son Charles VI. As a courtier (a man who attends the court of the king), he was a first-row observer of courtly behavior and speech, as well as the patterns of courtly love expected of nobility. He offered the following verse in recognition of what he viewed as a knight's virtues:

You who long for the Knightly Order,
It is fitting you should lead a new life;
Devoutly keeping watch in prayer,
Fleeing from sin, pride and villainy;
The Church defending,
The Widows and Orphans succouring.
Be bold and protect the people,
Be loyal and valiant, taking nothing from others.
Thus should a Knight rule himself.
He should be humble of heart and always work,
And follow Deeds of Chivalry.
Be loyal in war and travel greatly;
He should frequent tourneys and joust for his Lady Love;
He must keep honor with all,

So that he cannot be held to blame.
No cowardice should be found in his doings,
Above all, he should uphold the weak,
Thus should a Knight rule himself.

# Robin Hood and Marian

The legends of Robin Hood and his merry men were extremely popular social vehicles, told in song and verse in taverns across England from the thirteenth century, read during and after the Renaissance, then viewed on television and film in the modern era. The original tales provided morality plays and comedies for the lower classes; in a way, they were the popular means of transmitting morals, ethics, and values to the both the literate and illiterate classes. While the Robin Hood legends say very little specifically about gentlemen or ladies, the virtues are clearly spelled out and celebrated.

Modern manifestations of the tales of Robin Hood differ from their originals. Like the myths of King Arthur and the Round Table, these legends expand and contract, based in part by the current needs of the society or generation retelling the stories.

For example, Robin Hood's original persona was not primarily a crusader of wealth distribution.[4] Although some early tales display Robin taking from corrupt officials and giving the money to the needy, the notion of generic robbing from the rich and giving to the poor was a later addition to the legend.[5] Robin routinely practices several of the key virtues of chivalry, including justice. Despite his role as outlaw, he doles out justice with great integrity. He is also a humble man, gracious in defeat. Several tales illustrate a nearly boundless generosity. And finally, he appears to be light of heart—he takes few things seriously and loves a good jest.

---

[4] We know this because Robin Hood was too manly to be a Democrat. He also stole from a greedy government's tax coffers and returned the money to the overtaxed. Clearly a Tea Partier.

[5] Perhaps introduced in Obama's top secret thesis paper at Columbia.

Unfortunately, Maid Marian was not a figure in the early tales of Robin Hood. Her addition did little to move the story and there is little about the concept of the lady in even late manifestations of the tales.

## Christian Writings

Early Church Fathers such as St. Augustine and St. Ambrose in the fourth century produced more codified notions of Christian virtue. The church continued its enormous role in regulating and specifying the specific conduct of men and women during the Middle Ages. One order of knights created and supported by the Catholic Church was the Company of the Star. *A Knight's Own Book of Chivalry* by Frenchman Geoffroi de Charny was written specifically for knights of this order. Like Llull's handbook, this autobiographical work contains many admonishments and rules for chivalric, noble, and virtuous behavior, such as the following:

> And make sure that you do not praise your own conduct nor criticize too much that of others. Do not desire to take away another's honor, but, above all else, safeguard your own. Be sure that you do not despise poor men or those of lesser rank than you, for there are many poor men who are of greater worth than the rich. Take care not to talk too much, for in talking too much you are sure to say something foolish; for example, the foolish cannot hold their peace, and the wise know how to hold their peace until it is time to speak.

Desiderius Erasmus was a Catholic priest and one of Martin Luther's arch-nemeses during the early sixteenth-century Reformation. One of his important works was the *Enchiridion Militis Christiani*, or the "Manual (or Dagger) of the Christian Gentleman" (1503). In this little volume, Erasmus outlines the views of the normal Christian life, as well as how Christian men should conduct themselves personally. He specifically refers to the virtues to which men should aspire.

## Sinful Virtue?

There is significant evidence that the courtesy and chivalry of the medieval age stemmed in part from a desire of the noble classes to separate themselves from the non-noble classes. Because of medieval Europe's broadening economy, the merchant class (burghers) rose in economic and social status. According to historian David Herlihy, this "challenged [the nobles'] position," who wished to maintain their lofty status in a society that was exceptionally conscious of class and rank. The practice of chivalry, with its courteousness and etiquette, created a clique of sorts, in which learned behaviors set nobles and others who practiced chivalry apart from the new working class. In spite of the newly found economic status of the merchant class, they were not privy to the social learning and modeling of courtesy and etiquette to which the nobles were privy.

The practice of chivalry in royal courts gave nobles an advantage. Chivalrous nobles set up and then lived by ideals that they felt kept them in the upper echelons of medieval society. According to Herlihy, this "had the function of providing to . . . [the nobility] a justification for its privileges and position."

In a way, nobles behaved like Dr. Seuss's sneetches, whose fraternity of starred creatures wanted to separate (elevate) themselves from those who had "no stars upon thars." Rather than acknowledging and being content with their equal value before God, the noble class simply had to be *more* special than the rest—then prove it with a complex and rigid system of behaviors. Sometimes our sinful desire to be like God can be masked by even our most sublime efforts.

## Monarchy-Supported Virtue

Many kings used the chivalric code and its behaviors for similar purposes. King Edward III of England, one of the monarchs most closely associated with the development and practice of chivalry, is a prime example. Because England was at war with France, he required a healthy number of battle-ready knights at his disposal. In order to supplement the knights' financial reward for their faithful service to the king, Edward encouraged the social elevation of the nobility by encouraging the chivalric code. Knights, then, could aspire not only to land but to esteem.

Whether this psychological strategy was explicitly planned or merely accidental, he seemed to have understood the innate human desire for prestige, glory, and status.[6] One part of this plan compelled Edward to create his own knightly order: the Knights of the Blue Garter. As the head of this order, Edward created a powerful measure of prestige and structure by which nobleman could climb to greater glory and elite status.

## Chivalry's Elevation of the Lady

In many ways, the noble class in the Middle Ages was very much like a fraternity; the chivalric code, then, was its rule book. Being a nobleman or an aspiring knight necessitated significant motivation. The knight's primary motive—at least explicitly—was to serve God. However, the chivalric code encouraged a second, hardly subordinate motivation: devotion and service to a lady.

Colman Andrews, author and creator of *Saveur* magazine, suggested

> it can be argued that the ancient codes of chivalry helped render women powerless by placing them on pedestals, turning them from flesh-and-blood into ideals—but it can also be argued, I think, that in an age and a milieu in which women were, for the most part, powerless (for whatever reasons), chivalry was the perhaps essential discipline that forbade the gentleman, and everybody else, to take advantage of them.

A second Frenchman, Andreas Capellanus, created his own set of rules of courtly love in the twelfth century. As one can see, these thirty-one romantic principles provide a mix of godly principles for marital love with guidance for the romantic inklings of a man whose

---

[6] Making Edward III one of the first social psychologists.

passion burns for another man's wife! To a degree, this devotion to women crossed over the line into idolatry.[7]

1. Marriage should not be a deterrent to love.
2. Love cannot exist in the individual who cannot be jealous.
3. A double love cannot obligate an individual.
4. Love constantly waxes and wanes.
5. That which is not given freely by the object of one's love loses its savor.
6. It is necessary for a male to reach the age of maturity in order to love.
7. A lover must observe a two-year widowhood after his beloved's death.
8. Only the most urgent circumstances should deprive one of love.
9. Only the insistence of love can motivate one to love.
10. Love cannot coexist with avarice.
11. A lover should not love anyone who would be an embarrassing marriage choice.
12. True love excludes all from its embrace but the beloved.
13. Public revelation of love is deadly to love in most instances.
14. The value of love is commensurate with its difficulty of attainment.
15. The presence of one's beloved causes palpitation of the heart.
16. The sight of one's beloved causes palpitations of the heart.
17. A new love brings an old one to a finish.
18. Good character is the one real requirement for worthiness of love.
19. When love grows faint, its demise is usually certain.
20. Apprehension is the constant companion of true love.
21. Love is reinforced by jealousy.
22. Suspicion of the beloved generates jealousy and therefore intensifies love.

---

[7] Mirroring one of the errors of radical feminism: shifting from one extreme to another.

23. Eating and sleeping diminish greatly when one is aggravated by love.
24. The lover's every deed is performed with the thought of his beloved in mind.
25. Unless it please his beloved, no act or thought is worthy to the lover.
26. Love is powerless to hold anything from love.
27. There is no such thing as too much of the pleasure of one's beloved.
28. Presumption on the part of the beloved causes suspicion in the lover.
29. Aggravation of excessive passion does not usually afflict the true lover.
30. Thought of the beloved never leaves the true lover.
31. Two men may love one woman or two women one man.

## Lady Light in the Dark Ages

Readers will notice that the vast majority of material produced during the Middle Ages about the virtues—call it "medieval moral propaganda"—focused on men. One of the primary reasons for this is that almost all purveyors of popular culture—authors, troubadours, and others—were men. Simply put, there were few public female voices in Europe speaking to women or about women.

There were notable exceptions. Christine de Pisan, for example, was well known for her love ballads and heroic poetry, the two most important literary forms supporting chivalry. Her most famous works, *The Book of the City of Ladies* and *The Book of the Three Virtues*, celebrated women for their virtues and accomplishments. The German Hrostvitha of Gandesheim[8] held up the lives and virtues of specific Christian women. Finally, Heloise of Argenteuil was a French nun and author. Her *Problemata Heloissae* was a tract that implored nuns

---

[8] Fun fact: if you say "Hrostvitha" out loud, it sounds like you are speaking backward.

to occupy their time diligently and fruitfully, to dress in a manner that reflected their spiritual goals, and to eat in moderation.

Still, women's voices were more muted than those of their male counterparts, leaving the concept of the lady trailing behind that of the gentleman. Another reason for this is the fact that women had primarily been without individual power for most of recorded history. Often referred to as *chattel* (derived from *cattle*) and merely the property of her father, then husband and lord, a woman owned no property and had no money or possessions of her own. Also, because universities admitted only men, women who wished to become educated had one choice: become a nun. Unfortunately, by the end of the Middle Ages, women in the church had all autonomy, instruction, and independence taken away from them. The narrowness of women's roles—make babies, work the fields, knead the bread—held very little room for expansion or exploration. They also required few virtues.

However, there is no doubt that the Middle Ages' introduction of chivalry introduced a transformation for women. The romanticism of chivalry—combined with the increasing and formalized Catholic adoration of the Virgin Mary—witnessed a birth of idealism regarding women. This ushered in a radical alteration in the public view of the woman. She was, in some ways, elevated from the baby-making, barley-picking, and bread-kneading laborer into an object of adoration, the impetus for great deeds and achievement, and the motivation for a whole code of courtly love. Granted, women remained objects, but they became multidimensional objects of somewhat greater value than in previous generations.

## Renaissance Ideals

William Shakespeare was not well known for his personal virtue. However, many of his plays and poems were deeply concerned with the definition of the lady and the gentleman, as well as the role of the virtues. Many of his plays and sonnets mention virtue. For example, sonnet 142 begins, "Love is my sin and thy dear *Virtue* hate" (italics added). In *Romeo and Juliet*, Capulet, the patriarch of Romeo's archenemy, speaks glowingly of Romeo's character:

> And, to say truth, Verona brags of him
> To be a virtuous and well-govern'd youth:
> I would not for the wealth of all the town
> Here in my house do him disparagement

Later in the play, the Friar says to himself, "Virtue itself turns vice, being misapplied, And vice sometime by action dignified."

It is crucial to see the literature of the Renaissance era in the context of changing views of men and women, particularly in the reign of Queen Elizabeth I. Her refusal to marry and bear children was considered by many unnatural, yet it also challenged the status quo of what made a lady. After all, if Elizabeth could be the primary lady of England, should this not alter her subjects' view of the essentials of ladyhood? Elizabeth herself spoke of her own unique set of virtues:

> Though I be a woman, yet I have as good a courage answerable
> to my place as ever my father [King Henry VIII] had. I am your
> anointed queen. I will never be by violence constrained to do
> anything. I thank God I am indeed endowed with such qualities,
> that if I were turned out of the realm in my petticoat, I were able
> to live in any place of Christendom.

Writers of the day, such as Shakespeare, would have risked more than their careers if they dared to portray the virtues of womanhood in a narrower sense than that of the sovereign. As Queen Elizabeth extolled virtues from the crown—such as courage, magnanimity, and self-sacrifice—so they were transferred to paper by the era's writers. While this influence was most certainly not direct—as suggested in the film *Shakespeare in Love*—the current political state likely challenged Shakespeare to offer his female characters a dimensionality with which they could break out of their silent, submissive, and self-suppressed bonds. Arguably, this allowed for Lady Macbeth's prodding her husband's "vaulting ambition," Cordelia's righteous vengeance against her evil sisters, and Katherine's fierce independence and refusal to submit to narrow cultural norms.

Another clearly direct link between the reign of Elizabeth I and the works of art she inspired was *The Fairie Queen* by Edmund Spenser. This epic poem, which was written explicitly to glorify England and her queen, focuses on heroes and heroines who exhibit virtues such as holiness, temperance, chastity, justice, and courtesy. Historians suggest that Queen Elizabeth was quite fond of Spenser's work and no doubt spoke highly of it to her courtiers and courtesans, creating a virtue "trickle-down effect."

Another fascinating and influential Renaissance woman was Isabella d'Este, often referred to as the First Lady of the Renaissance. She seemed to encapsulate a balance of ladylike femininity with a vigorous command of finances and other occupations traditionally held by men. She was forced in a way to become expert in the male-dominated world, having been married to the prince of Mantua; after his death, she ruled in his stead.

In Julia Cartwright's biography of her, entitled *Isabella d'Este: Marchioness*, she is described as "a typical child of the Renaissance, and her thoughts and actions faithfully reflected the best traditions of the age. . . . She was beyond reproach. . . . She had a strong sense of family affections and would have risked her life for the sake of advancing the interests of her husband and children or brothers." Later in life, she commissioned many works of art that had the express purpose of "disposing the mind to pure and noble thoughts." She patronized works that displayed the virtues.[9]

Of course, not all medieval works supported the concepts of the lady and gentleman. At the same time, the chivalric code was woefully inadequate in addressing the inequality of the sexes; it fell far short of matching the Bible's simple admonishment to "love your neighbor as yourself." Still, it seems apparent that every generation attempts to recodify and specify the virtues, and label men and women who reasonably display those virtues.  ★

---

[9] A practice we should all consider when examining how we allocate our time and entertainment dollars.

# Chapter Three

★★★

# The New World

*Bad men cannot make good citizens. A vitiated state of morals, a corrupted public conscience are incompatible with freedom.*

—PATRICK HENRY

*He therefore is the truest friend to the liberty of this country who tries most to promote its virtue, and who, so far as his power and influence extend, will not suffer a man to be chosen into any office of power and trust who is not a wise and virtuous man . . . .The sum of all is, if we would most truly enjoy this gift of Heaven, let us become a virtuous people.*

—SAMUEL ADAMS

*Let us go home and cultivate our virtues.*

—ROBERT E. LEE

## Virtue in Colonial America

The transition from monarchy to republic required and allowed a shift in responsibility, a transfer from the state to the individual. Early individuals such as the Pilgrims left the hierarchical, patriarchal systems of Europe, fleeing to a new world where they could determine their own methods of worship, as well as establish their own systems of conducting business and personal affairs. Marriages and families—the basic structure of the society—became wholly voluntary, rather than arranged for purely political purposes.

## Founding Fathers

Despite what the modern cadre of self-loathing, revisionist American historians would like to believe, the founders were, by and large, men of stellar virtue. Chapter Four deals with the undisputed star of the American Revolution, George Washington, but without doubt, the beliefs, attitudes, demeanor, and behavior of the entire *dramatis personae* of America's founding can easily be viewed as civil, honorable, and virtuous. Similarly, many women in the early American history—including the wives of the founders—provide excellent models of ladylike virtue and behavior.

In *Search of the Republic: Public Virtue and the Roots of American Government*, Richard Vetterli and Gary Bryner argue, "The idea of virtue was central to the political thought of the founders of the American republic. Every body of thought they encountered, every intellectual tradition they consulted, every major theory of republican government by which they were influenced emphasized the importance of personal and public virtue."

Of course, the founders were human; they were tarnished by sin just like the authors and readers of this book. We must take caution not to elevate the founders to idol-like status. However, we would be wise to take stock of their beliefs, virtues, and behavior in order to understand how this nation was founded not just on principles but on the character of the men and women who believed and lived out those principles.

## James Madison

At Virginia's convention to ratify the Constitution, Madison attempted to convince his colleagues that if they aimed to achieve a sustaining self-government, they must have a virtuous people:

> But I go on this great republican principle, that the people will have virtue and intelligence to select men of virtue and wisdom. Is there no virtue among us? If there be not, we are in a wretched situation. No theoretical checks—no form of government can render us secure. To suppose that any form of government will secure liberty or happiness without any virtue in the people is a chimerical idea.

Madison makes the *critical* point that a democratic republic cannot survive without a virtuous people. He is not referring to a people with exacting manners, European etiquette, or strong physical characteristics. Madison here speaks of morals, ethics, and civility. In essence, he asserts that a representative republic such as ours requires that both the governors and the governed possess virtue and that, without it, the republic will not survive.

If Madison is correct—and Madison was the Founder who was the most expert on the history of republics—it follows that any nation with dwindling virtue must attend to an increase in those virtues. This is the condition in which we currently find ourselves.

## Dolley Madison

The name of Madison's wife is often misspelled (the dessert company dropped the *e*), and her contributions to the behavior of ladies—especially that of subsequent First Ladies—is often underestimated. Dolley Madison was an exceptionally active and committed First Lady. Appearing to relish the role and all of its facets, she considered herself a political figure, even though she did not hold office. Subsequent First Ladies are measured by how like they are to Mrs. Madison.

Mrs. Madison was well versed in all of the fineries of ladyhood. She was a stellar hostess, quite able to throw an elegant and impressive party. She was keenly skilled at dialogue with politicians of all stripes—she seemed particularly able to utilize her impressive charm, knowledge, and eloquence with politicians' wives. Some believe that this skill not only aided her husband's popularity but also helped encourage the power of persuasion between spouses.[1] In essence, Dolley Madison brought all of her ladylike skills to bear in her marriage to James Madison—both in the personal and professional realms.

## Elizabeth Monroe

James Monroe's wife, Elizabeth, could hardly present a greater contrast to Mrs. Madison, playing a far less active role. As Elizabeth's education as a lady was deeply rooted in European convention, she was taught the traditional social graces, etiquette, and manners, as well as the established skills ladies were expected to master: sewing, dancing, fine arts, and literature. Also well known for her stunning beauty, flair, and sense of high fashion (she was particularly enamored with French style), she was dubbed *la belle Americaine*.

Mrs. Monroe exhibited a fairly detached approach to her role as first lady. This earned her a somewhat undeserved reputation for aloofness. Rather than disinterested, a fair reading of history suggests that she simply prioritized family rather than the prescribed expectations established by her more outgoing and active predecessor. By all accounts, she maintained a profound but muted support of her husband's varied roles and duties.

Mrs. Monroe was not idle or without courage. While living in France, she singlehandedly secured the release of Adrienne de Noiolles de Lafayette, the wife of French revolutionary leader Marquis de Lafayette. Mrs. Lafayette had been imprisoned when her husband, a close personal friend of George Washington's, left France. This resulted in a charge of treason—which carried a potential death penalty for both the marquis and his wife. Elizabeth risked both

---

[1] It is difficult to imagine a modern-day version: Michelle Obama encouraging "pillow talk" at the Boehner home in order to convince the speaker to raise taxes.

personal and political danger by riding to Paris directly to the prison, where she demanded a visit. The French government, not wanting to risk offending the fledgling United States, soon released Madame de Lafayette.

## Ben Franklin

Not normally regarded as a man of impeccable virtue, Ben Franklin was deeply and consistently concerned with the question of proper behavior and demeanor, as well as discipline of the virtues. He was also an incredibly self-disciplined man. From the age of twenty, he consciously and proactively sought to live out the following virtues, codifying them, grading himself daily, and recommitting to a perfect expression of each virtue the following day. Here are the thirteen virtues Franklin determined to perfect throughout his life:

- *Temperance*: "Eat not to dullness; drink not to elevation."
- *Silence:* "Speak not but what may benefit others or yourself; avoid trifling conversation."
- *Order:* "Let all your things have their places; let each part of your business have its time."
- *Resolution:* "Resolve to perform what you ought; perform without fail what you resolve."
- *Frugality:* "Make no expense but to do good to others or yourself; i.e., waste nothing."
- *Industry:* "Lose no time; be always employed in something useful; cut off all unnecessary actions."
- *Sincerity:* "Use no hurtful deceit; think innocently and justly, and, if you speak, speak accordingly."
- *Justice:* "Wrong none by doing injuries, or omitting the benefits that are your duty."
- *Moderation:* "Avoid extremes; forbear resenting injuries so much as you think they deserve."
- *Cleanliness:* "Tolerate no uncleanliness in body, clothes, or habitation."

- *Tranquility:* "Be not disturbed at trifles, or at accidents common or unavoidable."
- *Chastity:* "Rarely use venery but for health or offspring, never to dullness, weakness, or the injury of your own or another's peace or reputation."
- *Humility:* "Imitate Jesus and Socrates."

Most amateur historians rightly note that Franklin was less than perfectly self-disciplined with at least two of these virtues—notably chastity and temperance. However, he was humble enough to admit this fact. He also found joy and solace in the process of striving itself: "Tho' I never arrived at the perfection I had been so ambitious of obtaining, but fell far short of it, yet I was, by the endeavour, a better and a happier man than I otherwise should have been if I had not attempted it."

Furthermore, Franklin understood the importance of educating children in proper moral character and virtue:

> I think with you, that nothing is of more importance for the public weal, than to form and train up youth in wisdom and virtue. Wise and good men are in my opinion, the strength of the state; more so than riches or arms. . . . I think also, that general virtue is more probably to be expected and obtained from the education of youth, than from the exhortations of adult persons; bad habits and vices of the mind being, like diseases of the body, more easily prevented [in youth] than cured [in adults].

## George Washington's Mother, Mary

We will discuss our first president in great detail in Chapter Four, but for now, suffice it to say that Washington was a man deeply concerned about honor and all things gentlemanly. His mother, Mary, should be given proper due, since it is in large part her training of young George that resulted in the man of stellar virtue and character. There are few accounts of her life; the only surviving text was penned by Martha Washington's grandson.

Mrs. Washington governed her home with strict discipline. Young George was explicitly taught the virtues of restraint, moderation, duty, and industriousness. He was raised to behave in a civil manner in all circumstances. From her demeanor and teaching, George learned the essence of civility: balancing the warrior and peacemaker.

Mothers, remember Mary Washington. Without her, George Washington would not have become the father of this great nation. For this, we owe her a deep debt of gratitude. Be encouraged that you are raising men and women who, through God's grace, will go on to mighty deeds. Your efforts are not in vain.

## Samuel Adams

Not just famous for his contributions to making beer, the cousin of John Adams was one of the most vocal proponents of the American Revolution. A master propagandist, he stated, "While the People are virtuous they cannot be subdued; but when once they lose their Virtue they will be ready to surrender their Liberties to the first external or *internal* Invader. . . . If Virtue and Knowledge are diffused among the People, they will never be enslaved."

## The Civility of Two Enemies

It is difficult for some to imagine that one of America's shining examples of virtue and gentlemanly behavior during the nineteenth century was Abraham Lincoln's mortal enemy. But indeed, Robert E. Lee was a man of no less honor, gentility, and courage than his Union counterpart. Both men were prototypes of what we call the "virtuous warrior"; both maintained a profound respect for the other.

In *A Life of Gen. Robert E. Lee*, John Esten Cooke crystallizes history's assessment of the man who could marshal the violent inclinations of a thousand men, rally them to ferocious battle, but then command these same men thusly:

Soldiers! We have sinned against Almighty God. We have forgotten His signal mercies, and have cultivated a revengeful, haughty, and boastful spirit. We have not remembered that the defenders of a just cause should be pure in His eyes; that 'our times are in His hands,' and we have relied too much on our own arms for the achievement of our independence. God is our only refuge and our strength. Let us humble ourselves before Him. Let us confess our many sins, and beseech Him to give us a higher courage, a purer patriotism, and more determined will; that He will hasten the time when war, with its sorrows and sufferings, shall cease, and that He will give us a name and place among the nations of the earth.

As a deeply religious man, Lee understood that "the battle is the Lord's" and that even a warrior is called to both civility and to virtues beyond that of skilled brutality.

Another proof of Lee's impeccable civility and virtue was given by a Union soldier, who, at the end of the Civil War, noted Lee's graciousness:

Soon after his return to Richmond, in April, 1865, when the *immedicabile vulnus* of surrender was still open and bleeding, a gentleman was requested by the Federal commander in the city to communicate to General Lee the fact that he was about to be indicted in the United States courts for treason. In acquitting himself of his commission, the gentleman expressed sentiments of violent indignation at such a proceeding. But these feelings General Lee did not seem to share. The threat of arraigning him as a traitor produced no other effect upon him than to bring a smile to his lips; and, taking the hand of his friend, as the latter rose to go, he said, in his mildest tones: "We must forgive our enemies. I can truly say that not a day has passed since the war began that I have not prayed for them."

Lee's faith and virtue were sufficient to allow him to put away all bitterness and to be eager to forgive.

Abraham Lincoln was no less a gentleman. He was also one of the more intellectually honest presidents America has witnessed. Lincoln was keenly aware that all policies could—and should—be traced to a philosophical belief system, a set of larger ideals, or presuppositions.

On the one hand, he was skeptical of orthodox Christianity. He did not appear to rely, in stark contrast to Lee, on a transcendent Almighty but solely on an Enlightenment reason.[2]

One of Lincoln's chief virtues was integrity; he strongly emphasized uniting the real and the reputation. Lincoln quipped, "Character is like a tree and reputation like a shadow. The shadow is what we think of it; the tree is the real thing." Lincoln, like Lee, evidenced an eagerness to forgive. He did not want to punish the Southern states after the war, but prioritized the reunification of the Union.

## Pioneer Virtue

"We did not notice any difference in the service to any person. . . . Civility and kindness seemed to be in the air in those good old pioneer days." These are the words of Emily Grey, a daughter of former slaves, describing her time in the black enclave in Minnesota during the 1850s.

Life on the American frontier was decidedly different than that in New England, especially in the cities. Men and women in the Wild West were not judged by the same standards as those in more "civilized" society; they were not expected to behave like traditional gentlemen or ladies. Early historian Frederick Jackson Turner wrote of the unique character of the pioneer in his 1893 essay *The Significance of the Frontier in American History*:

> To the frontier the American intellect owes its striking characteristics. That coarseness and strength combined with acuteness and inquisitiveness; that practical, inventive turn of mind, quick to find expedients; that masterful grasp of material things, lacking in the artistic but powerful to effect great ends; that restless, nervous energy; that dominant individualism, working for good and for evil, and withal that buoyancy and exuberance which

---

[2] Although Enlightenment thought eventually results in intellectual and spiritual dead ends, Lincoln's life demonstrates that nonbelievers *can* both believe in and behave with gentlemanly and ladylike virtues just like their Christian counterparts.

comes with freedom—these are traits of the frontier, or traits called out elsewhere because of the existence of the frontier.

Clearly, the pioneer spirit was coarser and less refined than that of the East coast, where European sensibilities, gender roles, and expectations held a firm grip on men and women.

One such rough-and-tumble man was Jim Bridger, a well-known character in the early 1820s. The respect he earned from his fellow pioneers had nothing to do with refinement. Instead, he was described as "a very companionable man, over six feet tall, spare, straight as an arrow, agile, rawboned, and powerful of frame . . . hospitable and generous, and always trusted and respected." Physical strength, generosity, trustworthiness, and a hearty constitution were what made a pioneer gentleman.

Still, some men maintained a gentlemanly demeanor and temperance. Famed trapper and mountain man Jedediah Smith was known for his refusal to drink, or use tobacco. He did not take mistresses, refrained from cussing, and bathed regularly—somewhat of an anomaly in those parts.

## The Church and Virtue

In the first half of the nineteenth century, the United States witnessed a massive religious revival. Designated the Second Great Awakening,[3] the movement manifested various emphases across the country. Some geographic areas tended to refocus their efforts on theological concerns, but many denominations and individuals began considering the social consequences of the gospel and how it related to the infant Constitution.

Virtues were redefined as stemming from Scripture as their foundation. Christian writers and preachers extolled the virtues of industriousness, temperance, and civility. Temperance movements abounded; abolitionist groups sprang up in churches, especially in the North. Suffrage movements were born as well.

---

[3] The original Great Awakening had occurred in the early eighteenth century.

## History of Finishing Schools

The notion of finishing schools sounds quaint and completely out-moded to the twenty-first-century mentality. However, they were an important part of the development and maintenance of societal norms for ladies from the middle of the nineteenth century. Given two cultural facts—the transition from private to public school and the reality that women generally did not work outside of the home—finishing schools were instituted to offer young women an education that would primarily prepare them for domestic duties, including marriage, raising children, and running a household.

Finishing schools in large urban areas and that housed students from wealthier families tended to focus on etiquette, entertaining, and other skills that a lady could utilize to assist her future husband's professional or political aspirations. Most schools were started by organizations with affiliations to a church and had a strong emphasis on moral and civic ideals.

## Twentieth-Century Remnants

While there were growing exceptions, the arts and most cultural icons tended to continue reinforcing ladylike and gentlemanly characters and virtues. Many figures from popular culture, such as sports and movie stars, TV personalities, politicians, war heroes, and religious figures provided excellent role models for educating a generation of ladies and gentlemen. Examples from several spheres of public life follows.

## Television's Golden Age

In television's first half century, there were many shows that reinforced ladylike and gentlemanly characters and virtues. Just as any art form both alters and reflects society's beliefs and norms, television's "golden age" reflected the relative innocence, justice, mercy, courtesy, graciousness, and many other character traits that its viewers espoused. Arguably, the characters and story lines provided models for at least two generations to emulate. A few excellent examples personify how a medium in its infancy could be utilized both as art and as a means to an end—teaching, fostering, and upholding virtue.

Comedy and variety shows such as *The Red Skelton Show* and *Your Show of Shows* provide a stark contrast to today's biting, sarcastic comedic celebrations of the depraved. It is truly awe-inspiring to witness how true creative geniuses can produce laughs without dropping f-bombs or dragging the audience through the gutter.

Family programs like *Leave It to Beaver* may seem quaint and silly to modern viewers, but the characters were three-dimensional. The boys weren't Pinocchio-like robots who always did the right thing. They got their hands dirty, showed amazing creativity, and were endearing even in their foibles. They regularly goofed up; rather than simple mistakes or misunderstandings, they often revealed sinful, dishonorable inclinations. However, the Cleavers practiced mercy, patience, forbearance, and justice. The boys showed genuine repentance and learned real lessons; likely, the show's viewership did as well.

Children's shows like *Kukla, Fran, and Ollie* or the *Mickey Mouse Club* reveal a great deal about the baby boomer generation. Patience, innocent fun, respect for authority, and creativity were clear values reflected in these shows and their creators.

*Bonanza* and *Gunsmoke* were early Westerns that acted as simple but profound morality plays. One of the key themes in both shows was an intolerance toward defying the law. Sure, people did bad things, but they paid the penalty. Justice was upheld at all costs. At the same time, there was a sense that those who flaunted the law or defied proper authorities were dirty, even anathema. Additional virtues professed by central characters were the sanctity of marriage, personal sacrifice, and the centrality of God in one's life.[4]

## Virtue in American Athletics

Lou Gehrig was nicknamed "The Iron Horse" for his amazing strength and durability. The Hall of Fame first baseman played through dozens

---

[4] Today's Hollywood simply could not produce a show with Bible-believing characters, unless it was a vulgar comedy.

of injuries without complaint or drawing attention to himself. Lou was a man's man, but without the machismo shown by some modern-day athletes. Edward Herrmann, who portrayed him in film, opined, "There was nothing effete about him—he was just a quiet, sensitive man in need of emotional release. . . . What a gentle, powerful, decent man he was. No show, no razzmatazz."

Playing in Babe Ruth's shadow, Gehrig pushed himself to become a better player throughout his career. By all accounts, he was a team player, dedicated to winning and unimpressed by personal achievements. Sportswriter Marshall Hunt described Gehrig as being "unspoiled, without the remotest hint of ego, vanity, or conceit." With his Boy Scout aura, Gehrig inspired writers to describe him as a paragon of virtue in contrast to Ruth.

Gehrig did not need to brag. Playing by the old warrior's code, he allowed his talent and efforts to speak for themselves. He also let the sportswriters provide the acclaim rather than try to gobble up the attention and glory to puff up his ego. Would that more of today's sports heroes emulated Gehrig's humility, strength, courage, persistence, and simplicity . . .

## Musicians

There were many patriotic musicians in the early half of the twentieth century—just as there are today.[5] One gentleman who was well known for his charm and civil nature was Perry Como. Not only did his voice smack of virtue—as did his musical choices, including his famous rendition of *Ave Maria*—but his humility was ironically legendary. Contrasted with many artists of that and later eras, Como often underreported the number of albums he sold, so as to avoid being a braggart. He even refused to have several of his albums certified as achieving gold-record status.

Composer Ervin Drake said of the well-respected Como, "Occasionally someone like Perry comes along and won't 'go with the flow'

---

[5] For some reason, today's patriotic musicians seem to be concentrated primarily in the country genre.

and still prevails in spite of all the bankrupt others who surround him and importune him to yield to their values. Only occasionally."

Como and his wife[6] reportedly had a peaceful marriage; they remained married until her death at age eighty-four, which reportedly devastated him. Perry Como was a true gentleman.

## A Gentleman's Agreement

It is difficult to imagine Bob Hope or Charlie Chaplin experiencing "wardrobe malfunctions." It is equally difficult imagining Louis Armstrong suing Ticketmaster. Of course, artists concerned themselves with being paid fairly, but in many ways Armstrong was particularly gentlemanly. For example, he kept the same manager, Joe Glaser, for his entire career. Their relationship began with a handshake and was never consummated with a pen stroke on a dotted line.

Armstrong was well known for being a "clean performer." That is, while he enjoyed colorful jokes in private, he never cursed in front of children or in public performances. In fact, he adored children, never refused to sign autographs or encourage them, and even invited them to his home! He was also a prolific letter writer, often responding to fans with lengthy, handwritten letters, despite having no personal knowledge of the person. Armstrong seemed to adore and deeply appreciate his fans; indeed, it seemed that he had a deep love and respect for all humankind.

## Calvin Coolidge

Sometimes, being a gentleman means doing and speaking less. If that is the case, President Coolidge was the consummate gentleman. Known during his presidency (1923–1929) as "Silent Cal," Coolidge was a reticent man who tended to listen more than speak, and favored efficiency rather than verbosity when it came to dialogue. "The words of a president have an enormous weight," he once suggested, "and ought not to be used indiscriminately." Legend has it that

---

[6] First and only wife—it's sad to have to clarify that.

author Dorothy Parker once challenged "Silent Cal" at a party: "Mr. Coolidge, I've made a bet against a fellow who said it was impossible to get more than two words out of you." Without cracking a smile, Coolidge replied, "You lose."

Mr. Coolidge's presidency was marked by a decency that makes modern politicians appear filthy in comparison. After his son died in 1924, Coolidge understandably became grief-stricken. He pressed on with his campaign for reelection, however (election, to be more accurate; he became president when, as vice president, Warren Harding died in office). From all accounts, Coolidge never once said anything disparaging about his Democrat opponent, John W. Davis. In fact, he never referred to Davis during the campaign. Instead, he spoke of his own policies, his theory of government,[7] and his specific platform.[8]

Although Coolidge believed in limited government, he was not sedentary. One of his more active bursts stemmed from a crucial plank of his platform: a genuine support of civil rights. He actively appointed blacks to federal positions, fought for anti-lynching laws,[9] granted full US citizenship to American Indians, encouraged the formation of the Negro Industrial Commission, and frequently spoke out against racial and religious discrimination. His administration bravely took on the Ku Klux Klan, actively suppressing the group's influence—incredibly powerful during that period—and speaking eloquently in favor of those groups the Klan had been attempting to subjugate and disenfranchise.

Coolidge was a gentleman, possessing great courage and intellect, coupled with a measure of quiet civility.


## Early Film Star

Many readers know of Shirley Temple, one of the most famous stars of early film and one of the most endearing child stars of all time. She

---

[7] Smaller government, lower taxes, fewer regulations, more personal liberty: essentially the Tea Party platform.

[8] Coolidge won in a landslide.

[9] Vigorously opposed by Southern Democrats.

was a remarkable young lady with more grace, charm, and virtue than many of her adult contemporaries—and certainly more than many modern child stars. By all accounts, she was incredibly industrious, mature, and proud of good work.

Film directors were constantly impressed with her work ethic. Temple, for example, often protested and sometimes even refused to allow stunt doubles to perform her stunts for her. She trained with the adult actors for long hours in order to perform her own.

She owed much of her success to the strict discipline exacted by her parents, which she eventually internalized. After being punished for being silly or otherwise wasting a director's time, she was put in a black box—a sort of "sensory deprivation time-out." As cruel as this sounds, Temple recalled the value of early discipline: "This lesson of life was profound and unforgettable. Time is money. Wasted time means wasted money means trouble. Time spent working is more fun than standing in an icy black box and getting an earache."

After retiring from the movie industry, she forayed into politics. She did a stint as a representative at the United Nations, then was appointed ambassador to Ghana and then Czechoslovakia (being selected by both Democrat and Republican presidents). Eventually, because of her charm and civility (one diplomat called her "a walking charm school"), she became the first female to be appointed chief of protocol of the United States. Finally, Temple was one of the first women to speak publicly about breast cancer—and to reveal having had a radical mastectomy.

Shirley Temple isn't just an innocent drink for children. She was an innocent child who was and remained a true lady.

## On the Brink

Of course, there were numerous uncivil, ungentlemanly, unlady-like Americans in every sphere of life, from the birth of these United States through the modern era. Arguably, however, our nation seemed content to expect and encourage civility and people who lived honorably, while we openly discouraged individuals who rejected virtue or who displayed ungentlemanly or unladylike behavior. There seemed to be a consensus that civility and virtue were essential elements of the American character.

All of that changed in the latter half of the twentieth century. The foundations were already crumbling, although the destruction would not be fully realized until our lifetime.

## PART TWO

# The Quintessential Gentleman and Lady

NOW THAT WE HAVE established the historical development of the gentleman and the lady, we turn to examples of each in order to paint a good picture and to inspire us to honor and virtue. Remember, virtues cannot and should not simply be abstract, lofty principles to study or blindly admire. They are useless until beliefs, feelings, and thoughts compel one to action.

Still, one cannot learn how to cook by simply knowing a recipe's ingredients; one must watch a master chef create a masterpiece with that recipe. Similarly, the best way to learn and inspire virtue is through example. Luckily, God has not left us to invent our own virtues; they have been modeled for us by many men and women. Examples of virtuous gentlemen and ladies abound in great works of literature and in the annals of history. We can and should learn from them all.

Choosing a man and a woman for the roles of "quintessential gentleman" and his female counterpart was daunting. It forced us to consider the essential qualities of gentlemen and ladies, as well as determine which negative traits should automatically disqualify. For example, King David, despite his amazing persona, impressive faith, and heroic deeds, didn't make the grade. Forcibly committing adultery and arranging the death of the woman's husband was just too much.[1] Other choices, such as Martha Washington, were decent choices, but were simply too mundane or nondescript.

Other choices could be argued. We encourage others to contradict us and offer their own choices. We presume (and hope) that

---

[1] We call it the "Kennedy Disqualifier."

some will answer that their mother or father was the consummate gentleman or lady. Such debate should encourage further discussion about what makes a virtuous man or woman, and we hope that similar discussions will foster a common language among adults and between generations in order to define and support the virtues. ★

*Chapter Four*

★ ★ ★

# What Would Washington Do?

## (THE QUINTESSENTIAL GENTLEMAN)

*On the whole, his character was, in its mass, perfect, in nothing
bad, in few points indifferent; and it may truly be said, that never
did nature and fortune combine more perfectly to make a man
great, and to place him in the same constellation with whatever
worthies have merited from man an everlasting remembrance.*
> —THOMAS JEFFERSON REGARDING
> GEORGE WASHINGTON, *WRITINGS*

### Don Quixote

If you haven't read *Don Quixote* since high school, you may recall that
the novel's hero sets off on a great quest that is somewhat similar to

ours. Over time, he becomes obsessed with chivalry and envisions himself a warrior of virtue. He constantly reads books filled with stories of heroes whose deeds of superhuman strength and courage inspire him. The stories propel him to pursue heroic deeds and practice his virtue. Under a new name, he sets off on a general quest to seek adventure and any opportunity to live out his desire to be a noble, virtuous gentleman.

Don Quixote's quest and perceptions may seem a bit extreme to modern readers. In fact, the English language now uses the term *quixotic* to describe something or someone extravagantly chivalrous or impractically romantic. People just don't act like that. Better yet, no one *wants* to act like that. As virtuous as Don Quixote was, his extreme and absurd character could hardly inspire men to gentlemanly deeds.

What about someone a bit more realistic? A real human being, perhaps?

## No Man/Woman Is Perfect

Remember, no one person encapsulates all of what a gentleman or a lady is. Jesus is the only living example of perfect virtue. If we only considered flawless men and women, our cause would be hopeless. All men and women have stains on at least one section of their life's quilt or in at least one chapter of their life. Consider the tainted resumes of the following men who are considered great by most standards:

- Martin Luther King Jr. was a chronic philanderer.
- Mahatma Gandhi's actions resulted in the death of tens of thousands of his countrymen.
- John Adams's otherwise illustrious career was marred by pride, moodiness, and jealousy.
- Franklin Delano Roosevelt's stellar reputation was sullied by his internment of 120,000 Japanese and his rejection of black athletes after the 1936 Olympic Games.

Fortunately, we have been blessed with men and women throughout history whose lives reflect most of the character traits that we described in the previous chapter. Their biographies are enhanced by towering excellence in multiple virtues. Equally important, the blemishes on their life story are few and underwhelming.

We examined many men and women for this chapter. All of them had excellent resumes; several of them could arguably have been chosen. Two stood out above the rest: George Washington and Abigail Adams. This chapter examines the virtuousness of Washington, the man whom Americans were describing as "the Father of the Country" since before he was even that country's first president.

## George Washington

Before heaping praise on George Washington, we must take a moment to recognize that he was not a perfect man. The chief complaint frequently lodged against him is that he owned slaves. Despite wrestling with this issue throughout his life—and witnessing some of his fellow patriots free their slaves—he persisted in using slavery, no doubt in part to maintain his relatively comfortable lifestyle. There is no question that Washington did not behave with impeccable integrity regarding a practice that most would now consider abhorrent and anything but virtuous.

Shouldn't this disqualify him from our reverence and as a person to whom men should aspire? No. It would be unfair to judge Washington too harshly for this admittedly grievous sin. First, he was a product of his culture and his time. Most eighteenth-century Americans before the Revolution accepted slavery; it was, by and large, taken for granted. Slavery had, in fact, existed for thousands of years with little criticism. Washington was first and foremost a Virginian farmer; as such, his views on society and the necessary ingredients for seeking profit were no different from that of his fellow Virginians.

Second, Washington found the practice despicable. Many sources reveal that Washington desperately wanted to end the general practice of slavery. He also made plans during the last half of his life to free his own slaves after his death. He was the only well-known member of the Founding Fathers who were major slaveholders who freed his slaves. Thomas Jefferson did not; neither did Patrick Henry nor James Madison.

In the meantime, he was also known to have treated his slaves quite well, amply providing for their physical health and for their education after his death, so that they could obtain meaningful work after they were freed. He often gave his slaves extra food and financial bonuses for successful work, and offered them freedom to visit friends and relatives in nearby towns. He allowed more days off than most slave owners and expected less-grueling work. He relied less on corporal punishment and more on positive reward to induce a strong work ethic and good behavior. He was also one of the rare slave owners who permitted his slaves to keep arms, which they could use to hunt for additional food to eat or sell for profit.

Should Washington's persistent slave ownership prove a blemish on his resume? Absolutely. On the other hand, a thorough study of George Washington reveals a character of innumerable commendable qualities and impressive virtues. In John Rhodehamel's study of Washington's role in early American consciousness, *The Great Experiment: George Washington and the American Republic*, he concluded that

> the real source of Washington's greatness lay in his moral character. Washington was a man of virtue, but this virtue was not given to him by nature. He had to work for it, to cultivate it, and his contemporaries knew that he did. Washington was a self-made hero, and this impressed an eighteenth-century enlightened world that put great stock in men controlling both their passions and their destinies.

Pulitzer Prize winner Gordon Wood goes even further, suggesting that Washington

> did come from another world. And his countrymen know it almost before he died in 1799. Washington was the only truly classical hero we have ever had. He was admired as a classical hero in his own lifetime. . . . He was well aware of his reputation; that awareness of his heroic stature was crucial to Washington. It affected nearly everything he did for the rest of his life.

*Physical Appearance*: We have already made the argument that a man's physical appearance does not make him a great, good, or virtuous man. However, an impressive physical stature can certainly augment his reputation, provided that it is consistent with his internal character. Consider it the sprinkles on a cake's frosting.

A fellow officer described Washington's physical appearance in this way:

[S]traight as an Indian, measuring six feet two inches in his stockings, and weighing 175 pounds. . . . His frame is padded with well-developed muscles, indicating great strength. His bones and joints are large, as are his hands and feet. He is wide shouldered but has not a deep or round chest; is neat waisted, but is broad across the hips and has rather long legs and arms. His head is well-shaped, though not large, but is gracefully poised on a superb neck. A large and straight rather than a prominent nose; blue gray penetrating eyes which are widely separated and overhung by a heavy brow. His face is long rather than broad, with high round cheek bones, and terminates in a good firm chin. He has a clear though rather a colorless pale skin which burns with the sun. A pleasing and benevolent though a commanding countenance, dark brown hair which he wears in a cue. His mouth is large and generally firmly closed, but which from time to time discloses some defective teeth. His features are regular and placid with all the muscles of his face under perfect control, though flexible and expressive of deep feeling when moved by emotions. In conversation, he looks you full in the face, is deliberate, deferential, and engaging. His voice is agreeable rather than strong. His demeanor at all times composed and dignified. His movements and gestures are graceful, his walk majestic, and he is a splendid horseman.

The Marquis de Chastellux, a French officer who knew Washington well, noted that "[T]he strongest characteristic of this respectable man is the perfect harmony which reigns between the physical and moral qualities which compose his personality. . . . It is not my intention to exaggerate. I wish only to express the impression General Washington has left on my mind, the idea of a perfect whole."

Again, none of this made Washington a gentleman, but his physical appearance certainly intensified his reputation as an impressive man and magnified all of his other magnificent traits.

*Commitment to Family*: When Washington was twenty-six, he married Martha Dandridge Custis, who had been widowed two years prior and had two children. It was apparent that his marriage was of the utmost importance to him, as he wrote twenty-five years later, "I have always considered marriage as the most interesting event of one's life, the foundation of happiness or misery." While only one letter between the two has survived, several of Washington's letters to others refer to his wife in nothing but the most caring and tender terms.

In terms of Martha's two children, George immediately adopted them as his own. Not a distant father by any means, he was intimately involved in decisions regarding their education, health, and other matters. He personally interviewed the children's tutors. He also referred to them lovingly in letters.

There is evidence that Washington's patterns of amusements significantly narrowed upon marriage and fatherhood. For example, he no longer attended cockfights and rarely joined hunting expeditions. The family, instead, spent time together exploring the countryside, especially the mountains and springs of Virginia.[1]

Washington's familial care extended past his nuclear family. He managed and provided for the financial care of his aging widowed mother. There are several letters of correspondence between him and his brothers that make clear his concern for them. Finally, he included his adopted grandchildren in his will: "The two whom we have reared from their earliest infancy, namely: Eleanor Parke Custis, and George Washington Parke Custis."

Given his position of power and his overwhelming responsibilities, plus the tendency during that era for most fathers to be somewhat distant and uninvolved, it would be understandable if he had committed less of his time and devotion to family. But a consummate gentleman puts his family first. Such is Washington's legacy.

*Graciousness*: Washington's faith in God[2] and his reliance on the Bible in developing and guiding character helped form his practice of

---

[1] Quality time indeed.

[2] Washington was definitively a believing and practicing Christian, not a Deist, as has been proposed by many secular—and hopelessly biased—biographers.

forgiveness. One of his specific criticisms of King George of England was that the king was neither able nor willing to forget or forgive. There are several chastening examples of Washington's gracious heart, all of which increased his reputation as both a great and a good man.

Before the war, Washington had a childhood friend named Bryan Fairfax. During the Revolutionary War, Fairfax sided with the Tories (those allied with King George, often called Loyalists) against Washington, who took it as a personal and political affront. After the war, Fairfax asked Washington for forgiveness. Whether his plea was born from genuine repentance or self-preservation, Washington eagerly forgave him.

Washington's stepchildren's tutor was a protestant minister named Jonathon Boucher. The man whom he entrusted to teach his children verbally criticized their stepfather; on a handful of occasions, the criticism were withering and personal. Washington gently confronted Boucher, corrected some of the reverend's misperceptions, and humbly asked him to reconsider his perception. In the end, Boucher begged Washington's forgiveness; by all accounts, forgiveness came swiftly and eagerly.

Finally, the Reverend Jacob Duche, who had led the first Congress's prayer, utterly rejected Washington's patriotic leanings and refused to support the Revolution. True to form, Washington forgave him without reservation. The two maintained a peaceful relationship after the war.

One story in particular demonstrates the depth of his graciousness. While Washington was commander-in chief of the Continental Army, an infamous Loyalist named Michael Widman was captured and brought into camp. Widman had long been suspected of carrying aid and information to the British. During his court-martial, it was determined that his influence had been particularly damaging to the American army. He was found guilty of spying and was sentenced to be hanged.

The evening before the scheduled hanging, a well-known patriot named Peter Miller requested an audience with Washington. Washington accepted the request. Mr. Miller asked Washington to pardon Mr. Miller, despite the fact that he had been found guilty of treason.

Washington was initially shocked, recounting for Miller the damage that Widman had done to the patriot cause. Washington insisted that it would not be wise to show leniency with traitors, even if the request was to save Mr. Miller's friend.

Mr. Miller quickly corrected General Washington's misconception, telling him that Widman was no friend but was his bitterest enemy, having persecuted Miller, beaten him, and spit in his face. Washington expressed his confusion, asking why he should forgive such a wretched enemy. Miller's response was that because Jesus had forgiven him so much, he wanted to reflect that forgiveness to someone who had grieved him.

One recounting of this episode suggests that Washington turned away, walked into the adjacent room, and within seconds returned with a written pardon for Michael Widman. Handing it to Mr. Miller, he added, "Thank you for this example of Christian charity."

Even in the midst of war, where killing and executing justice are behaviors reflecting high virtue, Washington did not reject virtues of equal (or greater) importance.

*Manners and Courtesy*: From childhood, Washington committed himself to behaving with impeccable manners. Rhodehamel suggested that "he was obsessed with behavior in a proper and dignified manner." As a young man, he was blessed to have access to a sixteenth-century French essay translated into English that enumerated the behaviors that men should emulate as their code of personal conduct. He copied these into his *Rules of Civility*.

Here are some examples:

- Every action in company ought to be with some sign of respect to those present.
- Show not yourself glad at the misfortune of another, though he were your enemy.
- Being to advise or reprehend anyone, consider whether it ought to be in public or in private, presently or at some other time, also in what terms to do it; and in reproving show no signs of choler, but do it with sweetness and mildness.
- Use no reproachful language against anyone, neither curses nor revilings.

- When another speaks, be attentive yourself, and disturb not the audience. If any hesitate in his words, help him not, nor prompt him without being desired; interrupt him not, nor answer him till his speech be ended.
- Speak no evil of the absent, for it is unjust.

A quick scan of the current political environment reveals that many of our leaders fall far short of these standards.

*Honesty*: Every student knows the story of George Washington and the cherry tree. Because he "cannot tell a lie," he risks his father's disappointment and wrath. Whether this tale is all myth or it contains a germ of truth, it reveals a perception of Washington as a man of stellar truthfulness. One of his life's mantras was "For there is but one straight course, and that is to seek truth and pursue it steadily."

One of the most important evidences of a man's honesty is his enduring reputation. If any fault could damage a man's ability to secure and maintain the respect of his peers, it is a tendency toward falseness. Washington's reputation—which was formed and fed by all the Founding Fathers, as well as friends and enemies on both sides of the Atlantic—was impeccable. All of Washington's pronouncements were regarded as true. Even his one-time enemy Jonathan Boucher admitted that "in his moral character he is regular, temperate, strictly just and honest."

By the end of the Revolution, his stellar reputation preceded him in every relationship and endeavor. His reputation endures long after his death. Despite scores of historians scouring letters and the reports of his contemporaries, no scandal has tarnished his reputation as a man who never bore false witness. There is no "Mt. Vernon-Gate" or "Valley Forge-Gate" on Washington's resume.

*Masculinity*: There was nothing effeminate about Washington. He was a man's man. While he was accomplished at dancing and horsemanship—two activities considered masculine at the time—his wrestling skills were legendary in his home state of Virginia. His diaries fondly describe episodes of hunting, fishing, canoeing, and other competitive, typically manly pursuits. He was also trained as a swordsman.

*Courage*: Washington was not famous for his military prowess during the Revolution. In fact, many historians have suggested that his raw skills as a general were underwhelming at best. No one, on the other hand, ever questioned Washington's bravery. Of the many virtues that Thomas Jefferson praised, he extolled this in Washington: "He was incapable of fear, meeting personal dangers with the calmest unconcern."

The man who eulogized Washington, Fisher Ames, wrote that from his earliest days,

> the soul of Washington [was] exercised to danger; and on the first trial, as on every other, it appeared firm in adversity, cool in action, undaunted, self-possessed. . . . We have seen him display as much valor as gives fame to heroes, and as consummate prudence as insures success to valor; fearless of dangers that were personal to him, hesitating and cautious when they affected his country; preferring fame before safety or repose, and duty before fame.

Years before Washington became known as the father of our country, he was a Virginian soldier with a growing reputation. He was a trusted aide of famed British general Edward Braddock and survived several significant battles. In attempting to push the French army out of Pennsylvania, he reportedly had four bullets pass through his coat and had two horses killed under him. He reputation as a highly courageous soldier did not come from polishing buttons or digging trenches.

*Self-control*: Washington was known as a deliberate, careful, even stoic man. His reputation for speaking at a measured pace, as if he were constantly filtering his words, was legendary. People who were unfamiliar with him sometimes wondered if he was hiding his true emotions. But Washington's deliberate nature was neither accidental nor inherited. It was practiced and honed over decades. His deep passions were always under strict, disciplined control. Almost always.

Biographer Paul Zall writes in *Washington on Washington*, "His dignity and self-esteem were such that to a superficial observer he appeared to be cold. Actually he was emotional, tender, and capable of outbursts of violence. An iron discipline, which he imposed upon himself all his life, kept a leash on his passions." One fellow soldier noted, "His infrequent outbursts of anger were legendary."

Washington himself proclaimed the importance of deliberation before action: "To deliberate maturely, and execute promptly is the way to conduct it to advantage. With me, it has always been a maxim."

*Humility*: Washington lived in the same era as Napoleon—a military general who became emperor following his military success. He and the rest of the world were keenly aware of the many examples of victorious generals—such as Julius Caesar and Oliver Cromwell—who refused to give up power. It took an abiding sense of humility to willingly give up power after winning the Revolutionary War. He could easily have ridden the winds of power and support he had from the people and set himself up as king or dictator.

Instead, Washington eagerly ceded power and returned to his home. Pulitzer Prize–winner Gordon Wood called this "the greatest act of his life, the one that made him internationally famous." (*The Radicalism of the American Revolution*)

But Washington sincerely desired for all those in his military to return to a peaceful existence. Even the humiliated and defeated King George III predicted that Washington's relinquishing power would make him "the greatest man in the world." His compatriot Thomas Jefferson declared that "the moderation and virtue of a single character . . . probably prevented this revolution from being closed, as most other have been, by a subversion of that liberty it was intended to establish."

Another important example of Washington's humility was how heavily he relied on his peers for advice when making difficult decisions. There was no pretense with Washington that he knew everything or was above asking for help. There are many occasions in which Washington struggled with a moral, ethical, or political decision, reaching out to friends and political confidants.

Finally, Washington was not a braggart. He was accused by some of being shy, but he never appeared eager to recount his exploits or accomplishments as a war hero. One friend recalled: "Most people say and do too much. Washington . . . never fell into this common error."

*Service*: There is no doubt that a big part of Washington's heart was that of a servant. His roles as Founding Father, military leader, father of a new nation, and father of his stepchildren all reveal a heart for service. Washington went a step further.

To Washington, performing his Christian duties was the pinnacle of his virtue. "While we are zealously performing the duties of good Citizens and soldiers, we certainly ought not to be inattentive to the higher duties of Religion. To the distinguished Character of Patriot, it should be our highest Glory to add the more distinguished Character of Christian."

There was a point in Washington's military career when he saw little hope of a prosperous commission in the king's army. His attention shifted to serving his fellow countrymen and earning their respect. In a letter to his friend in 1755, he wrote,

> For here, if I gain any credit, or if I am entitled to the least coun-
> tenance or esteem, it must be from serving my country without
> fee or reward; for I can truly say, I have no expectation of either.
> To merit its esteem, and the good will of my friends, is the sum
> of my ambition, having no prospect of attaining a commission.

*Faithfulness*: Is there any doubt that George Washington was a faithful president, husband, father, and friend?

Even before his involvement in the Revolutionary War, Washington demonstrated remarkable faithfulness in his duties. As a colonel and commander-in-chief of the Virginia militia, he often found himself with too few men to defend his state from Indian raids. At one point, he became ill and dejected. Still, he wrote that "no man that ever was employed in a public capacity has endeavored to discharge the trust reposed in him with greater honesty and more zeal for the country's interest."

After the Revolutionary War was won and he had retired to Mount Vernon, Washington was begged to head the Virginia delegation at the Constitutional Convention. He became violently ill shortly after.

In the end, Washington recognized that this was an opportunity as well as a duty—to participate in something far greater than himself and his own comfort. Not only did he play a key role in the convention but his presence had an enormous effect on the opinion of his peers and the general public. James Madison concluded about him:

"To forsake the honorable retreat to which he had retired and risk the reputation he had so deservedly acquired, manifested a zeal for the public interest that could, after so many and illustrious services, scarcely have been expected of him."

After the Revolution, many of the soldiers who had fought and never been paid determined not to relinquish their arms until the fledgling government kept their promise to provide for them. Alexander Hamilton wrote, knowing Washington quite well, that "his virtue, his patriotism, and firmness would, it might be depended upon, never yield to any dishonorable or disloyal plans into which he might be called; that he would sooner suffer himself to be cut to pieces."

George Washington always kept his word and his obligations.

*Self-sacrifice*: All of the Founding Fathers sacrificed when they decided to declare independence from England. All knew that they not only were sacrificing financially and risking financial ruin but were literally risking their necks. Washington's risk was no less than his fellow countrymen.

After the Revolution, Washington could easily have become king. In fact, many Americans—even some fellow patriots—wanted him to become just that. But Washington was not at all interested in such an increase in power. By declining to (understandably) feed his ego, he evidenced his greater desire for a peaceful republic. He retired from his nearly all-powerful post to retire from politics.

Of course, he was brought back into the political maelstrom to help lead the Continental Congress, which was busy forming the new government and the constitution of the United States. As exhausting as this work was, Washington felt it was his duty. Throughout his life, he evidenced a singular commitment to carrying out his duties.

*Integrity*: Integrity is behaving in accordance with one's beliefs. This most difficult of virtues was something for which Washington strove throughout his life. It was what gnawed at his conscience—what he called "that little spark of celestial fire"—and drove him to will his slaves free after his death.

Washington sought to align his private and public character; he was often willing to sacrifice his political or personal gain in order to earn the respect of his peers, superiors, and soldiers. In fact, he took it as a great insult for someone to question whether his public character matched his personal character.

## A Personal Note

Studying the life of George Washington has not only been educational; it has humbled me (Dr. Paterno). While I always knew he was a great man, I had not been keenly aware of how noble and good a man he was. I hardly expect to be called into service as crucial as Washington's, and I doubt I will have the opportunity to achieve a fraction of his greatness. Yet his qualities—especially courtesy and self-discipline—move me.

As a Christian, my standard is Christ; I am called to become more Christlike and to rely on God's sanctifying grace to equip me. Part of that equipping, I am convinced, comes from witnessing heroes of virtue and modeling my life after them. Studying Washington's words and deeds has convinced me to work harder to emulate several of his virtues.

## What Would Washington Do?

Washington, throughout his life, was a man guided by principles—carefully selected and long-practiced. Our leaders would do very well to mirror his leadership, which was, even in Washington's day, filled with division and fierce competition. One of these principles in particular speaks to our current political culture. In a letter to Boston Selectman, Washington wrote:

> In every act of my administration, I have sought the happiness of my fellow-citizens. My system for the attainment of this object has uniformly been to overlook all personal, local, and partial considerations: to contemplate the United States, as one great whole: to confide, that sudden impressions, when erroneous, would yield to candid reflection: and to consult only the substantial and permanent interests of our country.

Washington was not inclined to use his positions of power to dole out personal favors, as is common in our current political landscape.[3]

In another letter, Washington wrote,

> Having undertaken the task, from a sense of duty, no fear of encountering difficulties and no dread of losing popularity, shall ever deter me from pursuing what I conceive to be the true interests of my country.

Washington did not focus on political polls; rather, his singular focus was on service of God and his fellow countrymen.

Imagine what our nation would be like if our leaders had such a singular focus. ★

---

[3] Waivers for "Washington Care" would have been unthinkable.

*Chapter Five*

★ ★ ★

# Abigail Adams: Trailblazer of True Womanhood

*Great necessities call out great virtues.*

—ABIGAIL ADAMS

*If particular care and attention is not paid to the ladies, we are determined to foment a rebellion, and will not hold ourselves bound by any laws in which we have no voice or representation.*
—ABIGAIL ADAMS, LETTER TO JOHN ADAMS IN 1776

## Mrs. President

Today, heroes are few and far between, especially for women. Historically, though, many women come to mind, but none quite so "bull's-eye" as the understated, eloquent, poetic, long-suffering, outspoken, passionate, patriotic Abigail Adams. Her life was a virtual dichotomy of situations, and the irony of her personality is, in every sense of the word, intriguing.

She married her third cousin, John Adams, who became the second president of the United States. She was the mother of John Quincy Adams, the sixth president, as well. She was the first Second Lady of the United States, and the second

Abigail Adams

First Lady of the United States. She was so active in her husband's presidency that many referred to her as "Mrs. President."

A prolific letter writer, she imparted her strong opinions to her husband, even rebuking the nature of men in her letter to him as he contemplated the Declaration of Independence. Her letters also provide an up close and intimate perspective on the American Revolutionary War that exists nowhere else. Her mother died young of smallpox, and Abigail was too ill to attend school; thus, she took her education upon herself, utilizing books in the home to self-direct an education rivaling any aristocratic education of her day. Her unschooled, erudite knowledge of poetry, literature, government, and politics was what drew John to marry her initially, and what kept him seeking her help with political matters throughout his career.

## Feminist or Femme Fatale?

She could be labeled a feminist, but not without recognizing her submitted spirit to her important role as wife, and mother, and traditional homemaker. When her husband was away for months at a time, she fiercely attended the harsh duties of the farm while raising her own children, and even her grandchildren at one point. The photos of her lavished in elaborate silks and linens stand in sharp contrast with the image of her baling grain, cleaning stalls, fertilizing soil, and other gritty necessities. She demonstrated the flexible and transformative nature of a real lady—able to move gracefully from one role to the other; Abigail was the quintessential multitasker.

Abigail took her role as First Lady very well in stride. In spite of her self-education, many would argue that she was the more intellectually elegant member of the dyad. She used her eloquence to encourage rather than strive against the political success of her husband. She demonstrated a command of the written word, an understanding of sovereignty, a submission to her role of servant-leadership, her willingness to rise up as John's helpmate, and her absolute obedience and allegiance to her God in this new role. Her words to her husband inspire as he accepted the nomination for president of the United States, on the eighth day of February, 1797:

> The sun is dressed in brightest beams, to give thy honors to the day. And may it prove an auspicious prelude to each ensuing season. You have this day to declare yourself head of a nation. And now, O Lord, my God, thou hast made thy servant ruler over the people. Give unto him an understanding heart, that he may know how to go out and come in before this great people; that he may discern between good and bad. For who is able to judge this thy so great a people? Were the words of a royal sovereign; and not less applicable to him who is invested with the chief magistracy of a nation, though he wear not a crown, nor the robes of royalty.
>
> My thoughts and my meditations are with you, though personally absent; and my petitions to Heaven are, that "the things which make for peace may not be hidden from your eyes." My feelings are not those of pride or ostentation, upon the occasion. They are solemnized by a sense of the obligations, the important trusts, and numerous duties connected with it. That you may be enabled to discharge them with honor to yourself, with justice and impartiality to your country, and with satisfaction to this great people, shall be the daily prayer of your A.A.

Her life was pregnant with experiences many of us will only ever dream of, but it was far from the stuff of fairy tales. Abigail experienced life richly, but none of this came without personal sacrifice. Her life was full and complex, pitted with the holes of a life of risk, submission, and true obedience to God. Her risks cost her greatly, as risks often do. In history books, we read about triumph and victory, but in her quiet moments, she must have had to re-commit herself again and again through diligent prayer to maintain her pace and passion.

## Complexities

Abigail endured tragedy and grief as a mother, in addition to the pride of raising a future president of the United States. She had six babies in ten years, only three of whom survived for long into adulthood. One baby, Elizabeth, died at birth, while another, Susanna, lived only two years. Her namesake, nicknamed "Nabby," died a prolonged and painful death of breast cancer in young adulthood.

Life was not always the luxury portrayed in photos of Abigail Adams. Living as a single mother for much of her childbearing and childrearing years, one can only wonder how she managed the farming, educating, homemaking, corresponding, policy-making, and playing the role of helpmate to the most powerful (and some would say the most cantankerous) man in the country as he worked diligently to establish and organize the fledgling United States.

Grace is manifested in many ways; some are mentioned above. Grace also means dignity in the face of betrayal. Abigail Adams described great disappointment when her friend and correspondent, Thomas Jefferson, ultimately betrayed her and her husband by opposing her husband politically. Every political wife knows this betrayal, though the history books often overlook her role. Mrs. Adams demonstrated her graciousness once again when she, in later years, forgave, then reestablished, her friendship and correspondence with Thomas Jefferson despite his earlier painful betrayal.

She fluently transformed from farm wife to First Lady like a consummate professional. She was the first First Lady to occupy the White House, where she not only helped develop and design the White House (then called "The President's House") but also took an active role as policy advisor during her husband's administration.

When her husband lost the election to Thomas Jefferson after his first term, she continued her activism through her writing and speaking out on the issues of the day, including women's rights, slavery, property rights, and her abiding faith in God.

Abigail Adams's fame is justified for many reasons, but perhaps her outspoken nature on the topic of women is the most well-known. Young blogger Madeleine Macaulay had the following to say about her hero:

> Abigail Adams is known, to this day, for her knowledge and dedication regarding politics and freedom. Many times, in our History classes, we hear about the letters she sent to her husband, President John Adams, while he was away. The vast majority of her letters were filled with input concerning the welfare of the Colonies, and though many of her letters were filled with great incite, there was one in particular that her independent and revolutionist spirit was greatly exhibited.

On March 31, 1776, Abigail Adams sent her husband a letter. She began by asking him about his whereabouts and the political situation, and then protested about the decisions coming into Virginia. Abigail, at that time, carried her writings to the discussion of the smallpox epidemic, letting John know that their family was not hit by it, but that she was a bit worried. She then went on telling him about the current state of affairs in their town, giving him a "better than expected" report.

After Abigail finished telling John about the family's welfare, she then segued to a new topic, one that sparks much interest in my mind. She discusses women's rights. It was at that point she made it clear that she was aware of the deals that were going on, regarding the Declaration of Independence, and she was sure to give a shout-out to women. But little did she know that those few lines would go down in history, referred to as "Remember the Ladies." She wrote:

> I long to hear that you have declared an independency—and by the way in the new Code of Laws which I suppose it will be necessary for you to make, I desire you would remember the Ladies, and be more generous and favorable to them than

your ancestors. Do not put such unlimited power into the hands of the Husbands. Remember all Men would be tyrants if they could. If particular care and attention is not paid to the Ladies we are determined to foment a Rebellion, and will not hold ourselves bound by any Laws in which we have no voice, or Representation. That your Sex are Naturally Tyrannical is a Truth so thoroughly established as to admit of no dispute, but such of you as wish to be happy willingly give up the harsh title of Master for the more tender and endearing one of Friend. Why then, not put it out of the power of the vicious and the Lawless to use us with cruelty and indignity with impunity. Men of Sense in all Ages abhor those customs, which treat us only as the vassals of your Sex. Regard us then as Beings placed by providence under your protection and in imitation of the Supreme Being make use of that power only for our happiness.

Abigail courageously took a fair hammer to a man's pride and did not hesitate to make an explicit threat of a women's rebellion. She took it even further, using her husband's words against him, saying, "We will not hold ourselves bound by any Laws in which we have no voice, or Representation." The trained ear will recognize this phrase's similarity to what her husband would encourage Jefferson to list as a grievance in the Declaration of Independence: "No Taxation without Representation." Abigail certainly made a strong case. Utilizing logic and common sense, she dared to call out the hypocrisy that was being exposed.

Abigail Adams was valiant. When the government told her to sit down and be quiet, she refused to be silent, and when most women were scared, she displayed her independent spirit. Abigail Adams was a woman of integrity, honesty, and fearlessness. She was an influential voice in the women's suffrage movement, because although it was hundreds of years before women's suffrage, she surely planted a seed, a wanting, and a vision for independence. After a hundred years of lying dormant, that seed began blossoming into liberty and equality for women.

Ultimately, her husband did not take her advice, rejecting Abigail's "extraordinary code of laws" for women. However, he later validated her input when he wrote, "We have only the name of masters, and rather than give up this, which would completely subject us to the despotism of the petticoat, I hope General Washington and all our brave heroes would fight." Though it is impossible to know the extent of the political pressure flow of the day, one can only imagine that Abigail's involvement shaped what was an otherwise unspeakable suggestion for women's roles in the political fiber of America.

## Political Activist

Mrs. Adams also understood freedom in ways many of her day would deny in the face of slavery. She took bold, strong stands for freedom, even assisting a young black boy in enrolling in school despite objections of the political establishment of her day. She expressed sincere doubt that most of the Virginians had the "passion for Liberty" they proclaimed to have, as they "deprive[d] their fellow Creatures" of freedom. She argued that he was a "Free man as much as any of the young men and merely because his face is black, is he to be denied instruction? How is he to be qualified to procure a livelihood? . . . I have not thought it any disgrace to my self to take him into my parlor and teach him both to read and write." Her son John Quincy would take up the bitter fight against slavery, representing black slaves in the famed *Amistad* case.

In an age of legalism, especially regarding the role of women in the church, again, Abigail was careful to point out that faith needed to be relational, a heart issue between God and man himself. "When will Mankind be convinced that true Religion is from the Heart, between Man and his creator, and not the imposition of Man or creeds and tests?" Note that she did not obsess, as some women do, over the word *man* or the submission to her Father God. She took such menial detail in stride; instead, she looked to see her own failures when held to the standard of Christ himself. Instead of dabbling in the menial activity of changing words like *man* or *father*, she looked at the big picture of how she could uplift and edify rather than tear down and rip apart for selfish, legalistic reasons. Rather than question the submission to her husband, as decried in the Bible, she looked at where she could give more, serve more, make a difference for freedom, and set the bar for women in America and beyond, *in* their roles as wives, mothers, politicians, helpmates, teachers, activists, advocates, and even communicators.

## Endings and Legacies

Abigail Adams died on October 28, 1818 of typhoid fever at the age of seventy-three. Even in her passing, her eloquence and honor were passed forward in her last written words: "Do not grieve, my friend, my dearest friend. I am ready to go. And John, it will not be long." Loving to her friends in her passing, urging them not to grieve, and passing along her faith in her ultimate arrival into eternal life with her beloved, John, must have given such comfort to those who lost their strong maternal figure that day. That was, perhaps, the strongest testimony to her honor—that she cared to comfort even at the end of her days, and beyond, and to leave a legacy of love and eternal faith in what is good. Would that God would bless us all with similar courage and grace.

Contemplation of the life of Abigail Adams can't help but elicit thoughts of the Proverbs 31 woman, who led and followed, served and set standards, indulged and abstained, spoke and refrained, all when appropriate. Such discipline is rare today. We have become victims to the messages the media imposes, sometimes to the degree that we cannot even see the error of our ways. Perhaps what sets Abigail Adams apart was not so much her ability to do the right thing but rather her ability to know when to do what—her discernment. There were network news outlets to tell Abigail Adams what to think; perhaps that offered her an advantage. Maybe therein lies our challenge as a society today. Perhaps we need to sharpen our critical thinking skills most of all so that we can know when we are called to be activists, when we are called to be still, and when we are called to step outside our comfort zone and transform into the image of God's latest call for our lives.

I cannot pretend to know, but it is my guess that Abigail would first warn about legalism, or man's interpretation of God's Word. She would warn against using our children, our struggles, or our situation in life as an excuse not to be politically active, as well. She understood that beneath her duty to her children and her husband, and at the very essence of her love for God, was activism and civic engagement. She pushed herself and gave all she had to fight for what she believed in.

Again, I can't know, but I suppose that Abigail would not claim she was right on every political position. I think she would instead say that she prayed that her relentless pursuit of the truth was her greatest moral victory. My guess is that if she were to claim righteousness in any area of her life, it would be in that she knew her flaws well, and did her best not to inject them into the lives of those she tried to serve.

Last, if we were able to ask her, I think Abigail would encourage us to live boldly, to take risks. She certainly did, and her life is a legacy because of that. Our lives should be lived to the fullest, giving all we can, when we can, wherever we can, to whomever we can. This is the legacy of a lady.

We can all be inspired by the gift of a life well lived in that of Abigail Adams. She loved faith and freedom, while applying her passion to her work in that regard. She enjoyed the beauty of art and interior design, and the indulgence of poetry, and yet she could philosophically articulate the rigors of politics and public policy, probably often with a diapered or nursing baby on her hip. However flawed and sinful, she used all her strength to advance the notions and principles she believed were right, and to leave a legacy behind for those who loved her, and even those who would never hear her name. That, I believe, best defines a true lady.

# PART THREE

## The Exodus of the Lady and the Gentleman

WHAT HAPPENED? WHAT DREW our nation away from believing in virtue, supporting it, transmitting these ideals to their children, and sharing a common vocabulary when discussing them? How did the term *gentleman* become so debased? How did the notion of the *lady* get twisted into a dirty word? Something grabbed our nation by the throat and squeezed the words out of our collective voice box.

Our central thesis stems from the belief that our nation was founded on two competing principles. First, our nation was designed to support virtue, without forcing it. Second, our nation has consisted more or less of virtuous people, whose deep flaws, combined with a natural benign self-interest, encouraged a drift away from virtue. Our civic leaders, then, must be people of virtue, who must create and execute laws to contain our deep flaws and self-interest. At the same time, our society must work independently to foster the morality and virtue of our people. If it does not, government will be forced to either enact greater measures to control the people or, conversely, acquiesce to the virtueless whims of the people. Our nation is witnessing both of these phenomena to a growing extent.

Our primary argument is that three ideas, forces, or movements have contributed to this decline: atheism, liberalism, and radical feminism. These are not utterly distinct, insofar as they all arise from the same presuppositions. They are facets of the same three-sided coin—a currency that must be rejected and replaced with truer and healthier ideas. ★

# Chapter Six

★ ★ ★

# Atheism: The Crack Cocaine of the People

*At that time the humans still knew pretty well when a thing was proved and when it was not; and if it was proved they really believed it. They still connected thinking with doing and were prepared to alter their way of life as the result of a chain of reasoning. But what with the weekly press and other such weapons, we have largely altered that.*

—C.S. Lewis, *The Screwtape Letters*

*I had no idea, then, quite why so many of the older generation had set their faces so hard against religious belief. I was quite shocked when I later discovered the true state of affairs. They did not know half the things they claimed to know. Their faith in science was an attempt to replace the Christian faith, ruined by wars and disillusion, with a new all-embracing certainty.*

—Peter Hitchens

## Atheism Defined

For the purpose of this discussion, it is important to be clear what atheism is and is not. Formal *atheism* specifies a lack of belief in any and all gods—essentially, a lack of theism. In modern lexicon, atheism can also denote a positive disbelief in or rejection of a particular god, such as the God of the Bible. We should also mention that *agnosticism*, a close cousin of atheism, normally refers to the conviction that one cannot be certain about the existence of any god.

## Carl Sagan Throws Down the Gauntlet

Carl Sagan was an astrophysicist who produced and wrote a television series entitled *Cosmos: A Personal Journey*. Airing on PBS in 1980, the thirteen-part series was one of the most watched television programs of all time, reaching just short of a billion people. While atheism had certainly existed in the public sphere beforehand, *Cosmos* elevated atheist dogma and its materialistic view of the universe into public view like nothing ever had.

In the introduction, Sagan pronounced that "the cosmos is all that is or ever was or ever will be." This chapter aims to highlight the consequences of this belief. Specifically, we argue that an atheistic worldview and its corollaries have resulted in a degradation of humanity and the virtues inherent in ladies and gentlemen.

## Why Does Atheism Exist?

We believe that the primary motivation for a belief in atheism parallels the primary motivation for *all* sin: a desire to be one's own god or master. The first sin of our forefathers was hatched from a desire to experience this: "Your eyes will be opened, and you will be like God, knowing good and evil" (Genesis 3:5). The serpent's temptation offered Adam and Eve something they believed they did not have, but should. After all, who would want their eyes closed to something as wondrous as the special knowledge that had been reserved for Almighty God? The temptation included a rejection of the limits essential to obedient submission to a greater authority.

Satan knew human's greatest weakness—the desire for unrestrained freedom, unfettered access to all things, and unlimited sovereignty. We are and always have been fooled by the promise of elevated pleasure and status, dissatisfied with our position before God. Atheism's hollow claims of nihilism promise such freedom, access, and self-sovereignty. Francis Schaeffer wrote of the dire consequences of this in *A Christian Manifesto*:

> The materialistic-energy, chance concept of final reality never would have produced the form and freedom of government we have in this country . . . but now it has arbitrarily and arrogantly supplanted the historic Judeo-Christian consensus that provided the base for form and freedom in government. The Judeo-Christian consensus gave greater freedoms than the world has ever known, but it also contained the freedoms so that they did not pound society to pieces. The materialistic concept of reality would not have produced the form-freedom balance, and now that it has taken over it cannot maintain the balance. It has destroyed it.

Schaeffer understood that a materialist view of the world (a logical extension of atheism) might appear to result in more freedom—even absolute freedom—but this freedom is actually a mirage, which turns out to be not a blessing to humanity but a curse.

In *Manliness*, Harvard professor Harvey Mansfield's influential and scholarly work on masculinity, he attributes the work of both Charles Darwin and Frederick Nietzsche for the culture's emboldened movement to reject all universal or objective moral codes.

> Nietzsche declared, and spread the news like a counter-apostle, "God is dead." By this he meant all ideals, everything transcendent or spiritual, as well as God in any religion. The only response to this news, if you believe it, is an assertion that man must go on without God and must make his own ideals to pursue, his own idols to worship, his own substitute God. Thus manliness gets a license from science and philosophy to boast and to act without restraint.

Atheism has, along with its offspring—social Darwinism and materialism, conspired to craft a virtue "Emancipation Proclamation."

Sexual freedom offers a prime example of radical emancipation. No one could deny the explosion of freedom in the realm of sexuality in Western culture over the past century. From the invention of contraception to the expanding legal freedoms for homosexuals, in addition to the mushrooming availability of pornography (now available to younger and younger children), the dam has broken and the floodgates have opened. It is no coincidence that many prominent leaders of the sexual revolution of the 1960s were atheists.[1]

What has this increased sexual permissiveness and experimentation, all under the guise of freedom, benefitted our society? Does our society have more internal peace? More joy? More cohesiveness? Are we safer? On the contrary, the consequences of this unfettered sexual liberty have been nothing short of disastrous.

A prime indisputable consequence of unfettered sexual freedom has been the tragic spreading of HIV/AIDS and the increase in the rate of other serious sexually transmitted diseases. We are not arguing that atheists directly conspired to generate the entire HIV epidemic or that materialism produced every case of chlamydia ever contracted. Plenty of Christ-followers and other theists are guilty of immoral behavior and have made shameful contributions to both epidemics. Still, society's permissive sexual mores—which actively encourages sexual exploration and deviance—are directly encouraged and openly practiced by those who reject God outright. Additionally, the immoral behavior of a theist does not reflect poorly on that individual's morals, his moral code, or on the God who established those morals. Rather, the immorality of a theist reflects solely on the person's continued state of imperfection (i.e., sinfulness)[2] and the unique timing of God's redemptive plan.

Who can argue that unconstrained sexual autonomy and experimentation have made for a joyful, peaceful people? We have become

---

[1] Betty Friedan, Herbert Marcuse, Harry Hay are just a few examples.

[2] The fact that many Christians are influenced more by decadent cultural mores than by their stated beliefs is often misinterpreted as proof of the impotence of the beliefs. The truth is that our failures—from Adam and Eve to modern day—occur in spite of our beliefs. That is, it is because we deny, ignore, or forget them.

like toddlers in a candy store who are told, "Your parents don't exist. There are no rules now, other than those you determine for yourself. You can have whatever you want, whenever you want, however you want."[3]

Another example is the chronically elevated divorce rate. Mirroring our society's desire to divorce itself from God, the drive to divorce has resulted in economic calamity, with far fewer children parented by both parents. Even if one considers divorce a necessary evil, undoubtedly the seeds sown from this radical personal sovereignty have not grown a harvest of joy or peace but of personal misery.

Yet another example manifests in parents' inability to establish a proper hierarchy in the home. The movement toward a humanistic, egalitarian view of childrearing blossomed with the baby boomer generation. Encouraged by experts like Dr. Benjamin Spock,[4] parents adopted a permissive parenting style that proved disastrous. Parents who wanted to avoid dominating their children determined that external constraints would deny liberty and stunt their children's emotional and spiritual growth. But children did not hear the benign message. The message children received was far more malignant: "You are mini-gods who should have no limits, boundaries, or external controlling authority."

Atheism entirely misses the objective of liberty. Because God's law is good, His people can find liberty *in* Him and His laws. The drive to establish freedom *apart from* Him is not altogether fruitless; unfortunately, the fruit it bears is wretched poison. Just like Eve handed the forbidden fruit to Adam, atheists continually offer their fruit to every successive generation—in schools, via the media, and in the presuppositions they use in scientific inquiry.

## The Psychology of Atheism

Karl Marx's notable accusation of religion being "the opium of the people" is often used to suggest that a hurting people cling to religion

---

[3] If a comparison to toddlers is too insulting, imagine instead an adult in a supermarket or mall being given the same unrestricted freedom.

[4] To his credit, Spock thoroughly repented of his child-rearing views later in life.

to soothe their pain. Marx's fuller statement states, "Religion is the sigh of the oppressed creature, the heart of a heartless world, and the soul of soulless conditions. It is the opium of the people." Marx contended that religion is a creation of man, in the absence of any objective truth: "It is the fantastic realization of the human essence since the human essence has not acquired any true reality."

Marx perceived no objective, universal meaning, truth, or reality. He looked toward economic and political struggle for his sense of meaning and purpose in life—his true reality. To Marx, religion is a man-made tool used by the wealthy ruling class (bourgeois) to subdue and fool the poor working class (proletariat). The poor cling to their God,[5] which allows them to essentially ignore or tolerate their deplorable condition and the economic abuse of their wealthier counterparts. Economic subjugation is thereby perpetuated.

Sigmund Freud was another ardent atheist. Rather than attributing economic and political meaning, Freud sought to explain religious belief in the context of the intrapersonal. Freud determined that the human psyche was both vulnerable and imaginative enough to spawn the creation of god or gods. Specifically, Freud was aware of humanity's existential conundrum: the knowledge of our mortal, finite nature. He believed this terrifying prospect forced humans to either cope or live in a chronic terror state.

According to Freud, the solution became God. Human beings project onto nature the closest thing they understand, which is a fatherlike being who, because he is greater than nature, can provide protection from nature's consequences (i.e., death). In man's creation of God, this fatherlike being provides an escape from mortality and finite nature, in the form of heaven.

It is critical to note that theists admit that there is, like all great lies, a kernel of truth to these theories. Even Satan was correct when he slyly said, "Your eyes will be opened . . ." It is a natural, God-given part of His design for us that we desire immortality and perceive it.

---

[5] Clinging to God is often described by nonbelievers as a habit of desperate, pathetic people—never a behavior of the wise.

We are designed to fear death and separation from God, at least until we comprehend that our earthly death is the gateway to eternal existence in God's heavenly presence.

One of Freud's enduring lessons is that all defense mechanisms are coping responses to an intolerable thought or emotional state. There is no doubt that religion can be reduced to one such defense mechanism; a massive projection of a supernatural fatherly being can certainly be used as a solid defense against the intolerable realization of one's mortality and the terror that realization produces. Most Christians would admit that they would rather imagine an eternity with God in heaven than an eternity of nothingness. This bias is real; it is silly to deny it.

However, atheists lie to themselves and others when they deny the opposite bias. The truth is, terror is an understandable, healthy, even godly response to the proposition that a real God exists who has real expectations and real wrath prepared for those who deny Him and His holy will. There is nothing courageous about thumbing one's nose at God.

There are two possible responses to this set of facts. One is belief; the other is denial. Denial is the atheist's primary defense mechanism. It allows the individual to avoid feeling shame and guilt connected with failing to acknowledge a legitimate authority in thought, word, and deed. It also removes any anxiety that could naturally besiege a person facing that authority's judgment. This is the fundamental "benefit" of atheism.

A second critical defense mechanism the atheist utilizes is rationalization. The atheist creates an arbitrary set of ethics, morals, and rules for himself, which he knows he can attain, and accordingly, if he fails, he fails only himself and no one of greater authority or power. This way, the mind and soul breaks free of the chains of objective meaning and morality. The perception of radical freedom hyperstimulates the atheist, who runs headlong into an eternal, shallow, hopeless search for meaning and self-worth, ultimately ending in a vain hunt for power and pleasure.

Atheism, secularism, naturalism, and materialism are the crack cocaine of the masses.

## What Atheism Presupposes about Humanity

Rather than freeing humanity, atheism devalues and debases humanity. According to scientific materialism, human beings are simply a more highly evolved species of animal. As impressive as that might be, it allows no special human nature. There is no inherent value that separates humans from other animals or any other life form.

Extend this to its logical conclusion. If humans are no more special or valuable than other animals, animals are no more special or inherently valuable than other life forms, such as plants. If plants are no more special or inherently valuable than rocks or mud, then humans are no more valuable than fish, worms, sand, or water. Human beings, then, have no special value whatsoever.[6]

In fact, all matter is debased. Materialism posits that matter is simply stuff. All living and nonliving things are made up of atoms. These atoms move and connect, creating different forms. Some of these forms make up animate objects; some make up inanimate objects. But atoms in any form or combination are just atoms—nothing more, nothing less. There is nothing special about them.

Because of this reality, humanity (life) has no objective or necessary value. Its value comes only from what humanity proposes for itself. That is, humans decide their own value—individually and corporately. Considering a more dangerous scenario, one person or group of persons will decide the value of another group of persons. History witnessed nothing less than this during the existence of Hitler's Third Reich; we witness the same phenomenon in many contemporary atheistic nations.

## Morals and Ethics in Atheism

Atheists chafe at the notion that atheism is immoral, and that by extension atheists are less moral than theists. They create straw men

---

[6] Or the converse, espoused by groups like PETA, which suggests that all animals be elevated to humanlike status. Of course, if humans are nothing more than atoms, this makes their argument meaningless, since animals too would be degraded.

by asserting that theism has plenty of immoral characters on its roster[7] and that plenty of atheists are reasonably moral. The power of this clever moral-equivalency argument is revealed when the theist is often forced to acknowledge these blindingly obvious facts and then defend them, thereby distracting from the core realities about atheism. Before we get distracted, let us dismiss this moral-equivalency nonsense.

Theism does not necessarily produce creatures of superior morality. Specifically, belief in God is the result of the Holy Spirit's chastening—His gracious message to us about our broken moral compass. Once a person believes in God, the presumption is that that person will become more moral. For sure, some experience a radical, sudden change in heart, mind, and soul. Others seem to change within, but their sanctification appears to progress at a snail's pace. Yet others improve in some areas of obedience, but struggle with troublesome issues their entire lives. The point is that theists (Christians in particular) are and will remain deeply sinful until God completes His sanctifying work in their lives.

Of course, this does not mean that atheists are necessarily any less moral than theists, nor does it mean that atheism is a particularly immoral philosophy. There are plenty of atheists who subscribe to a moral code consistent with God's commandments; the Bible asserts that God weaves His moral code directly into each person's heart (Romans 2:15). The truth is, however, that they do not have to. Nothing about atheism necessitates morality, whereas everything about Christianity necessitates it. In the end, it is more accurate to say that atheism is amoral; it has no inherent, universal moral or ethical code to which its adherents must subscribe.

The logical extension of this is that each atheist is free[8] to establish whatever ethical or moral framework suits him or her. The individual

---

[7] The critical error here is the presumption of causality. Theism does not *produce* immoral people; rather, it is *for* immoral people (i.e., everyone).

[8] Notice the appeal to man's desire for liberty and freedom, to which they contrast theism, which atheists generally assert minimizes or even eradicates one's personal freedom and liberty.

becomes the sole arbiter of right and wrong. Of course, the atheist is usually intelligent enough to know that immoral behavior will often—although not always—result in uncomfortable punishment. This is often the only justification for avoiding certain behaviors that are forbidden in a civilized society.

*The Humanist Manifesto* of 1933 is a statement created by the group that would later coalesce into the American Humanist Association, a collection of atheists attempting to increase the political presence of atheists in the United States. Updated in 1973, the manifesto states, in description of their nonreligious foundation, "As nontheists, we begin with humans not God, nature not deity." Later in the document, its assertion on ethics reflects the fruitless search for meaning without a necessary, objective, universal code.

> We affirm that moral values derive their source from human experience. Ethics is autonomous and situational needing no theological or ideological sanction. Ethics stems from human need and interest. To deny this distorts the whole basis of life. Human life has meaning because we create and develop our futures. Happiness and the creative realization of human needs and desires, individually and in shared enjoyment, are continuous themes of humanism. We strive for the good life, here and now.

Human life has meaning merely because human beings create and develop their futures? This vapid claim for meaning lacks any substance or logical force and opens the possibility for one person's experience to create a set of morals and ethics that profoundly contradicts another's experience and set.

For example, if I were to use this reasoning, I could just as legitimately determine that killing babies and putting their heads on spikes is perfectly moral as another person could insist that it is morally reprehensible. If my experience informs me that killing babies and putting their heads on spikes brings me happiness and brings me closer to my life goals (and even furthers the human species), then it couldn't possibly be wrong. Furthermore, no one can judge my behavior, because each person creates his or her own ethics or morals.

*The Humanist Manifesto* claims to believe in "maximum individual autonomy consonant with social responsibility." What if I believe that it is irresponsible to share resources with adults with dementia or children born with other developmental disabilities? What if my experience suggests to me that it would be best to rid society of "undesirables," such as severely wounded veterans, because they do not sufficiently produce? The slope becomes profoundly slippery.

Atheists do not like to admit this, but these are the logical consequences of an absence of an objective, universal authority. What authority determines the boundaries of "social responsibility"? The only virtues that are supported are those that match the current zeitgeist of the majority or ruling class. Certainly, some countries' ethical codes would decry killing babies. Others do not. China, for example, is an atheist nation that believes that killing some babies for the common good is essential. It is not a far cry to suggest that they could legitimately determine that killing dissidents, the elderly, theists, the infirm, or others could be justified by a subjective view of "social responsibility."

In an atheistic society, virtues could change, based on the prevailing winds or rulers. Peter Hitchens, brother of the late atheist Christopher Hitchens, shows in *The Rage against God* how an absence of an absolute code that exists outside of humanity will degrade itself and its fellow man, in part by avoiding the selfless example of Christ in loving "thy neighbor as thyself."

> In a society where the absolute code has been jettisoned and we have all become adept at making excuses for shirking such duties, selflessness of this kind will become less common, nursing less dedicated, wives more inclined to leave their babbling husbands in care homes to be looked after impersonally by paid strangers and perhaps encouraged gently down the slope of death, and soldiers readier to save themselves while their comrades lie in pain within reach of the enemy. And there will always be a worldly relativist on hand to say that this is only sensible, to urge that we do the easy thing, and to say that it is right to do so.

We have witnessed all of these realities in recent decades, and then some. Even the term *duty* sounds quaint and distant to many.

Men abandon their spouses and children when they feel they are missing out on fun, women claim "choice" to end pregnancies that are nothing worse than inconvenient, children have no concept of duty toward their elders, and politicians seem driven more by narcissistic advancement and protection than a sense of duty to constituents and higher principles.

## Theism As Crutch?

Other than being compared to an opiate addict, there is no greater insult to theists than the idea that their belief is a crutch. The notion supposedly insinuates that theists are emotionally crippled and simply cannot cope with the anxieties and responsibilities of existential crises with the same grace and aplomb as their atheistic counterparts. This is really just a regurgitation of Freud's theory using some clever imagery.

Does the theist's belief in God represent a crutch? To be perfectly honest: yes. Is that crutch necessary due to some unique weakness? No! Theists—Christians in particular—recognize the need for support because they recognize that they are broken and are temporarily disabled. Our spiritual disability necessitates outside aid. There is nothing weak or pathetic about a person disabled by a broken leg using a crutch. Why would it be shameful to admit to needing God for a spiritual crutch?

Part of the answer lies in Frederick Nietzsche's concept of the *Übermensch*. Nietzsche's atheism was relatively honest; he did not play games with logic, as do many modern atheists. His solution to the meaningless of existence was to strive to be the *Übermensch*, which is a quasi-mythical, theoretical man who is beyond the constraints of this world. Man need not look without to some supernatural being for solace or meaning. Instead, he creates a new meaning for himself, bravely accepts reality, and sets to work a new, creative force that affirms life in the present, rather than in a mythical future.

The *Übermensch*'s self-contained ego is self-sustaining. He does not require any crutch. In contrast, Nietzsche believed that Christians and other religious people were too weak to face the truth. Atheists truly do perceive theists as weak and foolish. For the believer, that is fine. We know that "the foolishness of God is wiser than man's wisdom, and the weakness of God is stronger than man's strength" (1 Corinthians 1:25).

## If God Really Were Dead . . .

What would society look like if atheism and secular humanism reigned? Our imagination need not scan far, since nearly half the world subscribes to an atheistic philosophy. As we mentioned earlier, Communist nations have as their foundation an atheist worldview. One of the prime examples of a failed atheist state is the Soviet Union.

Peter Hitchens describes Stalin's Russia as a humanist cult, centering on the tyrant's manic desire to be worshiped as a godlike figure. Stalin attempted to transfer the faith of all Russians from God to himself—not because he believed in God but because he knew how to use the trappings of religion (in concert with ruthless violence, mass-scale larceny, and intimidation) to win people's allegiance. Over the following decades, the leaders of the USSR attempted to remove all vestiges of religion and religious belief from society. The result was one of the most lifeless, loveless, compassionless, empty societies in recorded history.

How ruthless was Stalin? Estimates of people killed by Stalin range from eight to sixty million. Even a conservative estimate makes one shudder. Regardless of the number, it is clear that one of the motivators of Stalin's mass murders was his atheistic worldview and resultant self-worship.

While we are on the topic of violent atheist regimes, the other massive Communist/atheist state birthed in the twentieth century was the People's Republic of China. Conservative estimates suggest that Mao Zedong was responsible for the mass killing of at least forty to sixty million people. Most of these murders were done under the guise of Communist crusades with benevolent sounding names like "Land Reforms," "Great Leap Forward," and "Cultural Revolution." These are staggering numbers, for sure.

Yet another regime, Germany's Third Reich, has been described as atheist or pagan. For the purposes of this argument, we presume that Hitler's Third Reich actively rejected belief in a personal god to whom they must be accountable. Estimates of mass killings from "The Final Solution" range from four to six million.

These estimates only describe the murderous inclinations of sovereign states in recent history that have held to an atheist worldview. This does not include the following additional atrocities:

- Mass forced abortions
- Abolition of churches, worship, religious literature
- Political imprisonment
- Economic inequality
- Raping, pillaging, forced marriages, divorces, and adoptions
- Forced belonging to dominant political party

These are not mere consequences of a coincidental group of psychotics. These are the normal, natural behaviors of leaders who espouse a worldview that says that there is no god. They are completely consistent with the morality and ethics of an atheistic, materialistic society that degrades and devalues human beings. Smaller Communist nations are failing to mimic the Soviet Union and Communist China only in degree. Fidel Castro, Hugo Chavez, and Kim Jong Il have fewer people to kill, fewer acres to steal, and are less hidden from the world media, but they are no less ruthless and immoral.

## Atheism and Virtues

We have seen that an atheistic philosophy does not and cannot support the virtues espoused by George Washington and other Founding Fathers. Modern philosophy and literature's alternative ideals, such as Nietzsche's *Übermensch*, also reject the idea of God as a provider of a universal, objective, authoritative set of morals, ethics, and virtues.

If virtues have as their foundation an objective, universal reality, then it seems counterintuitive to attempt to teach children virtue outside of the framework of that reality. Removing prayer from public classrooms is simply one way to separate virtues from their foundation.

A nation that rejects God as the undergirding reality of its foundational beliefs—as expressed in our Declaration of Independence and the Constitution—will soon find those beliefs eroding. If we are not endowed by our Creator with unalienable rights, then the government is the sole authority of our rights. This is precisely what the framers of our constitution sought to avoid and what their forefathers fled from in Europe. Our rights are only unalienable if they are endowed by a real Creator with real authority. Otherwise, they are meaningless.

We do not need less discussion of Christian morality in the public sphere; we need more of it. We do not need God spoken of less in classrooms; He should be front and center in our children's academic lives. We do not benefit from judges who claim that the separation of church and state means that God must be evicted from public discourse or buildings. We do not need political leaders to shy from their personal faith, as if admitting the influence of God in their life establishes a state religion.

Lastly, we do not need the media channeling their atheistic, anti-God propaganda into our minds and into the minds of our children. Rather, we should support specific media, personalities, and outlets that acknowledge God and espouse the virtues He destined for His people. ★

*Chapter Seven*

★★★

# A Wall of Separation between Morality and State

*We will remember not the words of our enemies, but the silence of our friends.*

—MARTIN LUTHER KING JR.

*There is no such thing as being non-political. Just by making a decision to stay out of politics you are making the decision to allow others to shape politics and exert power over you. And if you are alienated from the current political system, then just by staying out of it you do nothing to change it, you simply entrench it.*

—JOAN KIRNER

*Be faithful in small things because it is in them that your strength lies.*

—MOTHER TERESA

# When Words Don't Matter

What's in a name? "That which we call a rose . . . By any other name would smell as sweet." (Shakespeare, Romeo and Juliet (II, ii, 1-2). That fits for liberals, or progressives, or agnostics—all of whom love to quibble over labels, all the while ascribing labels of their own to conservatives. I won't bother with dictionary definitions of liberal, or progressive, or even conservative. Yes, the classic liberal was one who understood liberty—that seems self-evident—as all variations come from the Latin *liber,* meaning "free." But the definition is irrelevant to the modern liberal; that definition has gone the way of the dinosaur!

The definition may not matter, but the history does. The history matters because at its very inception, modern liberalism sought to undermine, or at least ignore, God. John Locke, the "Father of Modern Liberalism," wrote in his 1690 statement called "Two Treatises" that government derives its power from the governed and not from God or other supernatural beings.[1] This idea dominated philosophy over the next century as the populace wrapped its counter-religion in a culture of intellectual orgy. The period of Enlightenment threw out tradition and ultimately sought to dismantle religion based upon its role in the monarchies that had become unpopular for their unlimited and unscrupulous power in the eighteenth century.

This idea of sovereignty and personal rights were the basis for the American colonization, and ultimately the Declaration of Independence and the Bill of Rights, among other foundational American documents.

In 1776 Adam Smith wrote "Wealth of Nations," in which he applied classic liberalism to the field of economics, and pointed to the natural laws that a truly free market would offer. The laissez-faire economy took the world by storm and sparked a debate that would later be embraced by conservatives. This liberalism was changed once and for all when it was redefined by the British when they overthrew a monarchy in Ireland, and allowed voting by a secret ballot.

---

[1] Despite Locke's deep influence in Jefferson's development of the Declaration of Independence, Jefferson retained the notion that governmental power and the people's rights come directly from their Creator.

When the proletariat (working class) became concerned about food prices, liberals began to look to the government to provide for the poor via welfare, pensions, health care, and other things. Simply put, they wanted free stuff.

This basic demand for "free stuff" by the working class ran rampant in the twentieth century, and resulted (as it always does) in Communism. The Russian monarchy was lost in 1917 after three centuries of rule. The Bolsheviks, led by Lenin, took over, declaring war on capitalism, which had been the basis for the original concept of liberalism.

When the 1930s ushered in the same poverty and demand for "free stuff" in the US, Communists took advantage of the political landscape and spread their propaganda in the US. John Maynard Keynes argued that real freedom came not in the free market but in free disbursement of jobs, free access to social welfare, and full employment. President Roosevelt brought Keynesian economics to full fruition in his New Deal, which brought a level of security to a limping economy that had reached 23 percent unemployment. Massive government spending later resulted in massive debt (120 percent GDP).

The question ultimately becomes: "What *is* liberty?"

The classic liberal would be appalled at the modern application of the idea. To them, liberty was never "the freedom to have everything you need" but rather "the freedom to have the opportunity to achieve it." Put simply, modern liberal Thomas Hill Green said, "If it were ever reasonable to wish that the usage of words had been other than it has been . . . one might be inclined to wish that the term 'freedom' had been confined to the . . . power to do what one wills."

Modern Liberalism, as I see it, is based on a few simple ideas. First, that freedom means guaranteeing equality to all, and that, for the common good. It also must assume that all people are truly equal—not in terms of value or respectability, but economic *outcome*—and that the role of government is to ensure this equality. It cannot in any way account for varying levels of ability, competence, competition, or justice. Therefore, government has become more than "of the people" as originally defined by liberal ideology. It must be "of the power, over the people, in order to establish their equality." Government must be the great equalizer, in order to provide freedom for everyone to have what everyone else has. Government, in other words, must oust God because it must **be** God.

## "You will know them by their fruits . . ."

Before there was Chicago Community Organizer Barack Obama, there was Chicago Community Organizer Saul Alinsky (1901–1972). Alinsky is considered by many to be one of the patron saints of modern liberalism.[2] Perhaps the necessary eradication of God from all things should not surprise us when the heroes of the liberal movement are those like Alinsky. He began his famous book *Rules for Radicals* with a "quote" from Satan in his (Alinsky's) own words:

> Lest we forget at least an over-the-shoulder acknowledgment to the very first radical: from all our legends, mythology, and history (and who is to know where mythology leaves off and history begins—or which is which), the first radical known to man who rebelled against the establishment and did it so effectively that he at least won his own kingdom—Lucifer.

Alinsky taught several tenets of power-grabbing that even conservative giant William F. Buckley called "genius." He also suggested that liberals focus on the "appearance of morality" as opposed to the establishment, or genuine possession, of personal virtue.

His rules—and our brief commentary of each—are as follows:

*RULE 1*: "Power is not only what you have, but what the enemy thinks you have." Power is derived from two main sources—money and people. "Have-nots" must build power from flesh and blood.

*There are always plenty of people, and if you are government, there is always plenty of money. If you know how to use money to get people, and you know how to use people to get money, you have absolute power.*

*RULE 2*: "Never go outside the expertise of your people." It results in confusion, fear, and retreat. Feeling secure adds to anyone's backbone.

---

[2] Hillary Clinton not only met Alinsky as a teen but wrote glowingly about him in her senior thesis at Wellesley College.

*This is why organizers speak to their membership in simple, emotionally charged sound bites. The objects of their attacks become bewildered by their focus on issues that seem ancillary. This is intentional on the part of the organizers. Organizers will only focus on simple emotional phrases in their attacks so that their membership understands and doesn't retreat.*

RULE 3: "Whenever possible, go outside the expertise of the enemy." Look for ways to increase insecurity, anxiety, and uncertainty.

*That is why liberals attack on issues that are nonissues to conservatives over and over. They attack conservatives as racist when the issue is jobs, or greed when the issue is taxes. This confuses conservatives and unites the liberal voting base.*

RULE 4: "Make the enemy live up to its own book of rules." If the rule is that every letter gets a reply, send thirty thousand letters. You can kill them with this because no one can possibly obey all of their own rules.

*How many times do liberals scream "liar" when conservatives make promises? They are often not held up to their promises because they don't campaign on moral specifics; their base doesn't demand virtue, but the conservative base does.*

RULE 5: "Ridicule is man's most potent weapon." There is no defense. It's irrational. It's infuriating. It also works as a key pressure point to force the enemy into concessions. *This is classic bullying, and why bullies do so well in politics.*

RULE 6: "A good tactic is one your people enjoy." If people enjoy an activity, they will come back.

*This is part of the psychology of elitist domination of the have-nots They give away hunting paraphernalia to their members, while using their dues to promote politicians trying to decimate their Second Amendment right to even own the gun they just gave them. They give away sports tickets to keep their members distracted, entertained, and focusing on the mundane—the opiate.*

RULE 7: "A tactic that drags on too long becomes a drag." Don't become old news.

*Every savvy politician knows that a good volunteer is a used volunteer. Tyrannical personalities will exploit this natural tendency of the servant's heart personality so that they can dominate that person.*

RULE 8: "Keep the pressure on. Never let up." Keep trying new things to keep the opposition off balance. As the opposition masters one approach, hit them from the flank with something new.

*This is the "Attack! Attack! Attack!" approach that has been employed by many a militia, and many a union, and many a movement. The simple strategy is based on the understanding that if one's target is constantly on the defensive, it never has time to develop an adequate offense.*

RULE 9: "The threat is usually more terrifying than the thing itself." Imagination and ego can dream up many more consequences than any activist.

*This tactic is applied throughout the liberal media, especially blogs. You will see a headline like "Candidate X says he is conservative, but we have information that will destroy him." Or headers like, "Uh oh! Tea Party is dying." Who says? And based on what data? None! But they don't have to prove anything because there are plenty of emotional, dramatic people who will publicize their headline and create a narrative that is baseless. This puts conservatives at a distinct disadvantage because many conservatives base their morality on the Judeo-Christian Ten Commandments, of which "Thou Shalt Not Lie" is a real boundary. This gives the left an obvious advantage in the game of war and politics.*

RULE 10: "If you push a negative hard enough, it will push through and become a positive."

*The Occupiers used this rule well. They complained, ridiculed, mocked, and even participated in vulgar behavior, and then Hollywood came in and made them look legitimate. Ultimately, they were funded, and activists were paid to organize and push the Democrat machine, without even affiliating with the Democrat party, per se. This was convenient for all, and ultimately an effective attack on anyone perceived as "1%"—namely Romney and business in general. For all the "oh, but they fornicated in the streets and defecated on police" protests of the Right, they were ultimately effective based upon this rule.*

RULE 11: "The price of a successful attack is a constructive alternative." Never let the enemy score points because you're caught without a solution to the problem.

*Unions use this all the time. Unions say "we want free health care and full pensions" and then they accept a substantial raise as a "compromise."*

RULE 12: "Pick the target, freeze it, personalize it, and polarize it." Cut off the support network and isolate the target from sympathy. Go after people and not institutions; people hurt faster than institutions.[3]

Anyone watching current politics can see that the Left has applied Alinsky's tactics as fluently as Castro speaks Spanish. The question for the conservative quickly becomes, "Do we embrace these uncivil, ungodly tactics in order to win the war?" Should conservatives fight fire with fire?

The answer to the question lies in the abject rejection of the credo of atheists and agnostics (many of these folks being liberal)—that there is no God, or if there is, He might be a "she" or an "it," but in any case, God doesn't belong in politics. If we believe in and are accountable to the God of Abraham, we are instantly going to have a problem with the "Playground Politics" advocated by the likes of Alinsky, Barack Obama, and his closest supporters.

Add to this equation the reemergence of the Cloward Pivens strategy to overload our social welfare roles to the point of collapse, in a stated effort to establish a mandatory government-provided salary for all (socialism), and you have a picture of how the Left continues to chip away at the basic framework of the American Constitution and ideology. And it might be easier to collapse this once unshakable superpower than we thought, because the poor are being enslaved and paid to do it:

Howard Phillips, chairman of The Conservative Caucus, was quoted in 1982 as saying that the strategy could be effective because "Great Society programs had created a vast army of full-time liberal activists whose salaries are paid from the taxes of conservative working people"

(Robert Pear [1984-04-15], "Drive to Sign Up Poor for Voting Meets Resistance," *The New York Times*).

I suppose little of this would matter if the once-freedom-loving movement had not morphed into Communism and the need for

---

[3] http://sleepless.blogs.com/george/2009/08/alinskys-rules-for-radicals-for
-dummies.html

tyranny to "equalize" things. The Marxist upbringing and ultimate indoctrination of Barack Obama is well documented in my "Cousin" Trevor Loudon's blog[4] Ultimately, he not only traces his roots, contacts, and cronies but also documents the strategy currently underway based upon dismantling our economy in his first term, and the hopeful ushering in socialism as *the answer* in his second term. Whether or not Obama and his cronies were successful at his second term, they are invigorated for the surprising victory they managed to pull off in his presidential election, and they are alive and well working through various community organizing cells throughout the United States.

Their policies fail again and again throughout history, and yet they persist as if the rest of us are too stupid to recognize their previous failures and transcendent truths. This is why learning US History and the US Constitution, and studying about the Founding Fathers and foundational documents is so important. If we don't know the history, we will be tricked by their tactics. If we know history, then we can identify their trickery and choose to call them out, or beat them at their own game.

The whisper campaign among the ruling elite establishment is the creation of "useful idiots." Useful idiots must be fed, clothed, spoken to in simple terms, provided basic medical needs, and entertained. They need as many useful idiots as they can find to protest, to vote, and to be taxed or forced to pay union dues to their campaign coffers. They want us all to be useful idiots. We aren't, because we have seen those tactics before.

The execution of liberalism results in the calculated or inadvertent challenge and even debasement of the virtues of our culture, and the God ordained freedom He intended for all of us. Liberal policies devalue life, squash personal responsibility, and create childlike dependence rather than mature interdependence.

In the end, we know that Alinsky's celebration of Lucifer is a farce, because it does not end well. We all know who wins in the end, and who the true Victor is. It has been written since the beginning of time. "There is nothing new under the sun" (Ecclesiastes).

---

[4] www.trevorloudon.com or www.keywiki.org.

## Micro and Macro Playground Politics 101

Everything I never needed to know I learned in sixth grade—on the playground.

It becomes more evident as liberals scramble for a way to combat the self-evident truths of Constitutional Conservatism that their age-old tactics are losing steam. This must be incredibly frustrating and disillusioning for liberals, but it has not seemed to thwart their commitment to the same old tactics.

Liberals wonder how it is that conservatives are beating them so consistently and winning the hearts and minds of the American electorate, and for me, it is very simple. We recognize and are pointing to the immaturity of their arguments more and more.

Does that sound pious? It might. I apologize for that. I just can't get over the relentless over use of the old lib playbook that isn't working any longer—that of playground politics.

Playground politics is so, well, elementary. We all know it when we see it, so we decided to create a dictionary of it just to help you organize it in your mind. I think if we educate liberals about the fundamental shortsightedness of their approach to winning in politics, they can catch on. After all, their ignorance can only go so far, right? They can't be completely brainwashed, indoctrinated, or uneducable . . . can they? If we can show them what we see when they think we aren't looking, then we will be less annoyed, and they will have to come up with some more, um, adult behaviors.

*"Takes one to know one."* The only group of true racists I have ever been around was the Democrat House Labor committee my husband served on as a minority member. One night, the committee was out with lobbyists at a restaurant near Capitol Hill, and very late into the evening, after many drinks, I learned what it really meant to be a racist. Though I had heard liberals accuse conservatives of racism again and again, I never really knew what it meant to be a racist until that night. Once the racial slurs began, I stood in shock as words I had never heard flew out of the very mouths of those who had accused so many conservatives of the same. I never forgot that night, and this is the first time I realized that racism is still alive, and in the Party it has been in since the war between the states.

*Attack the pretty girl* (or rich kid, athlete, whomever you are jealous of). It is easy (and the habit of all simpletons) to resent the success, beauty, and accomplishment of someone who has what you want. Girls are notorious at this, but political operatives use it all the time. Barack Obama used it when he said that all those who make more than $250,000 are "corporate jet owners" who really don't want to "pay their fair share." The left successfully brands the right as greedy, selfish, and uncaring for the poor in an effort to pit those who want for anything against conservatives who are accused of having it all. This is especially apparent in the rhetoric of the Left surrounding Sarah Palin. The vitriolic attacks on her family, her friends, and her honor are unparalleled in our history, with transparent resentment of her stunning good looks, charisma, personal success, and now her wealth and influence.

*I didn't do it (he did it)!* Every time I point to one of my children with an accusing glance, they react with a standard impulse. I call it the "I didn't do it!" reflex. The immature reaction to guilt is to blame another. While it is developmentally understandable for a preschooler to point the finger, when grown men and women do it, it tends to illuminate the path of the real fault. Remember when every time the Democrats or Obama were asked about the spiraling debt or the economic woes of the US and their answer was "we inherited this problem" or "the policies of Bush . . . (you get to fill in the blank)"? The finger pointing that takes place in the political world not only demonstrates the deplorable maturity level of our political class, but their leadership ability as well.

President Truman said, "The buck stops here." In this statement, he established his strong style of leadership in the face of responsibility and blame, and acceptance of both. This is honorable. Willingness to be held accountable, to take risk, and even subsequent blame for any failures while standing strong in the face of all of the above would be true leadership—the kind politicians shy away from like schoolyard children. This is yet another arena where an increase in honor would take this country a long, long way.[5]

---

[5] We are convinced that the approval ratings of any president who admits mistakes and takes blame would shoot through the roof. Why? Because of the graciousness of the American people.

*"Huh? I didn't hear you!" Or "What? I am confused."* Remember the kid in class who pretended not to hear the correction of the teacher? Well, not much has changed for many liberals, many of whom fancy themselves well educated but play dumb when it suits them. One prime example is the way President Obama goes deaf when conservatives speak to important failures like Solyndra and other monumentally wasteful spending items, or when the media points out the prevalence of crony capitalism. And who can deny the exceptional hairsplitting expertise of President Bill Clinton, when he responded to questions regarding sex with Monica Lewinsky with, "uh, it depends on what your definition of *is* is.[6]"

*When all arguments fail, name call!* Despite the fact that the left is largely the home of racism and phobias, liberals persist in pointing their fingers at the right, and calling us names (racist, homophobic, xenophobic, Islamophobic, bigoted, haters, anti-woman, anti-child, anti-peace, the list goes on . . .). One of the telltale signs of a debater's weakness is the use of the *ad hominem* ("to the man") argument, which is in fact not an argument but a personal criticism or attack on the debater's rival meant to distract from the argument itself. The most humorous part of this is that while liberals call us names, they are calling for "civil discourse" (as if we are the ones precluding such discourse).

*Be the biggest bully on the playground* The union bosses are really the masters of this tactic. If you take them on, prepare for death threats, intimidation, and even loss of livelihood as they will picket, cajole, and harass businesses that are not in lock-step with their view of politics. Not only that, like so many leftist activists, they will work against you politically, sue you, or in some way cost you personally or professionally if you don't agree with them. By and large, this tactic has served them well with both parties who seem afraid to really ever take them on.

Though conservatives continue to call liberals out on each of these items, liberals carry on as though the conservatives aren't on to them. Hope lies in the current political *zeitgeist*, which suggests

---

[6] Apparently, we missed the "It's virtuous and sexy to play dumb" memo.

that the general electorate is disgusted by liberal immaturity and bully tactics. According to one Gallup poll, minorities, Hispanics, and other minorities, along with much of the American public, not only recognizes the leftist Playground Politics Playbook, but has started to point it out and move away from those who would engage in school games of yesteryear. Most of the American electorate agrees that adult behavior is needed, and warranted at this time, and they are turned off by the blatantly obvious ploy of the left to divide people, use people, and engage in ugliness that gets us nowhere in these difficult times.

The good news is that since folks are seeing through this bad behavior, this is conservatives' chance to own the next election, and those to come. The reality is that if the Left refuses to cease and desist, they will only keep losing votes. No longer shielded by the mainstream media, the new media is poised to expose the left's hypocrisy and the lengths they are willing to go to control votes, money, and power. This is especially displeasing to intellectually honest liberals who are capable of critical thought. As they continue to jump ship on the politicians and media who refuse to abandon the ridiculousness of these playground politics conservative candidates and ideals will attract liberals and independents like flies to honey.

## Plantation Politics

The worst of their failed policy bullying doesn't take place on the playground but in a much darker, more secret place. I call it *Plantation Politics* because it uses people who are subjected to the elite "owners." They hand it out it like slave owners will, and call it social welfare. They subjugate the people and call them "working people." They take away freedom and call it "fairness." They emasculate men and call it "equality." They steal from people and call it "taxation." They steal even more, and call it "dues." They own people, and call it "organizing." They kill people, and call it "choice." Would someone explain to me what is more palatable about this than the plantation they all claim to abhor?

How long will the insanity continue? How can we teach the next generation to be discerning and wise?

Those of us who know, know. But we are unsure all of what we know, terrified to know what we know, and altogether unsure how to act upon what we know, we know. So where to go from here . . .

We start with knowing our founding documents and teaching them to our children. Public school certainly will not. We read the Bible, and important literature (see Appendix [Dr Gina Required Reading List]). We teach our children critical thinking, and logic, so they can discern truth from fiction, and articulate it well. We learn that primaries are the important elections, not generals. We learn about honor and civility, and make it our business to restore it, before it is too late.

## The New Rebel—The Fun Part

G.K. Chesterton wrote, "He is a very shallow critic who cannot see an eternal rebel in the heart of a conservative."

The Occupy movement and the radical "Flower Children" of the 1960's desperately wanted to perceive themselves as rebels. Perhaps they were, if one flashes back to the proletariat uprising of days long ago. America is unique in many ways, but one ironic element of that iniquity is her ability to prove old adages false. In America, it has become the standard that the bully on the playground, who is underweight, over ugly, or in some way feels slighted, grows up to be the liberal. To be a liberal, you cannot go around looking like a conservative, or you'll be put out to pasture. As a result, liberals spend a lot of time trying to collectively reject tradition. The only problem lies in that they *all* do it, thereby becoming the culture, rather than the rebels opposing it. So their attempt to look like rebels is humorously undermined by their inability to think for themselves, even when it comes to style. They all look the same.

This leaves the conservative in an interesting position. Does the conservative go out and establish some outward manifestation of her rebellion against those who are trying so hard to look original and rebellious?

As I was leaving for a Tea Party rally I had helped organize in St. Louis at the beginning of the Tea Party, I remember my husband commenting that he "loved when I got all protesty."

That was the first time I realized that smut dominates our culture, and that my opposition to the popular liberal culture is "protesty." I felt a need to dress in a style that communicated that I cannot be pushed into a box, and labeled, and set on a shelf! I wanted to express my opposition to the culture so dominated by liberal French and now American liberal culture. I looked around me and saw liberals like Hilary Clinton in "church lady" polyester suits. I saw Barack Obama in a well-tailored suit. I grabbed my *NOT* mom jeans, and determined myself to rock them. I wanted to stand out from the polyester suits.

I am a traditionalist in every sense of the word, except in the legalistic sense of the word. I think we have to be completely sure that we are living by God's law, and not mans. We also need to remember that preaching to the choir gets us nowhere. I have heard it said that more than 50% of Christians who sit in the pews don't make it to the ballot box. They talk it, look it, preach it, pray it, and then sit there in the pews when it really matters! This should stir up the righteous indignation of every Christian and indict every pastor who neglects to exhort his congregation to get involved in preserving this providentially established country.

I enjoy the fact that when a liberal meets me, they often have trouble distinguishing me as a "stodgy conservative" because I am not; I am a rebel against the pervasive liberal culture (i.e., I do wear colors other than black). I am also a rebel against the conservative box they would like to put me in—aka—no polyester suits, no mom jeans, no khaki pants, no cardigans, no prairie skirts, and no sweater vests[7]. I am a proud, unbridled, protesty conservative. Let freedom ring!

Mother Teresa's wisdom provides a stark alternative to the Alinsky model:

> People are often unreasonable, illogical and self-centered: Forgive them anyway. If you are kind, people may accuse you of selfish, ulterior motives: Be kind anyway. If you are successful, you will win some false friends and some true enemies: Succeed anyway. If you are honest and frank, people may cheat you. Be honest and frank anyway. If you find serenity and happiness,

---

[7] What works for Rick Santorum does not necessarily work for Gina Loudon.

they may be jealous: Be happy anyway. The good you do today, people will often forget tomorrow: Do good anyway. Give the world the best you have, and it may never be enough: Give the world the best you've got anyway. You see, in the final analysis, it is between you and God: It was never between you and them anyway.

The faithful, Godly model works. ★

# Chapter Eight

★★★

# "If Fish Don't Need Bicycles"

*Aw, man, I feel like a woman tonight.*
—SHANIA TWAIN, LYRICS, *I FEEL LIKE A WOMAN*;
MERCURY RECORDS

*Promise me you'll always remember: You're braver than you believe,*
*and stronger than you seem, and smarter than you think.*
—CHRISTOPHER ROBIN TO POOH (A. A.MILNE)

*We women talk too much; nevertheless, we only say half of what*
*we know.*
—NANCY WITCHER ASTOR, FIRST WOMAN TO SIT IN THE
BRITISH HOUSE OF COMMONS, 1879–1964

## Sin Is Sin Is Sin Is Sin

Ecclesiastes reminds us that there is "nothing new under the sun." When given absolute power, there will always be corruption. Traditionally, the first power was given to men. Men got to name animals, write laws, craft literature, determine job descriptions, and even pen the Word of God. Therefore, just as the very Word they wrote predicted, sin would find its way into the place of power and corrupt what was originally and naturally a beautiful thing—God's natural order.

At a certain time in American history, some men had gone too far, and women pushed back; they held the line. This wasn't progressivism or feminism in the modern sense. This was as traditional as it gets. The women's suffrage movement was a throwback to Esther, Ruth, and Deborah—true feminism in the most holy sense of the word.

Just as the male power brokers had polluted men prior to women's suffrage, the power women gained began to pollute women and their underlying cause. Women began to deny that men contributed anything positive to society and to exert their superiority over men. This contaminated the natural order of things, just as masculine domination polluted the original intent of creation.

The advancement of women in Western society—where they have demanded, achieved, and asserted their natural God-given rights—is a glorious achievement indeed. The twentieth century in particular has witnessed many contributions to the feminist cause, and it would be foolish to attempt to deny or minimize these contributions. However, there is a dark side to feminism—one that has been well-documented and must be recalled if we are to truly understand the degradation of virtue, civility, and honor in today's society.

The emasculation of men stands as the Hiroshima of radical feminism. Modern-day socially liberal women have asserted—either explicitly or inadvertently—that in order for them to have power, they must take on the male persona, and feminize or reduce men (emasculation). This absurd assumption is both immoral and sophomoric.

Just as God so perfectly designed the male and female bodies to fit together, and gave us pleasure in the process for celebration, He designed our unique ideas, purposes, drives, gifts, weaknesses, and even quirks to be woven together into interdependent and complementary wholes. This explains why the differences between men and women are so important and how these ideas are anathema in a politically incorrect leftist culture. If one were to acknowledge the interdependence of men and women distinct of our design, then radical victimization no longer applies. How can I complain that government doesn't equalize the playing field for me in work, sports, finances, or other areas if we are designed to be interdependent, and both genders are integral to the natural order of society?

Radical feminism completely denies all such differences and interdependence, and claims that women can live well (or even better) without the involvement of men whatsoever. Gloria Steinem popularized the phrase "Woman needs man like a fish needs a bicycle." Really? We wonder if all of the abandoned mothers and children living in squalor agree with the concept of man's unessential nature.[1]

In order for feminists to feel value, they must devalue men. In the perfect feminist world, where value is a zero-sum game, men are competition, an irritant, better to be cast aside, controlled, emasculated, and exorcised.

> *"A woman is the only thing I am afraid of that I know*
> *will not hurt me."*
> —ABRAHAM LINCOLN

> *Village life in Israel ceased, ceased until I,*
> *Deborah, arose, arose a mother in Israel.*
> —THE HOLY BIBLE, JUDGES 5:7

I consider my friend Debra. She has been married for ten years. Before she married, she had the ordinary trappings of any single red-blooded American woman. She had a great job, and got her hair foiled

---

[1] I suppose Ms. Steinem would agree that divorced men should refuse to pay child support based on their supposed redundancy? I wonder how popular she would be with feminists if this logically consistent consequence were exercised.

and her nails gelled; she owned a swank condo, wore cute jeans, and even drove a little red sports car. To the outside world looking in, she had it all.

Then she met Tom. He worked for a posh hotel chain, earned a good income, and shared her passion for orphaned children. Fast-forward ten years. They adopted twenty children from the "unadoptable list" that most of us would not have the skill or know how to adopt, let alone raise. Her chosen life may not sound political at first blush, but let me assure you—one does not adopt twenty children without a phenomenal amount of political savvy. She is more skilled at the political game than most politicians I have known in my lifetime. This is what Debra was born to do. To me, this is a brand of feminism in the strongest sense of the word.

> *What Britain needs is an Iron Lady.*
> —MARGARET THATCHER

## Margaret Thatcher

When I have asked women of all political pursuits and persuasions which woman they most admired, Margaret Thatcher has consistently been the hands-down winner. Most women express awe at how flawlessly Margaret functioned in a man's world, yet remained so feminine. I met Margaret Thatcher just after the Reagan revolution. I was struck at how personable she was one-on-one. Her reputation as a cold, distant, calculating politician seemed totally undeserved, judging from our meeting. She was warm, engaging, even embracing. This made me wonder at the disconnect between the "iron lady" projected in the media and the lady in my presence. Was this genuinely as it appeared? Was this intentional? Was this "distance" required of a woman to be effective in that political place and time? These are all questions we ask ourselves when gauging what it means to be a woman, or a lady, in today's society. Few would dispute that Margaret Thatcher was an eminently skilled political artist.

*Dear God, please take care of your servant*
*John Fitzgerald Kennedy.*
—Jackie Kennedy Onassis

## Jackie Kennedy Onassis

Consider Jackie O. The very thought of America's archetypal female political icon conjures pillbox hats and silver clutches, yachts, and fabulous sunglasses. We think she was warm, but why did she not give more of herself to us, her adoring public? Why was she so aloof? Was this mere protection, or was this what we, the public, demand, so we can fill in the gaps in our minds as we like?

Perhaps the modern-day lady is a bit aloof. Perhaps the mystery is compelling in a day with storming paparazzi, tabloid inundation, and social media. Despite her aloofness, she was adored, and is still held up as an icon on the subject of "feminine."

*Because the idea that a black woman from Birmingham, Alabama*
*ought to be a Soviet specialist is pretty farfetched, right?*
—Condoleezza Rice

## Condoleezza Rice

Condoleezza Rice seems to have the aloof thing down to an art. We know about her talents and abilities, but very little about her heart. Popularity polling would probably deem her a favorite pick for public office, but why? Is it merely because she is talented and we know nothing else about her? Does her willingness to share her heart matter to us?

She is strong, articulate, educated, and amazingly adept at conducting interviews that reveal very little about her personally. We know more about the White House dogs during the Bush administration than we do about the personal interactions of the Secretary of State. This is obviously by design. Why is it that when we know more about a woman (for example, Sarah Palin) we tend to ridicule her, and when we know less, we tend to hold her in high esteem? Does this speak to our *true* bias against women, or does this speak more to our desire for more traditionally feminine roles, such as meekness, gentleness, and a quiet spirit?

> *A woman is like a tea bag. You never know how strong*
> *she is until you put her in hot water.*
> *I think a woman gets more if she acts feminine.*
> —Nancy Reagan

## Nancy Reagan

What creates our reactions to other powerful women? What is it that photosynthesizes within us to become the "image" that burdens our female political icons?

I have already referred to my affinity for President Reagan. We spent time at his ranch as a family, and we witnessed first hand his love of country and his vision of the simple, beautiful America he bequeathed to us. We saw his love of humor with his Jelly Bellies, his jeep, and his jackalope in the den of Rancho de Cielo. His love of friends was evident in the welcoming, casual style of his retreat, with his photos and items of Western culture, as well as his personal reading collection. His love of God's creation was apparent in his sprawling ranch set quaintly in the mountains, his sweet horses, his gently buried, carefully marked pet graves, and his hand-tamed property that could have easily been groomed by servants, but was not. I love to remember that hardworking, loving, warm Reagan.

One other thing is evident about his love. He loved Nancy. He wrote her name in a little cave just behind the entrance to their ranch. He named their little canoe "Tru Love" and gave it to Nancy as a gift. Then there are the letters. Oh, he loved his Nancy all right. As much as many of us loved him, did we love his beloved?

I met Nancy years after the president passed, at a private dinner secretly arranged with Merv Griffin by our wonderful friend, Mike. To us, Nancy was the one piece remaining of the Ronald Reagan we loved. I was thrilled to meet the object of his heart. The setting could not have been more perfect. Tears filled my eyes and hers as I told her what their love meant to me, to all Americans.

I could tell the pain of losing him was still more than she could bear. Oddly, I only knew him publicly, but it was heavy for me too. I wanted to really like her, but I found myself struggling with some very "female" emotions, as I have come to see them now. I wondered why her public persona was so very different from that of other women damaged by "First Ladyhood." I believe these sentiments are more about us than her, and I believe women have something to learn herein. I wanted to know this! How is she different than Jackie O? Was her pain not just as agonizing in losing her Ron, as was Jackie's in losing her adulterous spouse? Jackie survived and moved on; we watched in anticipation for her success with Aristotle Onassis and others, always hoping she would find the love she deserved. Yet we idolize President Kennedy and prefer to remember him with her.

We remember President Reagan alone, without Nancy. While it is obvious that he drew much of his strength from her, there is little public discussion about that. All politics aside, why does the public not embrace this wife of an iconic president? After the years of private pain she has endured, where is our affection for her? Ultimately, what can women learn about the treatment of other women and images of self?

*I am not some Tammy Wynette standing by my man.*
—HILLARY CLINTON

## Hillary Clinton

Then there is Hillary. Some feel sorry for her for what her womanizing husband did to her, but in the hearts of many Americans, we think he (President Clinton) is nicer, and we like him more. Many perceived her as bitter when she was First Lady. Her popularity has ebbed and flowed in her public life with both republicans and democrats. Regardless of politics, do you really want to be her friend? Is there something in Hillary, just as a person, that people perceive as abrasive? Like Jackie O, Hillary was betrayed by her husband. Jackie O is the eternal victim. We imagine she might have been damaged beyond repair by the hurt she endured in her life, and we feel compassionate admiration for her. What about Hillary? Why is she so different? Might it be because she bounced back and went on as a strong, capable, scarred but not crippled woman? If we really believe in the strength of women to transcend their injuries and circumstances, why do we sometimes resent it when they do? Again, I submit to you that vulnerability—or meekness—is an admirable quality in our culture's idea of femininity.

> *Jealousy is all the fun you think they had.*
> —ERICA JONG

## Sarah Palin

Consider the polarizing figure of Sarah Palin. I first met Sarah after my own hard-fought primary where I was chided by my opponent and her pious crowd for wanting to run for office while I was the mother of five children, one with Down Syndrome. I found it particularly insulting since my husband held elective office for fourteen years with no one ever once peppering him with questions like those they asked me daily. I met the double standard head-on. So you can only imagine how well I could relate to Governor Palin as a woman in politics with five children, one with Down Syndrome.

I met her at her hotel room in St. Louis after waiting for her entourage with her husband (one of the sweetest guys in the world), Todd. I was shocked to hear McCain staffers cut her down and criticize every choice she made. She was criticized that day for "demanding" someone purchase a baby seat for Trig, which they found frivolous and self-indulgent. The irony was lost on them that if she hadn't had that seat, the whole campaign would have been grilled for taking a baby in the motorcade without a safety seat. Furthermore, God forbid there had been an accident and little Trig was hurt!

None of that seemed to matter to the McCain staffers who were controlling Sarah's every move, to the republican establishment who were still scratching their heads over McCain's choice for Veep, or to the press who was happy to point to her every shortcoming. To those who were jealous, tired, or frustrated that they were losing, she was an easy scapegoat. Some in the republican establishment labeled her a whiny country bumpkin who was upstaging their candidate and might be credited with winning the election when each of them believed they deserved the credit.

They hissed on with talk of how "shabby and podunk" a dresser the governor was, how she was not good enough for McCain, and how they could not let her within a mile of the blue bloods for certainty of a blunder. I took my seat next to her baggage handler, who wasn't saying much, but he seemed above all the clamor and felt safe.

I don't know what I expected when she walked in to the hotel, but there she was, looking just like . . . well, Sarah Palin. We stood. She approached a very tired Todd, the sympathetic baggage handler, and me with a warm, homey hug for Todd and sincere greetings for the rest of us. "Hi, I'm Sarah," she offered with a tired but sincere smile.

"It's an honor, Governor." I responded. She stood there with a baby bottle in her hand, baby Trig on her hip. She warmly reached down to quiet littler Piper, who was tugging at her sleeve, wanting something terribly important to a five-year-old. She talked to me as a mom. We talked about our children, specifically about the blessings of having a child with a special need. We talked about faith, family, and the perils of the campaign trail with children and detractors, as only we could. She was so honest. In a word, I think that honesty is her baseline. She struck me with her transparency like a bolt of lightning because I had never met a high-level politician who felt so authentic.

My background in psychology could barely register a politician with this air of authenticity—it just would not compute. While I furiously searched for what was wrong with this woman, I settled in to realize that I felt I had known her forever. What you see is exactly what you get, and while I believe that is her personal triumph, I also question if we as a public are ready for her level of authenticity. I wonder if we prefer the quiet aloofness of Jackie Kennedy or Condi Rice, who seem content to remain in the background, leading only as directed by a man.

The governor called me after an event to thank me for playing with her children. Again, I was struck by that honest, maternal reaction to something that seemed very normal to me. I have played with the offspring of dozens of lower-level politicians, and never had one call to thank me personally for it. What is it about Sarah Palin that is so threatening or upsetting to the electorate? Why do they feel the need to criticize her so harshly? Could it be because we see more of ourselves in Sarah than we want to see?

> *I don't care to belong to any club that will*
> *have me as a me as a member.*
> —GROUCHO MARX

We say we want "we, the people" commoners for politicians, and yet many conservatives clamor to criticize her. We say we want a non-ivy league, non-blue-blood, non-billionaire for a politician. Palin fits every one of those bills, and yet she is rejected. It makes me wonder if, although we want more women involved generally, we are really ready for them to lead in a serious way, if they are merely "one of us."

Or, could it be that we are jealous? After all, she does seem to have it all together. She is pretty, thin, smart, savvy, happily married, and has beautiful children and great parents who love her. I have seen many women in politics—just like in junior high school—hated for that, while the haters grasped for excuses to hate that pretty girl. Should all "beautiful warriors" gird their loins for the attacks, regardless of good intentions, preparation, or aptitude for the job?

A recent study published by Canadian researcher Tracy Vaillan-court said that women can be passive-aggressive with other women if they perceive them as "sexy and thin." She describes the competitive nature of women they perceive as a threat as having an "old brain in a modern context." While women purport to want more women in places of leadership, they spend too much time demeaning one another. It is ironic that while women say they want no judgment on the way they dress, they suddenly become pageant judges whenever a female politician enters their view.

Did we prefer the hard feel of Lady Thatcher or the mystery of Jackie O? Who is the political icon of our generation? What will we, as a public, demand? How can women be a part of the kinder, gentler day in politics if we say we want one set of values but demand another?

> *Jealousy is the tribute mediocrity pays to genius.*
> —FULTON J. SHEEN

When I began with the Tea Party, I loved the idea of a fresh, new, enlightened group of savvy adults changing the world in an outspoken, clear, no-frills way. One can imagine my disappointment when I saw that this child I had helped birth was growing up to be a carbon copy (or, in this computer age, a file/edit/select all/copy) of the Republican Party—warts, and all! At the heart of the matter were the same battles I thought we left behind in junior high—we hurt ourselves. In Republican politics, I had watched helplessly as one pro-life legislator killed a good pro-life bill not because it wasn't a good bill but because her name wasn't on it. I saw good efforts fraction over jealousies, and good alliances fall apart because there wasn't enough proverbial "air at the top of the tank."

Imagine how it felt to watch the GOP lose the presidency to Obama, help nurture this nascent movement called the Tea Party, then watch it struggle with the same maturity issues that caused me to turn away from the GOP in the first place. It was discouraging, but it was expected. Like a disappointed but understanding mother, I posted the following on New Year's Day in response to all of it:

OKAY! This one is for the girls. You know who you are. You are fighting for your children's futures. You are fighting for all that is right and good in this world, with a spatula in one hand and a "Don't Tread On Me!" flag waiving in the other. You understand liberty, and aren't willing to compromise even if it means that life is very inconvenient for you at times. Your children know the Pledge, the Bill of Rights, much of the rest of the US Constitution. They know Scripture, they know history. They know how a bill becomes a law. They are versed in battle and etiquette on equal levels. They can wear white gloves to a black tie event, and reload a rifle in the rain. They hunt (good practice for future skills of self protection). Your family chides you, your enemies envy you, and your friends challenge and motivate you. You are a millennial mother. Just doing the daily business of raising up a well-mannered warrior who can stand against the dark forces of evil, all in a day's work.

I will submit to you that we might be undermining our own efforts. For all of our big plans, grandiose accomplishments, and lavish accolades, we can be pretty petty. I see these political moms doing all the right things, and still letting envy, jealousy, and pettiness divide their efforts, and I just want to pull out my bullhorn and scream "WHY?" How small of us. How unfair to our children and our husbands who sacrifice greatly for us. How disloyal to our God, whom we claim to serve. And most pathetically, how self-defeating. We are stronger together.

I bet that like me, your ultimate dream is to walk up to the gates of heaven and have the Lord say, "Well done, good and faithful servant." But I bet that, like me, you are not always a servant. I am rather pathetic at it. I blame it on being an only child. We all have our excuses. I have mine, and I can rattle them off more quickly than I can recite my children's birth dates.

"She wants what I have. She might be BETTER than me. She might reach the finish line before me. She says she is my friend, but can I REALLY trust her? I have been hurt too many times by women just like her. She probably thinks she is better/thinner/smarter/richer/more Christian/more savvy than me! There might not be enough oxygen at the top of the tank for both of us! I know! I will get better lipstick! Gloss! Gloss."

Do we do this with men? If I think a man is better at something than me, why is that okay? Men are better at a lot of things. John is better at almost everything than I am and it only makes me love him more. I have found that I have many "guy" friends, and a few, solid (and very patient—THANK YOU) good girlfriends. Why? What kind of example am I setting for my daughters? I tell them to get along and forebear and love in spite of flaws, yet I am quick to get impatient with the woman who is too good at calculus (how COULD she?!), because I struggle with it (blood pressure rising quickly).

I love real New York–style cheesecake and real butter cream frosting. I do not like to share it. If she wants a piece of it, I will probably try to hide it someplace. Why?

Is it really any wonder that we are so insecure, when we have had, and ARE, bad examples of how to prop up other women?

Now, while I am rambling, I think it in order to clarify that I am not a feminist in a Pelosi/Hillary sort of a way. But I am pro-woman because I value the special gifts that God used to equip women in such amazing ways. We are so capable and necessary in public dialogue and political action, and in raising up the next generation. There is a perfect time for disdain regardless of gender. And the fact is that there are caustic people of both genders that we are better off without our lives. I don't think we should be any more tolerant of women than men.

My observation is the "scratchers and clawers" fail time after time. If women choose that route, we WILL fail. If we are really going to reclaim our world for our daughters and sons, if we are really going to make it in our careers, and if we are really going to be good mothers, we need to look inside deeply, and humble ourselves. Are we willing to do that to advance the causes we say we believe in and are willing to fight for? Are we REALLY fighters, or sissies? Can we really expect the men we work with to extend us credibility when we act like sissies? In our deepest hearts, should we be asking if we have earned, my dear sisters, the glass ceiling we keep blasting our head against?

As the New Year enters, I am going to guard myself against this self-defeating baby behavior I should have been past in junior high school—even if she is better in calc, or if she wants some of my cheesecake (do I HAVE to share the butter cream?). I can spare a little humility to share with a sister. Can you? Sisters, join hands!

We are stronger together.

*And he said unto them, "Ye will surely say unto me this proverb, Physician, heal thyself.*

—LUKE 4:23, KJV

Perhaps before we look at what we can do for society, we need to look deeply at our role in that society. That will cause us to focus on who we are, how we raise our daughters, relate to other women and men, and the messages we are sending to our generation via our own actions.

We will need to guard ourselves with the abject rejection that femininity must equal masculinity. It doesn't. Femininity (in its pure form) is its own unique brand of natural giftedness. Women don't need to reject their femininity, and women don't need the women's movement any more than fish need to ride bicycles. Women need to claim their own role in our culture and teach it to other women.

Whether it is activism or domestic duty, whether it's public or private, whether to your mother, your daughter, or your husband, I believe we are called to the chivalrous version of our womanhood. Simply put, *act* like a lady! ★

*Chapter Nine*

★★★

# From Into the Wild
# to "Girls Gone Wild"

*Children are being given a false picture of what it means to be human. We tell them to be good and kind, nonviolent and giving. But on all sides they see media images and hear and read stories that portray us as bad, cruel, violent, and selfish.*
　　　　　　　　　　　—RIANE EISLER, TOMORROW'S CHILDREN

*The United States is unusual among the industrial democracies in the rigidity of the system of ideological control—"indoctrination," we might say—exercised through the mass media.*
　　　　　　　　　　　—NOAM CHOMSKY

## Hell in a Handbasket

We are not the first culture critics to suggest that Western society—particularly in the United States—has been devolving for decades. From Robert Bork's *Slouching Towards Gomorrah* to Sean Hannity and Zell Miller's *Deficit of Decency*, many conservative authors have been lamenting the degradation of virtue in our culture. The Media Research Center, headed by Brent Bozell, excels in its role as media watchdog, policing the plethora of films and television programs that either advance or undermine ladylike or gentlemanly behavior and ideals.

Our first aim is to specify why and how the media in the past several decades have wreaked their havoc on these ideals. Second, we will list the most offending members—what we call the "Enemies of Virtue All-Stars." Finally, we recognize there are exceptions to this trend. After distinguishing them, we will call on people of virtue to support wholesome media that cherish the virtues and those heroes who exemplify them.

## Media: Cause or Effect?

Without question, the media have changed their stripes in the past several decades. Why? One hypothesis stresses the relative youth of certain media like film and television. Because they are less than a century old, some might say they are going through an adolescent rebellious period where they must break free of the restraints of their controlling "parents" (patriarchal studio heads, for example). If that were so, earlier film and television producers and writers were merely pretending to be kinder, gentler, and more virtuous, biding their time until they could get away with expressing a deeper, truer depravity.

We have argued that a general cultural shift away from God and toward godlessness, along with all of its logical consequences, is both reflected in the changing media *and* has propelled and quickened that cultural flight from virtue. We would also argue that people don't want to see virtue in their media heroes because that would make people feel bad. Modern Americans simply do not seem as able or willing to tolerate bad feelings.

The advent of popular psychology in the twentieth century shifted the focus from community, action, and duty to feelings, self, and avoidance of judgment. Sigmund Freud, Carl Rogers, and other icons in the field of psychology have wreaked great havoc on the virtues. Instead of responsibility to others, Freud's theories spawned a focus on the biological urges. The *id*, after all, is not immoral, but amoral.[1] Carl Rogers preached *unconditional positive regard*, which confuses judgment of behavior with a judgmental spirit, inadvertently sacrificing any critique of thoughts, words, or deeds at the altar of self-worship.

Compare and contrast the lists of film heroes later in this chapter. Heroes from yesteryear served others, perceived a sense of duty to others, and lived by a code of ethics that was handed down to them by their predecessors, to whom they usually submitted. More recent heroes have taken the value of rugged individualism to its extreme, glorying in the kind of frenzied rebellion that feeds their narcissistic wounds and insatiable appetite for aggrandizement.

Many of these heroes are admittedly engaging. Their powerful charisma can lead viewers to wonder if perhaps they, too, could be their own ruler, their own sovereign, their own god. Their message sounds eerily like that of the serpent in the garden: "When you eat of it your eyes will be opened, and you will be like God, knowing good and evil" (Genesis 3:5)

The perverse lies of liberalism, atheism, and radical feminism are thus transmitted through all the various media.

## Film

Compare several of the heroes of early film history with those of the last fifty years:

---

[1] *Immoral* refers to desires and behavior that are judged based on moral standards (e.g., how we treat people); *amoral* refers to that which is not subject to moral judgment (e.g., mathematics, biological mechanisms)

| Pre-1960 Film Heroes | Post-1960 Film Heroes |
|---|---|
| George Bailey (*It's a Wonderful Life*) | James Bond |
| Lou Gehrig (*Pride of the Yankees*) | Michael Corleone (*The Godfather*) |
| Alvin C. York (*Sergeant York*) | Tyler Durden (*Fight Club*) |
| Colonel Nicholson (*Bridge on the River Kwai*) | Thelma and Louise |
| Atticus Finch (*To Kill a Mockingbird*) | Ada McGrath (*The Piano*) |
| Father Flanagan (*Boys Town*) | Che Guevara (*Che*) |
| Juror #8 (*12 Angry Men*) | John Bender (*The Breakfast Club*) |
| Dorothy (*Wizard of Oz*) | R. P. McMurphy (*One Flew Over the Cuckoo's Nest*) |

So many heroes in modern film appear to fit the term *lovable scoundrel*.[2] Contrast them with the heroes from film's early decades. All of these early figures were men and women of solid, albeit imperfect, virtue. Almost all exhibited excellent manners, even during the most difficult circumstances. They treasured other people more than themselves, many acknowledged God, and they prioritized country and nobility. Much of their behavior was sacrificial; they elevated justice and the needs of others ahead of their own comfort (e.g., George Bailey saving his brother, Atticus Finch representing a black man in the rural South).

Modern heroes, in contrast, tend to be of highly questionable character. Michael Corleone is beloved not in spite of his ruthlessness but because of it. Thelma and Louise celebrate their feminist liberation by hurling themselves off a cliff. James Bond, while

---

[2] The exception being Che Guevara, who would be more aptly named *Loathsome Scoundrel*.

well-mannered, well-dressed, and arguably loyal to queen and country, evidences a ruthless and almost amoral sensibility. Tyler Durden celebrates humankind's more chaotic, animal instincts. John Bender, certainly a more sympathetic character, flaunts his ignorance and rejects authority, as well as anything refined or excellent.

## Popular Literature and Film's Warped View of the Gentleman

A perfect example of how heroes of literature and film can subtly alter one's virtues can be found on the blog www.howtobeagentleman.com. This anonymous blogger gives as his paragon of gentlemanly behavior none other than 007: James Bond. He supports his claim by offering the following evidence:

> Another reason we can consider him a gentleman is how he treats women. Although he is a womanizer he still treats women with respect. He's self confident [sic] but not arrogant. Charming and sensitive but still manly and tough. He is capable of courting a woman and still make [sic] her feel comfortable in the process. He is also appropriately and stylishly dressed for every occasion. Although James Bond acts a nice guy to women that's not all he does. He mixes the nice guy part with a little bit of naughtiness.

If the mainstream culture perceives a misogynistic cad who has no problem slapping women around as a "nice guy with a little bit of naughtiness," then we have slouched all the way to Gomorrah.

## The "Enemies of Virtue All-Stars": Media Division
### Talk Radio

| | |
|---|---|
| **1st Place:** | Ed Schultz |
| **Runner-Up:** | Alan Colmes |
| **Dishonorable Mention:** | Schultz called Laura Ingraham a "right-wing slut" on his program. Colmes mocked the Santorum family's choice to grieve for their stillborn child by bringing it home. |

## Cable News

| | |
|---|---|
| **1st Place:** | Keith Olbermann |
| **Runner-Up:** | Lawrence O'Donnell |
| **Dishonorable Mention:** | Olbermann has never enjoyed a reputation as a gentleman, but revealed a tarnished soul when he intimated that S. E. Cupp's parents should have aborted her. O'Donnell has a long history of interrupting guests, as well as name-calling and near-manic hostility. |

## Films

| | |
|---|---|
| **1st Place:** | *English Patient* |
| **Runner-Up:** | *Shakespeare In Love* |
| **Dishonorable Mention:** | Message of both films: it's perfectly acceptable to have affairs, as long as you can rationalize it.[3] |

## Books

| | |
|---|---|
| **1st Place:** | *Beautiful Disaster* |
| **Runner-Up:** | *Cider House Rules* |
| **Dishonorable Mention:** | Kylie Adams's teen novel creates characters who would make Madonna sick to her stomach. John Irving's novel glorifies a doctor led by moral relativism; in his world, piety is a vice, abortion is a virtue, and religion is for fools. |

## Television

| | |
|---|---|
| **1st Place:** | Donald Draper (*Mad Men*) |
| **Runner-Up:** | Samantha Jones (*Sex and the City*) |

---

[3] And your character is played by one of the Fiennes brothers.

**Dishonorable**

**Mention:** These two should get married; they'd likely cheat on each other during the entire duration of their marriage. Draper would be miserable, while Samantha would brag about it to her friends.

## Musicians

| | |
|---|---|
| **1st Place:** | Marilyn Manson |
| **Runner-Up:** | Ke$ha |

**Dishonorable**

**Mention:** Orcs are twisted and tortured versions of elves; Marilyn Manson appears to be a similarly tortured, effeminate man. One of Ke$ha's hits is "Sleazy." In fact, almost all of her lyrics and persona celebrate an extreme, depraved femininity.

## Sorry, Charlie, You *Are* a Role Model

In 1993, Charles Barkley starred in a TV commercial for Nike. In it, he emphatically asserts, "I am *not* a role model." He could not have been more wrong. One can empathize with Barkley; who would want to accept the responsibility for leading millions of children down a path of immorality and hooligan behavior? Granted, he was attempting to make the point that parents should be a child's role model; on that point, we heartily agree.

However, one does not have to sign on a dotted line to become a role model; it is not a volunteer position. The public chooses whether which public figures are role models. Barkley and other athletes are role models for many children and adults, whether they like it or not.

## Sporting Brats

Want to tickle your neighbor's funny bone? Make the claim that today's sports figures are more gentlemanly (or ladylike) than those of the first half of the twentieth century. It would be like suggesting that children are better behaved now than in previous generations or that the average Hollywood film is more family-friendly than ever before. Nobody in their right mind would buy it.

Almost nowhere is today's *virtue decay* more apparent than in the world of professional sports—and to a lesser but still profound degree college, high school, and even children's sports.

Here are the **"Enemies of Virtue All-Stars": Sports Division**.

## 1. Michael Vick

Most readers recall Mr. Vick's involvement in dog fighting. When police investigated a dog-fighting ring in 2007, Vick lied about it. Only when his "associates" decided to implicate him did he plead guilty. Not only did he finance the dog-fighting ring, he supported the hanging, drowning, and mutilation of many pit bulls that weren't considered sufficiently vicious fighters.

## 2. Tonya Harding

In 1994, Tonya Harding was one of the top figure skaters in the world. Prior to the US figure skating championships, she and her ex-husband hired a thug to break the leg of Nancy Kerrigan, her stiffest competitor. Badly injured, Kerrigan dropped out of the contest, allowing Harding to win the championship, which helped propel her to the 1994 Olympic team. Before long, she was forced to admit her role in concocting and then covering up the attack. Outrageously, when the US Olympic Committee attempted to remove her from the Olympic team, Harding threatened legal action and the committee relented. She placed eighth in the Olympics and was then banned for life by the USFSA.

## 3. John McEnroe

There was almost no more disrespectful individual professional athlete in the 1970s than tennis legend John McEnroe. He was brash, had a horrific temper, and evidenced little respect for the game's authorities. When expressing disagreement with a call, he would often throw his racket in disgust, and then berate the umpire, often with cuss words that were shown on live television. His temper tantrums often lasted for minutes.

## 4. Serena Williams

Ms. Williams has outdone her male counterpart with such vile and hateful rhetoric that many parents refuse to allow their children to watch professional tennis. After being penalized during a match in 2011, she called the umpire names, ordered her around like a servant, and ranted for minutes about how ugly a person the umpire was. She even made a veiled threat: "If you ever see me walking down the hall, walk the other way." Sadly, she was only fined two thousand dollars. Two years earlier, she exhibited a similar tantrum, threatening to shove the ball down the umpire's throat. After neither episode did she display remorse or make a genuine apology for her disgusting behavior.

## 5. Roberto Alomar

It is difficult to imagine anything more vile than spitting in someone's face. This is exactly what second baseman Alomar did to umpire John Hirschbeck after he committed a heinous crime toward Alomar— calling him out on strikes. Alomar immediately began arguing, and after the two jawed at each other for a few seconds, he let loose a big spray of spit—right in Hirschbeck's face. What is almost as disgusting is that Major League Baseball suspended Alomar for a mere *five games* (about 3 percent of the regular season) . . . with pay![4]

## 6. Roger Clemens

Even if Clemens didn't represent the sad number of professional baseball players who were likely steroid users, his behavior would still be lamentable. During Game two of the 2000 World Series, Clemens picked up a broken bat that had shattered from Mike Piazza. He whipped it right at Piazza, which started a bench-clearing brawl. Clemens claimed that because he was "pumped up" with nervous energy (i.e., "roid rage"), he mistook the bat for a ball.[5] Clemens now faces perjury charges for

---

[4] This is like punishing a child for rude behavior by sending him to bed early, but letting him take his dessert and video games with him.

[5] If he really thought it was a ball, why would he throw it at the base runner? Some lies are clever; others are evidence of either profound stupidity or desperation.

lying to Congress during their steroid witch hunt and is a defendant in a defamation suit brought by his former friend and trainer.

## 7. Ndamukong Suh

One of the best young defensive linemen in football, Suh already had a solid reputation as a malicious and dirty player when he was ejected from one game after slamming an opposing player's head into the ground, then stomping on his arm. He had the audacity to then make up a Clemens-esque story about it. Unfortunately, his own team refused to discipline him, instead allowing league officials to bear that burden, which resulted in only a two-game suspension.

## 8. Jerry Sandusky/Joe Paterno/Mike McQueary

In one of the most disturbing and disgusting stories in collegiate sports history, Jerry Sandusky has been accused of molesting and raping multiple boys over several years. Assistant Coach Mike McQueary witnessed Sandusky raping a boy in the locker room shower. Rather than intervening, he left the scene. The next day, he reported the incident to head coach Paterno (no relation, thankfully), who astonishingly held onto the information over the weekend, without telling either the athletic director or any other school official so as to not "interfere with their weekends."

## 9. Latrell Sprewell

During one argument with a teammate, Sprewell threatened him with a two-by-four and promised to return with a gun. In one famous 1997 incident, he got into an argument with his head coach, threatened to kill him, then dragged him to the ground by his throat. After "calming down," he returned and punched the coach in the face. Thankfully, the league suspended him for the entire season, which cost him millions. Off the court, Sprewell was accused of choking a woman nearly to death during sex.[6]

---

[6] Sprewell nears the apex of the "Top Ten List of People Who Shouldn't Babysit Your Children."

Some of these athletes' awful behavior is not surprising, since they grew up in and exist in a highly permissive culture that handsomely rewards outrageous, selfish, entitled behavior. Professional sports organizations have done a horrible job of negotiating contracts with their respective players' associations, which should allow the leagues *and* teams to properly discipline players when they exhibit intolerable behavior. Most leagues are hamstrung by silly rules, and the response to most bad behavior is nothing greater than a wrist slap.

Imagine how John McEnroe's or Serena Williams's on-court behavior would change if they knew they would be banished from their sport *forever* for their infantile, shamefully disrespectful behavior? The reality is that players like Alomar and Suh know darn well that they can essentially get away with out-of-control behavior because their teams think they need their skills and the team owners, media, and audiences want their services. They know any consequence will be minor, if anything. And so their inflated egos are trained.

Behavior like this brings to mind the gladiatorial age, where failure meant death and one's survival instincts elicited the most extreme barbarism and self-promotion. It makes one shiver to imagine that our culture has regressed that far.

We are not under the delusion that athletes have all been paragons of virtue until recently. There have always been hooligans in the sports world. Ty Cobb, for example, was profoundly racist. He was also brash, ill-tempered, and spiteful. He once attacked a man in the stands for taunting him with suggestions that his mother was half black. It turned out that the man had no hands and could not fight back. Cobb reportedly bragged about beating the man senseless: "I would have done the same if he had been without legs too." Nice guy, huh?

This problem is not limited to the world of men; women are following suit, as if the feminist movement ordered them to become as obnoxious and narcissistic as their naturally testosterone-enhanced counterparts. Not only are they catching up to men's athletic prowess, they seem to be trying to match their propensity for foul behavior and unsportsmanlike attitudes. This trend does not represent an evolution. It has been consistently, powerfully—albeit inadvertently— drilled into the minds of female athletes.

## Exceptions to the Rule

Although the general trend in the media has been deplorable, not every movie, book, magazine, or sport degrades the virtues of the lady and the gentleman. There are plenty of athletes, films, television shows, and other media that are consistent with nobility and its virtues. The following is just a small sample.

## Virtue on Talk Radio

Conservatives own the talk radio market. While many liberal radio outlets like AirAmerica have failed miserably, despite being well-funded and stocked with liberal celebrities, conservative talk radio hosts are a thriving bunch. From Dennis Miller to Sean Hannity, Laura Ingraham to Dr. Gina, the list of conservatives who champion virtue makes for an impressive roster.[7]

Many of these, such as Limbaugh and Mark Levin, are almost exclusively focused on politics. Others, like Ingraham, Dr. Gina, and Dennis Prager, spend a significant portion of air time focusing on morals, ethics, and virtues. The latter two also tend to comport themselves as a respectful lady and gentleman, respectively. This extremely important use of the airwaves helps conservatives stand out and model for listeners the complementary virtues of respect and strength.

## Virtue in Cable News

Arguably the most contentious medium, cable news programs—especially those that utilize commentary—invite outrageous verbal sparring in order to win over viewers—and as a result, advertising dollars. Apparently, people like to see two people engaged in gladiatorial bickering, in which both parties shout over each other, insinuate unflattering things about the other, without careful consideration of a word

---

[7] No doubt, there are also conservatives in talk radio—and in every medium—who are anything but virtuous in thought, word, and deed.

the other speaks. This is not how ladies and gentlemen engage in disagreement.

Still, some cable news personalities are more gentlemanly or lady-like than others. Sean Hannity seems affable and consistently keeps his jabs above the belt, while Monica Crowley does a superb job of attacking liberal orthodoxy while retaining her femininity.

## Virtue in Film

Two movies in particular come to mind: *The Incredibles* and *The Princess Bride*. In the former, several excellent virtues are elevated: family life, self-sacrifice, humble pride in one's gifts (and, by contrast, shunning mediocrity), and courage. In the latter, several virtues are exhibited, including courage (Inigo, Westley), humility (Fezzik), patience (the grandfather), faith (Buttercup), and faithfulness (Inigo).

The irony is that many of the films that extol virtue and elevate ladylike or gentlemanly behavior have been tremendously successful. In fact, of the fifty highest grossing films of all-time, only two were Rated R (*Passion of the Christ* and *Matrix, Reloaded*); of the top-ten highest grossing films, six are Rated G or PG and none are Rated R. The *Movieguide* report, a study that rates movies on their content—contrasting conservative versus liberal, Christian and moral versus liberal/leftist or immoral—found in 2012 that seven of the top-ten films of 2011 scored high on *Movieguide's* index and these films earned more than five times as much as those films that scored low on their index.

When will Hollywood understand that, deep down, viewers crave innocence, goodness, and virtue?

## Virtue in Books

Readers have a similar appetite for that which is noble. Of the top five best-selling English-language fiction books of all time, four are tales concerned with morality, virtue, and innocence (e.g., *A Tale of Two Cities*, *The Hobbit*, *The Lord of the Rings*, and *The Lion, the Witch, and the Wardrobe*). Likewise, all but one of the top-ten best-selling book series of all time are children's series; most have characters who could legitimately be labeled as ladies or gentlemen.

As a medium, nonfiction literature has been somewhat friendly to conservative values, virtues, and ideals. Books espousing conservative ideas tend to sell more books than their liberal counterparts, although there tend to be far more liberal books on the market.

There are many excellent examples to choose from, but one non-political book deserves special mention: *Bonhoeffer: Pastor, Martyr, Prophet, Spy* by Eric Metaxas. This stellar biography makes crystal clear both the humanity and virtuousness of one of the twentieth century's finest gentlemen and heroes. For children, William Bennett's *The Children's Book of Virtues* could not be any more self-explanatory.

## Virtue on Television

On television, two of the most successful programs in the latter half of the '70s were *Little House on the Prairie* and *The Waltons*. Both of these excellent shows illustrated a rural American family. These families were intact with a parent-first hierarchy, and showed respect between father and mother and children and their parents. Their characters also did the unthinkable: they worshiped God.[8] It has been a long time since a major television series focused on a family that lived out their faith in Christ.

We find it more than interesting that almost none of the heroines of modern television are married with children. Other than the aforementioned shows, one of the exceptions is the virtue-minded *Dr. Quinn, Medicine Woman* (although she did not marry until the end of the show's third season).

One of the best shows in recent times that appears to cherish and exemplify virtue is *Friday Night Lights*. The main character, Coach Taylor, is a *man*. He is masculine, tough, and ruggedly handsome. He works hard, believes in teamwork, and has high expectations for himself and others.

---

[8] In a Christian church, no less! And they owned guns! Someone alert the authorities!

Morally, he provides an excellent contrast to the sorry legacy of Sandusky and Paterno. One can only imagine what he would have done to his assistant coach had such disgusting acts been perpetrated on his watch. He likely would have wound up being arrested for a violent crime—a crime for which he would have been lauded.

Taylor loves his wife. He is an imperfect husband in many ways, but he is committed to his life partner and relies heavily on her. In fact, in one episode he states, "Marriage requires maturity. Marriage requires two people that will listen, really listen to each other. Marriage most of all requires compromise."

One of the virtues Coach Taylor extols is integrity-creating pride. He drives himself and trains his players to achieve victory, but what is more important to Taylor is giving his all to success and feeling pride in the process more than the outcome.

In sum, Coach Taylor is a gentleman—the kind of man most men would like to emulate.[9]

## Virtue in Magazines

Every child who has visited a pediatrician's office has seen *Highlights for Children* magazine. With a circulation of over three million, it has been part of fabric of American children's literature since 1940. Its feature cartoon, *Goofus and Gallant*, with its two diametrically opposed characters, have modeled vice and virtue, respectively.

Gallant is the boy who does everything right. He is virtuous to a fault. He is patient, he is kind, he is . . . yes, almost everything Paul describes in 1 Corinthians 13. More than withstanding any temptation—such as to touch something that isn't his—he doesn't even seem to be struck with temptation. He also seems to confront every situation with a humble smile on his face.

By contrast, Goofus always makes the wrong choice. He is impulsive, selfish, demanding, thoughtless, unrefined, and immoral. He is pure id, but somehow he does not seem happy with himself.

---

[9] According to Mrs. Paterno, he is the kind of man that most women would like to marry.

Certainly, these caricatures are not a nuanced look at the virtues, nor are they meant to teach new virtues. They do an excellent job, however, of teaching children about opposing choices, and showing that making the moral, ethical, and virtuous choice can result in a joyful heart.

## Virtuous Athletes

Not all sports breed disdainful and uncivilized athletes to the same degree. Arguably, professional hockey's code of conduct—other than the sanctioned fighting—is more gentlemanly than that of the

National Basketball Association. Golf likely employs fewer thugs than boxing. One sport in particular seems to have retained an all-around semblance of class, sportsmanship, mutual respect, and humility: rugby. Soccer has been dubbed "a gentlemen's sport played by ruffians"; rugby appears to be the ruffian sport played by gentlemen. The sport originated in northern Europe, where, in many places, virtues inherent in the gentlemen's code have been integrated.

Rugby's reputation as an intensely physical sport is well-earned. But its culture puts most American team sports to shame. For example, teams discipline their own. If one player disrespects an opponent or plays dirty, the other team withstands the temptation to exact revenge. Instead, the offending player is usually disciplined by his own team. Can you imagine Kobe Bryant benched by his own teammates for being disrespectful to an opponent?

Another example is that referees are always called "sir." In fact, the term has become so ingrained into the culture that "sirring" has become a verb synonymous with refereeing. If a player would dare to disrespect a referee, that team's coach and players would roundly rebuke him (or her; rugby is slowly catching on as a woman's sport in the United States).

After the match, the players demonstrate their mutual respect by applauding for each other, often with impressive genuineness. Finally, the home team demonstrates hospitality by arranging for a meal, usually at a pub or restaurant, and will even house the visiting team for the night.

Imagine if all little leagues trained their basketball, baseball, football, soccer, and hockey coaches and players to behave with this level of respect. Imagine if the parents, players, coaches, and referees all expected behavior and respect at a very high level and offered communal respect to those who exhibited them while rebuking and punishing those who did not. Imagine if they all used the term *gentlemen* and *lady* when describing appropriate behavior. This would go a long way to fostering a virtuous culture.

Finally, we would be remiss if we did not mention at least two figures in the world of sports who embody ladylike and gentlemanly virtue: Tim Tebow and Mary Lou Retton. Almost everyone knows about Tim Tebow, the exciting and talented young quarterback recently traded to the New York Jets. Whatever one's feelings about giving thanks in public for one's success in sports,[10] Tebow appears to be a man of integrity and faith. He will no doubt prove himself to be an imperfect human being, but we wager that most parents would prefer their children emulating Tebow than many other professional athletes. And who can forget the beautiful Olympic performance and equally precious smile of gymnast Mary Lou Retton? Not only a perfect ten on the floor exercise and vault, she has exhibited a sterling demeanor, ladylike manners, and warm spirit, both during and after her gymnastics career.

There are excellent role models out there. Unfortunately, they are the exception to the rule in most of the media and sports world.

---

[10] One could make an argument against public prayer, but Tebow's behavior does not appear pharisaical but simply desiring to give God glory for the gifts and success bestowed upon him.

# PART FOUR

# Reclaiming the Lady and the Gentleman

WE ARE NOT WITHOUT hope or recourse. As a people, we possess the same spirit, virtue, and sacred honor that urged the founders to Declaration, Revolution, and Constitution. Perhaps these traits have lain dormant in many of us, but they are not dead. They have certainly been squeezed out of many of our institutions, but people can change institutions. The poison can be removed. This section provides the antidote.

We envision a multifaceted, top-down and bottom-up countercultural trend that reclaims the virtues, returning our nation to its noble foundations. Culture change must be bipolar. That means that it must stem from both the individual *and* our public institutions. Flowing up from each individual's choice to commit to virtue and flowing down from our government officials, institutions, and media, systemic cultural change is a shared responsibility.

## Paterno/Loudon Hierarchy of Cultural Change

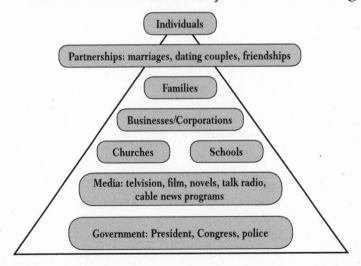

It would be far easier to teach our children the virtue of hard work if our government's policies reflected the virtues, especially civility. The little-league coach who benches his star player for cursing would not be considered a "lone wolf" if more professional sports teams held their players to higher standards of behavior. Teachers who implore their pupils to behave like ladies and gentlemen would not get quizzical looks if parents utilized similar language and taught the virtues inherent in those terms.

The last section of our book lays out a plan for this type of bottom-up, top-down cultural change. We encourage readers to consider their place in this hierarchy and examine the role(s) they can play in creating culture change. Beginning with individual virtue and calling for our leadership to exhibit personal virtue, readers can determine where they can make the greatest impact . . . then act. ★

*Chapter Ten*

★ ★ ★

# Sprinting Toward Gomorrah

*Labour to keep alive in your breast that little spark of celestial fire,
called conscience . . .*
—George Washington

*So let us begin anew—remembering on both sides that civility is
not a sign of weakness, and sincerity is always subject to proof.*
—John F. Kennedy

*We hear a great deal about the rudeness of the rising generation.
I am an oldster myself and might be expected to take the oldsters'
side, but in fact I have been far more impressed by the bad manners of parents to children than by those of children to parents.
Who has not been the embarrassed guest at family meals where the
father or mother treated their grown-up offspring with an incivility
which, offered to any other young people, would simply have ter-
minated the acquaintance? Dogmatic assertions on matters which*

*the children understand and their elders don't, ruthless interrup-*
*tions, flat contradictions, ridicule of things the young take seriously*
*sometimes of their religion insulting references to their friends, all*
*provide an easy answer to the question "Why are they always out?*
*Why do they like every house better than their home?" Who does*
*not prefer civility to barbarism?*

—C. S. LEWIS, THE FOUR LOVES

## The Few, the Proud, the Civil

Maybe it is our cultural obsession with youth? Maybe it is our frustration over the Alinsky tactics on the Left, and our subsequent use
of the same? Maybe it is just plain old sin? No matter how much we
ignore it, or try to deny the truth, Grandma told us to mind our manners. We must not hold Grandma in much reverence, because it takes
a while to think of any real pillars of virtue in the political arena these
days. Rogue is vogue. We enjoy a belligerent, passionate rant. It was a
rant that started the Tea Party. So where is the standard? Or, is it possible to recultivate a tradition of honor while fighting the epic battle
of this civilization? What happens if we don't?

I (Gina) am a conservative radio talk show host and political commentator. We all know that "if it bleeds, it leads." Sex still sells and
the squeaky wheel still gets the oil. So how does civility *ever* prevail?
In talk radio today, frankly, it doesn't, much. The shock-jock tactic
caught on for the Right as well as it did on the Left. Debased radio
shows might have started the denigration of civility, but those claiming conservatism have gladly taken up the mantle. I understand why.
On my show, when I get a liberal caller and take his or her idea and
shred it, I get more fan mail, many "atta girls" on my Facebook page,
and sometimes attention from other media for it. The lesson here
is simple—the audience today demands flair and showmanship. We
want to verbally steamroll our opponents. It is not enough to win in an
old school "Lincoln Douglass"–style debate. We want *moxy*.

I have noticed a distinction, though. Audiences shun those whose
approach is crass or shrill. Those celebrities pop on the scene and

provide a short-lived spectacle, but they fade quickly because they simply seem less credible to those looking for serious analysis, or real truth. I polled my audience to see who they think are the real ladies and gentlemen of media, politics, sports, and Hollywood. This is what they said:

| The good guys: | The bad guys: |
| --- | --- |
| Ron Paul | Bill Maher |
| Bret Baier | Michael Moore |
| Mike Huckabee | Rosie O'Donnell |
| Diane Sawyer | Whoopie Goldberg |
| Gary Sinese | Bobby Knight |
| Albert Pujols | Joy Behar |
| Sarah Palin | Jesse Jackson |
| Kurt Warner | Al Sharpton |
| Tony Dungy | Martin Bashir |
| Bill Clinton | Ed Schultz |
| Rick Santorum | Nancy Pelosi |
| Greta Van Susteren | Chelsea Handler |
| Oprah | Jon Stewart |

My audience loves the idea of a chivalrous war because that is where they believe we are. We agree. Civility is not about turning the other cheek; it is about warring with dignity.

## The Advent of Ladies and Gentlemen

Born of the heart of God, women were born of passion. Taken from the side of man, women were born to help. Chosen to bear the children of all futures, women were born to defend the futures of our children. Hand-selected to endure the peril of children and all parenting entails, women were born to create.

Born in the image of God, men were born of strength. Taken from the blueprint of God, men were born to protect. Chosen to lead the families of all futures, men were born to defend the futures of our children and serve the hand of their wives. Hand-selected to defend the very virtue of the holy plan, men were born warriors.

As creative, defensive, passionate helpmeets, women were born to start political movements. As strong, protective, servant warriors, men are to guard this "one nation under God."

How do we change a culture that seems hell bent? How do we change the political landscape that invites narcissistic personalities who find it quite difficult to live out ladylike or gentlemanly virtues?

Do you ever wish that you could make a difference in your local, state, or national government? Do you ever see a ridiculous law and wish you knew how to stop it? Do the red tape and bureaucracy make government seem distant and unreachable? Do you feel these battles are our last chance to save our culture? Have you ever considered running for office, writing a book, starting a radio show, or going to a protest in order to try to talk some sensibility into your government?

Or are you already knee-deep in the trenches, working every day, sacrificing all the spa visits, sporting events, and shopping sprees because you believe the very heart of our republic is at risk, and somehow it is your responsibility to change that? Do you run yourself ragged with deadlines and headlines and find yourself lying awake at night wondering if it is all worth it? I do.

Good news! More than ever before in our history, we have an opportunity to make sweeping changes in the cultural and political frontier. Your ability to affect what you don't like about government is more real and reachable now than it has ever been in our nation's history. Ladies and Gentlemen, this is our moment!

The reality is that if we are not involved now, we may never be able to be again. If there were ever a time when our unique endowment by our Creator was needed in the political dialogue, it is now. If there were ever a moment in our history when the voice of our ancestors will resonate, it is now. Politics needs you.

I (Gina) have been intimately involved in the world of politics for more than a decade, and I can tell you that I have never seen times like these. More people write books today than ever before, and their books sell more! More conservatives are in journalism—from television, to radio, to newspapers and blogs. The world of media is your playground today!

In this Internet age, anyone can start a blog or Twitter account or set up camp on Facebook. Patriots can pick up a camera and become a citizen journalist or pick up a pen and write an op-ed to their local paper. Reporters, candidate recruiters, and media conglomerates have confided that they are looking for conservatives to join their teams, to interview, or to run for office. Anyone can have their own Internet radio or television show; many of them have launched careers doing just that.

I believe we have come to this momentous place in history due to the natural talents and abilities we have as conservatives. I believe our unique endowment by our Creator has landed us with the skills necessary and useful for such a time as this. I believe that our passion and love for our God, country, families, children, and work have landed us in this place and time, which is unlike any other in our nation's history.

The age of the US and the abundance of information available provide a perspective never before in our history. The click of a button can call up almost any historical event recorded in great detail. Our ability to research and therefore look critically at information we are fed by mass media is unique to us. Our ability to look at the past, predict the threats of the future, and prepare the next generation is unique to us, in this place and time!

Although our ability to equip the next generation is incomparable, so is the necessity that we do! Never have the threats been so widespread and imminent. Never has our future felt so ominous. There seems to be a feeling of a freight train rushing past us, like never before, and in some ways it seems that it is up to us to divert the track.

While we can equip our children, we cannot *depend on* our children. Children are children, and they need to depend on us. We can talk more about this later, but cloistering ourselves in our homes in order to "equip" the next generation is not an option. There is no time for that convenient excuse, no matter how badly we wish there were.

I doubt you would argue that if each of us gave ten minutes of our day to a cause that we believe in, we could change the world. The cumulative effect of patriots on a mission has changed the course of history from the beginning of time. In my opinion, one mother on a mission can be as fierce as any tricked-out warrior.

This is a tumultuous time—we stand in dramatically shifting sands. Though we have never in our history perceived such a threat against our children's futures, we have never been so equipped for the challenge.

Many of those engaged in today's political battle truly desire righteousness and justice. They aspire to make a difference, but they doubt their own power to affect change. It might surprise them to know that many of the most brilliant people in politics are poster child material for ADD, and habitually late. For example, when my husband John was elected to the Senate in our state, I (Gina) remember how shocked I was to learn that the "Senate bell" meant that the Senate would arrive on the floor sometime within the next half hour, or so! That doesn't mean that you need to be ADD or habitually late to survive or succeed in politics, it simply means that we all have our weakness, and yours will be fine. Remember that even Einstein had difficulty remembering how to get home from work at night. It's a good thing he didn't let his weakness stand in the way of his work. Neither should you. Politics needs you like never before, and you can make a huge difference in the future if you are willing to enter the arena.

It is a mixed blessing. With every great privilege comes great responsibility. We believe most of us are feeling the burden of the blessing and the responsibility we have in cultivating a culture that can meet the challenges ahead. We believe that those who dare to act will be judged for their actions given our unique place in time. We believe that the next generation is waiting and watching us to see how we will use what we have been given.

Politics, and all the media and culture surrounding it, are working. The electorate is so frustrated they would like to just throw all the politicians out of office. People yearn for leaders. Businesses are hurting, our security is threatened, the wrong people are profiting, and our very future hangs in the balance.

The rules have changed and it's your game, now. As my cocktail napkins read: "Put on your big-girl panties, and DEAL WITH IT!" How could something so silly seem almost prophetic in this day and age?

# The Vision

Let me ask you this—if you really could not fail, what would you do with the rest of your life? Pause for a moment and answer that question. Don't worry if you cannot answer right away—we will get you there. If you think you know but are not certain, just start with the sketchy image you have of what you would do if you knew you could do it. Consider how you would feel and think and speak and what you would do in that position. The person you are looking at is *you*, minus fear and guilt. It's that simple. If it is what you want, why not make it your plan to get there? This book can walk you through the steps and provide the political secrets for you to get where you want to be, but your challenge is psychological. Our education is psychological, and much of our experience is political. We will help you combine the two to make the change you want, and achieve the results you could only dream of before.

# Options

There are virtually hundreds of options available to you if you want to be more involved in politics. There is the obvious option of candidacy, but there are so many other ways to change our culture. Some are listed here:

**Candidacy: Press:**
Mayor Citizen Journalist
Alderman News Reporter
School Board Writer
Fire Board Journalist
Police Board Blogger
US Senate Radio Host
US House of Representatives
   (Congress) Internet Radio or TV
State Senate Photojournalist
State Assembly (sometimes called
   State Representative)
Committeeman or woman

**Campaign:**
Fundraiser Staff
Strategist Publicist
Consultant Press Agent
Advisor (campaign or
   policy side) Manager
Vendor Pollster
Kitchen Kabinet (inner
   circle of advisors) Social
   Media Director

Or maybe you just want to volunteer or contribute? I have interviewed hundreds of politically interested people, and I can tell you with certainty that fear and guilt are your worst enemies if you want to be involved in politics. We will deal adequately with both. First, let's get to your goal. This is deeply personal, and requires a considerable amount of honesty you may not be used to feeling permission to tell. I (Dr. Loudon) have named this process *policology*—very simply, the nexus of psychology and politics.TP. This is both the study of why politicians do what they do, and why we perceive it as we do. This is the study of what works in politics, and what we need to change about the process.

> *Everything you've been taught, everything you believe, is upended by the artist in Philippe Petit: You don't engage in breaking and entering, you don't mount a major trespass, you don't risk your life, you certainly don't do it for no money, you don't dedicate your life to accomplishing something manifestly stupid and simultaneously beautiful. Most of all, you don't set out to do something impossible. Certainly not as a gift. Unless you do. And then you win.*
>
> —SETH GODIN, *LYNCHPIN*

## Motivation

If you love politics, do it. My PhD mentor, Marie Farrell, told me to study one thing I liked to study more than anything else because it would be all I would do for years. I chose to study love. I never got bored and I finished ahead of others. If you love politics, do politics. Don't watch from the sidelines and wish you were in the game. Politics might be your art or your poetry. The truth is, most in the game have a real love/hate relationship with it, myself included. But I do love to help people take risks and do what they love. So if it is what you love, then it must be what you do.

People generally enter politics for one of two reasons that may become blurred as they stay engaged. The first reason is personal power. There is no question that politics is a place to get things done. My husband served for fourteen years, and when his Senate term came to an end, I asked him, "What will you miss the most?"

His answer was simple. "I will miss the ability to help people so much." I knew that was what John would miss most because he is a servant leader. At first glance, that doesn't sound too akin to the power-hound, but the reality is that helping people requires power, otherwise everyone would just help themselves. Political power is unique and can be used for good or evil, much like any form of capital.

Consider this next story, though. John was blessed to be very young for his level of seniority in the State Senate. There was another young guy, "Rex Justice", who became a State Representative and began climbing quickly up the ladder of power. He decided to go for the powerful position of Speaker of the House, and I was elated because he was the beloved son of two Baptist missionaries, a dedicated father and husband, and a true Christian conservative. When his win for Speaker was eminent, but he was still counting his votes, I took a stroll from the Senate down to his office. I walked right in, then stood and leaned over him as he sat behind his desk. My "mama finger" began to wave. "Representative, I am here to tell you that you are a good man, and you love the Lord. John and I plan to support you. But I want to tell you one thing. If you ever change, I will find you, with my finger in your face, telling you and anyone who will listen that I think you have fallen. I will hold you accountable, my friend."

He slowly stood up from behind his desk as a warm smile spread across his face. He sauntered around his desk and gave me a big, sincere hug. "You do that, my friend. I know power can be addictive, and I don't want to lose who I am for this job. Please, Gina, you and John, hold me accountable."

Rex was elected, years passed, and Rex slowly began to get off course. The first thing I knew was that he was cutting deals that were outside what I knew he believed in. Then there were the dinners, the wine, the lobbyists, the women, the trips—we saw it all. Finally, he double-crossed John on a commitment, and I was getting my "mama finger" ready to go. The problem was that his entourage had him so untouchable that I could barely get close enough to confront him. I saw him out at night, but he was never sober enough to talk to. I expressed my concerns to friends quietly, but I should have done more.

Rex was indicted for a bizarre sex scandal I can scarcely comprehend, and in trouble for a lot of other corruption as well. His career is over. His wife left. Last that I knew, he lived with his daughter without a job, a family, or a future. I had chills when I read the transcripts from his court testimony. They asked what he would miss the most about being in politics. It wasn't the power, glamour, or money, or even the challenge.

"I will miss being able to really help people," he said.

The reality is that we all need to be needed, and feel like our work is valuable. If you did not have a need like that, you would probably find a different line of work. I believe most politicians, news media, bloggers, journalists, and others who change culture begin right where you probably are—with a sincere concern for their community, their state, or their country, and a desire to help people. Some level of power is necessary to do that. The problem is that power is as potently addictive as heroin.

The second reason people go into politics or media is they have a sense of justice, or an ideology. Many who start with that sense of ideology become frustrated with the drag of the process (it usually takes years to pass a really meaningful piece of legislation, or get your article or book published). That makes it tempting to compromise, or to begin to enjoy the spoils more than the fight for what is right.

The one thing you do not want to do is design your life in politics only to see it ripped away from you altogether. I have watched the path of destruction devour people over and over, and I have noticed the common stumbling blocks, and how some manage to lucidly avoid them. You can too. It is a matter of going into the arena in whatever capacity you choose, but with a focus, and a knowledge of who you are and why you are there. Sometimes it also means getting out at the right time, or switching roles.

Examine your heart as you consider your role, elected or not. Many of the same frustrations and temptations will tug at you no matter what your role is in politics or media. Careful analysis of your motives in this will help you avoid the pitfalls and safeguard your actions to remain true to your mission. First, you need to determine the right role for you. Even if you think you know, walk through these exercises, because the landscape is changing quickly, and you don't want to let your true calling pass you by.

To determine our role in the realm of politics, whether it is media, legislative, citizen activism, journalism, lobbying, or otherwise, we must first understand where we have been and where we are. What really tugs at our heartstrings?

I remember once standing on a corner in the freezing rain, my toes aching so badly that I knew if I could just persist a bit longer, they would be numb, and I would no longer feel the pain. I was working at a poll for a candidate whom I thought would fight for what is precious to me. I had tucked my face down in my coat to warm my nose, when I caught the smell of my child, who had been napping on me earlier that day. A yearning for him welled up in me from the core of my being and made me crave him in a way only a parent could know. I felt the sting of tears warm the lid of my eyes. I wanted to be with him.

But my life direction tells me that was a moment I owed to my son. I not only want to fight for the leaders that will lead in his lifetime, I also want to be a woman he knows will fight when my children are threatened. I want to be a woman he can admire for so many reasons. I am unconcerned with impressing him; that's not it. I want to show him my love for him. I want to raise him to look for a life partner who is a warrior in her heart—and one who will fight for my grandchildren when I am too tired for battle.

Children, my own and others, are my greatest inspiration. I love the quote on a business card holder that I bought for my young daughter for her first set of calling cards. It reads: "Strong women. May we be them. May we love them. May we raise them."

This is much harder done than said. Focus on each of the sentences above for a moment. We might be able to believe that we *are* them, but do we love them? Can women really love other women? We will talk more about that in chapters to come, but I submit that this is a great challenge for many of us. As I have gone through countless political battles alongside my husband, and we have forged alliances and occasionally parted ways with some, I have observed great differences between the way men typically handle the difficult people and the way women do. Men find it easier to be dispassionate, to separate the action from the actor. We women take things much more personally. We are much quicker to judge, compete with, step on, use, insult, and envy strong women than we are to *love* them.

And do we *raise* them? I know women who actually compete with their daughters more than they actively love them (and love *is* an action, not a mysterious apparition). Even if we control ourselves with our daughters, how well do we set the example for our daughters of loving other women? Do we help women in our social circles and love them? Do we love women who compete with us in the workplace? Do we love women who are in our family? Do we love our mothers? Do we love our mothers-in-law? Our sisters? Do we love women who are hard to love? Do we love women who hurt us? The next generation of daughters is watching.

The reality is that just as there is a hero in each of us, there is also a coward. We have to choose which place to draw from and do so with intention. We have to learn that despite our failures on some levels, we can keep our failures from defining us. We will devour this topic a bit later, but for now, let's play with my new word and take a step down the "policological" path.

## Motivations in Moscow: My Story

My heart swells when I consider the legacy of Ronald Reagan. I nearly burst with appreciation and adoration because he helped me realize what it meant to be an American. I remember lying awake, seized with terror night after night, wondering if "the bomb" was going to drop, waking to the nuclear winter depicted in movies. As a Cold War baby, I prayed for God to give our president the wisdom and courage to fight the Cold War so that one day I could grow to love, marry and have children, and have my shot at the American dream.

Twenty years later, celebrating Moscow with my husband, I was reminded of Reagan. We often joke that while on vacations there is no time for sleep; there is too much to see and do. That was especially true about White Nights. White Nights in Russia are very special—the time of year when it never gets completely dark. A mysterious fog and mist seem to descend on the cobblestone streets of

Russia. I found it wildly romantic. The mist and moonlight dances around each other, eliciting soulful thoughts and feelings. At two a.m. we were holding hands, laughing as we walked through the streets of Moscow in awe, contemplating how different things were than in the days of the Cold War. As we talked, we noticed two young women riding on horseback. "Hey! Can we rent your horses?" I called.

My husband swung his head to look at me, horrified. I have a habit of embarrassing him publicly with my wild ideas and impulses. But I didn't care; it was a moment of passion, and I somehow sensed that I had been waiting most of my life for this moment and was not going to miss it. As embarrassed as he was, he knew once he saw the untamed look in my eye that there was no stopping me, so he opted to cut his losses and hoped this was as crazy as it would get.

## Red Square

I wanted to ride into the center of Red Square on horseback to spiritu-ally mark our territory—and to acknowledge all that God had done in our lives, and in our world. We had enjoyed our day with a personal tour guide who showed us dozens of locations where the Communists had removed crosses and statues of Jesus. Invigorated to discover that they were being restored, one-by-one, we could mark the progress. Everywhere we looked, Communist hammers and sickles were being removed, replaced by the restored beautiful golden crosses. Churches had been turned into gymnasiums for the Communist elite and their guests all over the city, and they were also being restored to their full glory, piece by piece. I was shocked by the smell of victory of God and capitalism—still raw and wild—in the air, and I wanted to claim it that night.

"Hey! You! How much? How much we rent your [pointing, and holding out cash]? Please? Please! One chance in life. Please!"

Looking deeply at me, as if to decide whether or not I would steal her horse, she slowly dismounted and took my money. Her friend fol-lowed as they mumbled something in Russian. They nodded in my direction, relinquishing reins and half smiles.

"Where is Red Square?" I asked, as if I were on a life-or-death mission.

My husband gave me an "I am trying not to look at you like you are crazy, but you are" look, and tried to grin confidently for the sake of the young girls. The first girl pointed south to tell me the direction of Red Square. I hopped on her beautiful horse and began to ride away down the cobblestone street that had played path to kings and queens.

Images of Catherine the Great emerged in my mind as I held the reins in one hand and the majority of a cigar I had purchased at Churchill's Pub in the other. I didn't really like to smoke them, but it felt rebellious and revolutionary. It fit the moment—my moment. My horse was graceful and attacked the cobblestones as if they were a velvety green pasture. He knew his stuff.

I heard John trotting up behind me but noticed the rhythm of his horse was uneven. I glanced behind me to catch him mumbling something about the legality of what I was doing and the KGB having faster horses. I thought my horse could probably get me to my destination before they could catch me, so I rode on. It became painfully clear that John's horse was not so agile. ,

"It just figures I would end up on the dang gimpy horse" he yelled from behind. In pity, I slowed my graceful partner beneath with a gentle hold on his reins.

"Whoa, Gorgeous," I whispered in the silence of the White Night. "Let's wait for him."

The energy bursting from the strength and vigor of my animal was pulsing through my veins, and I could hear both of us breathing in anticipation of the run that awaited us. It was as though both of us knew a run was coming, and we had only to wait for John and "Gimpy" to catch up. We paused on the very edge of Red Square. We would wait for our friends to join us to venture to the center.

I was calling my horse "Vlad," and we exchanged whispers in the night. It was as if he knew that he was fulfilling a dream for me, and he appreciated the opportunity to be part of it. I wondered for a moment, amid the crowds and high-rises, if Vlad ever got to graze about a field or jump a creek. Though I couldn't imagine where or how, I knew that he did. I somehow felt that my passion was the fulfillment of his dream too.

John and Gimpy made their way toward us in one piece, although they almost fell twice en route. Old Gimpy just couldn't take the cobblestones and didn't have the will or good sense to care about our mission. "You look beautiful on that horse!" John said.

"This is Vlad!" I said. "Sorry you got Gimpy."

"Par for the course," he said. "Enjoy your ride." With that, Vlad and I rode to a full gallop in the misty moonlight of the White Night. I felt the little particles of wind and dew spray my face like a mist, and slowed as we approached the center of Red Square. I dismounted.

Standing in the center of Red Square, I could barely believe my eyes. I recalled the images of tanks and Soviet soldiers marching into this square during my youth. Those days were long gone. Few Americans realize that the Russians had actually retrofitted period-designed buildings to close the north end of Red Square to discourage those militaristic parades from ever occurring in Red Square again. My eyes welled with tears. How could this be? In a place where so many had lost their lives, the walls were now down. I felt as if I were standing in the middle of a very holy place, amid the handiwork of God. Never in my life was I so full of awe.

## Victories

Multiple fears weighed heavily on my mind: fears for the future of this beautiful country that had dazzled me, as well as for my own country that seemed somehow so close and vulnerable. I began to wonder how I could define this moment for my memory. I wanted to celebrate the victory of capitalism over Communism. I wanted to celebrate the victory of Christianity over the evil of tyranny. I wanted to commemorate the thousands whose blood was shed here, martyr and criminal alike. I wanted to thank God that I had been born in a different political era. I wanted to pray to God for this moment to forever be etched in my mind and prayers so that I could never forget what had been lost, what had been won, and liberty's fragility.

John and Gimpy hobbled up to join us. All was silent. The square was utterly vacant, though we sensed guards of some kind in the shadows of the monuments. It was three a.m.

In unison, and without a word exchanged, John and I fell to our knees. "Dear Lord," John began, "We are so unworthy and yet You are so merciful and full of grace we don't deserve. Thank You for preserving our republic. As two Cold War children, we thank you for sending us a president like Reagan to walk us through 'those perilous times to see that our flag was still there.' We pray, Lord, that you will make us an instrument of the same peace—peace through strength—and *your* peace that surpasses all understanding. We pray, Lord, that you will use us in mighty ways to expand Your territory for Your glory. In Jesus's name we pray, amen."

We stood in a teary embrace for a long time. I remember the smell of the horses, watching the night mist blow from their noses. I remember the rhythm of John's breath and the sound of his heart beating with my ear against his chest. I remember my silent prayers echoing his. I remember knowing that I would never forget this moment, and that I would always feel responsible to exert whatever power I had to preserve the republic that God had so graciously restored by His perfect placement of President Reagan at that moment in history.

## Memories

So many things passed through my mind at this time, one of them being the irony that I actually met my husband in the Winston Churchill Memorial. I thought of Winston Churchill's *"Sinews of Peace"* (better known as the "Iron Curtain Speech") when that great leader warned the world that an iron curtain was descending "from Stettin in the Baltic, to Triest in the Adriatic," spoken just yards from the spot where we took our vows. I remembered after our wedding in St Mary Aldermanbury's church and our honeymoon in the former East Germany, when we chopped pieces off of that "Iron Curtain" in Berlin, almost exactly where President Reagan did one week later.

Then I remembered returning to Missouri to meet the president as he dedicated a large piece of that wall on Westminster campus. I recalled the day my family spent privately at Rancho de Cielo, Reagan's "Ranch in the Sky" and favorite retreat where he and Mrs. Reagan caught their breath from the strenuous business of saving the world. "They loved horses too," I whispered to Vlad. I thought of my children, a world away, missing me, and hoped they were not too sad. I knew I had come here on a mission, and now I knew what that mission was. I remembered the poetry of this moment and vowed to never forget.

That day, I became a warrior in a great army of patriots who understand freedom and its high cost. I understood, more than I ever had, what Jefferson meant when he wrote in the Declaration of Independence "we pledge our lives, our fortunes, and our sacred honor." I prayed for the success of Russia's raw, untainted capitalism still in its infancy. I wished for another president like Reagan. Most importantly, I knew I had fulfilled my purpose that night, and that I would never, ever forget it.

## Your Story

That is my story. That was the moment I knew that I had to forfeit raising an army as a full-time mom in order to go out and fight to ensure they had a country to fight for one day. That was the moment that changed everything for me—when I went from mom *to* my children to warrior *for* my children.

What is *your* story? What has brought you to this moment? Why do you care so much? How far are you willing to go to make a difference? Is this the "hill you are willing to die on"?

Take some time in Appendix C to write your story. Try to get to the heart of what motivates you, even if it may seem less dramatic. What single defining moment or succession of events made you care? Honesty is the first step in trusting your own authenticity enough to depend on "you" to get you to your goal. Remember that God created you with all your passions and motivations. He can use them even if it is not clear to you just how He will do it.

## Scope

I am a student and analyst of human behavior and development. I think of life as if it were a shooting range. As I peer through my scope and adjust my view, I become certain that I am firing in the right direction. I see vision precision as critical before pulling the trigger in a long-range setting. I believe in setting the personal goal of civility and the means to achieve it before asking it of others. Eye on the prize, as they say.

## Tennis

When I was writing my dissertation, I was mentored by Dr. Marie Farrell. She was a member of the Harvard faculty, and since I did not attend Harvard, I was blessed to have her guidance during my doctoral work. She was part of the TV news program *20/20*'s exposé on Romanian orphanages that virtually revolutionized foreign adoption in our country, and inspired a lot of the work my husband and I did on legislation regarding adoption. She seemed to share my drive to constantly battle in the war of politics and policy. She did it all over the world as a nurse with the World Health Organization.

One day while wallowing in the drudgery of my dissertation, I was lamenting my state of being. She shared a story about the morning she realized she was really different—that she could never really fit in with most other women. On her way to the airport to catch a flight for Romania, she drove past the tennis courts and stopped to watch a match going on between two doubles players on the court visible from the road. She used to visualize herself playing tennis in the morning, instead of mentoring doctoral students, traveling the globe as a nurse, and tirelessly writing for professional journals. That day, as she pulled away from the tennis courts, she said she realized that she would never be one of those women playing tennis. She said her life was much more peaceful after she had accepted that reality.

I laughed despite my overwhelmed state, because there happens to be a tennis court within yards of my house. I almost never actually play, but I had always held out hope that one day I would be one of those women who played tennis. My guess is that if I did, I would quickly turn to gossiping or other bad habits I largely avoid now because I am always focused on a mission with no time to spare.

Are you like Dr. Farrell and me? Do you fantasize about playing tennis, crying over draperies, or matching your children's socks to their hair bows? Or are you lost in some of those details wishing you knew how to step out and change the world for your children, or someone else's children?

Margaret Thatcher said that "if you want something said, ask a man. If you want something done, ask a woman." You know if you are a doer. Someone else comes up with the idea of the party, and you make it happen while they take credit. If you are a doer, this scenario has repeated itself dozens of times in your history.

## Opportunities

Sometimes the issues and the politicians will evade you. Sometimes you may have to be the one who gets things started. Sometimes you may have to be the candidate, the major donor, the journalist, the consultant, or the activist trainer.

Our greatest triumphs are often born of our greatest frustrations. Before I opted to write this book, I was frustrated watching mistakes the new conservative movement was making. I feared those mistakes could result in ultimate failure. Realizing that while I shared their patriotism and admired their courage and passion, I could see the traps they were falling into because I had been in politics from the inside for so long.

I also saw people missing great opportunities in politics; my heart broke seeing the passion spent on efforts that I knew were doomed to failure. They were giving up their precious time and sacrificing for nothing—time that could be devoted to something with a far greater probability of actual results. I was not sure anyone would listen, but I knew I had to find a way to tell people what I knew.

## Heroes and "Hadda-beens"

Do people tell you that you should write a book? Maybe you should. Do people tell you that you should run for office? Maybe you will consider. Do people tell you that you should lead a movement? The next movement is waiting for someone just like you to come along and take the reins.

The truth is that you have a choice, and even if you feel the tug of a call to politics, you can say no. I can think of a million reasons I don't want to be involved, and yet I can tell you that it is an incredible way to make change in the future you are handing to the next generation. While political contributions are not tax-deductible, I have found political work more progressive and rewarding than my charitable work. I know one thing—whether or not you want to dive into politics, politics needs you! Someone once coined an important truth: "When good people do not lead, bad people will." If you have a heart to serve, you are needed in politics today. Many good people just can't withstand the rancor of politics, so they fall by the wayside. I see the way political bullies drive out the good guys so they can have absolute control. Don't let political slime blur your vision or quell your passion.

What if Reagan had said no? What if Palin had refused to blaze a trail? What if Lincoln had given up after he lost the fourth, fifth, or even tenth race? What if William Wilberforce had listened to his enemies and detractors and given up his battle to end slavery in Great Britain? There are heroes, and there are "hadda-beens." The heroes carry on despite detractors, enemies, personal pain, rejection, and unjust results. They remain civil throughout the process, even to those who slight them. The hadda-beens will never know that their touch could have changed the world. Seldom does anyone succeed without a path of failure behind them. Take up your cause and get in the game! They won't know what hit 'em!

## Pretty Is as Pretty Does

You can only imagine my awe to find those in my party (who criticized me only weeks before for running as a mother with a special-needs baby) cheering hypocritically at the first Sarah Palin rally held in my town. I was there to cheer for her too, but was amused at the irony and audacity of those who could criticize me for it only weeks before, then show up screaming like drunken concertgoers when Sarah arrived on the scene in identical circumstances. They know what they are, and they don't need me to tell them. This is where you can hang your hat: your detractors will always call themselves out. Be a person of honor who can say it all with a forgiving smile and a glance. This is a lady!

It is shocking to take inventory of all the things that can be done if there is no jealousy, no competing for air at the top of the tank, no greed, no competition within the ranks, and no need for credit. I can look at all the great political efforts I have known that have failed, and 99 percent of the time, they fail for those simple reasons. It always causes me to question if the "activists" are really as committed to their goal as they are to their own credit or gain.

Everyone owns their own battle. I have never found a person who, when you really drill down, doesn't have their own battle of some kind. Especially in my counseling work, I have discovered that the best athlete, movie star, model, politician, it doesn't matter—at the height of their career, they all cry; they all hurt. I believe—and have witnessed time and again—that those who contend at the top of their discipline battle the most ferocious demons of all. I think that is why you see movie stars who apparently have everything fall to drugs, alcohol, and suicide. If they have it all, what on earth do they want? They want peace. They want love. They want the same things you want. Their pain tolerance is no less than yours; their circumstances are just different. The fact that everyone has a battle is the key to avoiding becoming consumed with your own battles, often to the point where you destroy those around you who could have been your allies. You lose all the potential every time you step on a head to climb to the top. If you want to succeed in life, you must repeatedly resist this common temptation.

Just because you know that the world around you is full of sin and temptation and that you will likely walk through a battle every day does not mean that you can turn into a paranoid pessimist! Those are no good to any one, or any political cause. I see them every day, and their work is not very fruitful. They tend to be distracted, scared, and ineffective. You have no need to be paranoid or pessimistic, because you have done your work. The research and exercises you have done to this point are your armor, and you will be equipped for the call you have ahead. Much like the armor of God equips us against sin, we have all sorts of truths to focus upon to remain unfazed by the distraction and ugliness around us.

We are not only called to remain optimistic but to demonstrate grace under pressure. When you are in that place—and we all will be—where someone has said or done something to you that is unjust, press on. Keep your vision, and go back to the truth you know. When you are finished, tear out pages of this book if necessary so that you can remember what you need to know to keep your clarity of focus. And whenever possible, remain positive.

I have a good friend, Mary, who smiles almost all the time despite her circumstances. She has engaged in some of the ugliest political battles I have ever seen, yet she seems to maintain a cheerful demeanor that confounds her political rivals and often causes them to underestimate her. This is really funny to watch. Her smile is one of her best weapons.

On the other hand, my friend Dave, whose intentions are pure and good, always appears afraid and frowning. His suspicion of others is transparent, which likely encourages others to be naturally suspicious of him. He is really a very nice, quality person when you get to know him; the sad part is that few people see past the rough, scary exterior in order to get to know him.

Experience has taught me that, of all options, it is best to trust and hope for the best in others. This doesn't mean you trust people with your secrets, or things they can use against you. This only means that you believe the best in others until you know otherwise. This also means that war is hell, and sometimes hell is necessary. Even then, remember grace and the way that interpersonal strife can damage a mission. Sometimes this means looking at the log in your own eye before falling victim to the splinter in the eye of another. Sometimes this means examining your own sin and turning from it before it devours your soul. But you don't lose. Ultimately, the little stuff takes care of itself. You have a mission, and the prize is greater than all the little stuff. ★

# Chapter Eleven

★★★

# Images and Accidents

*Being powerful is like being a lady. If you have to tell people you are, you aren't.*

—Margaret Thatcher

*The more you act like a lady, the more he'll act like a gentleman.*

—Sydney Biddle Barrows

*Your dresses should be tight enough to show you're a woman and loose enough to show you're a lady.*

—Edith Head

## The Better Half?

You have learned all about the role of the gentleman in the renewal of our culture. But what about his partner—the lady? What is her role? How clear are the definitions of the lady? How personal is the journey toward that goal? How can you get there? How does one know when she has "arrived"? This chapter will prepare and equip you in your own journey, and give you clear, evidentiary markers to know when you have arrived! Get ready, ladies and gentlemen. We are going on a journey.

Definitions are dry, opinions are biased, and assumptions are dangerous. So how does one even know a lady when she sees her? How does a woman know how to *be* one? The most romantic images emerge as we contemplate the simple concept of "lady." But who wants to labor simply to match the image of the lady in her corsets and pinafores, sporting her itchy parasol and grievous girdles?

Is it possible to be a lady in a pair of torn-up jeans and faded T-shirt? The answer, in a word, is—yes!

The simplest and most concise definition of *lady* is a manifestation of the woman as God, the Creator of the Universe, designed her to be. Submission to God in its purest form defines *lady* for each of His daughters.

When does a little girl become a lady? No one knows, but we all know her when we see her. We knew when we saw Margaret Thatcher as she smiled and shook hands with Ronald and Nancy Reagan that she was a lady. We never doubted that Jacqueline Kennedy, as she held the hands of her children at her husband's funeral, was the quintessential lady. And we know when we watch Sarah Palin kiss the head of her little Trig or the lips of her husband, Todd, as she takes the stage to rally the troops that she matches the definition of *lady* at that moment. But how did they get there and what was the path? Did they gradually develop the grace, the confidence under pressure, and the courage to submit? Or did they one day mysteriously burst forth like a rose or a ray of sunshine? What takes a fat pink little baby, to a delightfully destructive toddler, to an awkward preteen, to a young lady?

We submit that many young women become a lady when she takes her groom's hand in marriage and vows to love, honor, and respect him all of the days of her life. On that day, she willingly submits because she doesn't really know at all what God might have in mind for her, and yet, she confidently accepts God's will as a bride for her lifetime. That brave and courageous public act may define the beginning of her journey into being a lady.

The flowers and white wonder make it easy to visualize the lady. But she is every bit the lady when, as she sweats and bleeds and squeezes her mate's hand, she propels her baby into this world. Again, it takes an amazing amount of faith and submission to trust God's will for the life of a child in today's world. It takes a lady to trust and submit to that level.

## "Even the Wind and the Waves Obey Him!" (Matthew 8:27, KJV)

Many modern women revile the concept of submission, at least initially. Certainly, the whiff of submission offends the woman who misunderstands the deeper meaning of the word. But like a quality stinky cheese, it tastes far different than it smells. The act of submission reflects the defining nature of courage. Anyone who has ever tried to control their own life rather than hand off the reins to a trusted partner knows that submission is at its core an act of true distinction and courage. Micromanagers and control freaks are a dime a dozen, while a woman who can relinquish the narcissistic and neurotic fantasy of control is a pearl of great value. What is it about the quiet assuredness of a Jackie O., the smiling confidence of a Phyllis Schlafly, or the sparkling resilience of a Sarah Palin that reveals some deep, mysterious, substantial, and significant knowledge that most women—most people—don't comprehend?

For you doubters out there (and I was one of them) who still don't believe in the amazing power of submission, consider a sailboat at sea. The captain can try as she might to fight the wind and the waves with her oars, her wheel, or her will, but not until she learns to submit to the powers of the sea can she truly navigate the forces of nature. She can smack the waves down with her oars, but they will swell again. She can curse the wind and steer the rudder, but nature will not relent.

Reality dictates that God's design provides our only true control in life. When a lady puts up her sails, grabs the warm hand of her first mate or crewmember, and faces the hurdles before her, she submits to a far greater power. She relinquishes the fantasy of control because there is no such thing in life—all is part of God's merciful design. Realization and acceptance of her role in life as a sailor—rather than a paddler, a wave swatter, or a curser—becomes her holy submission. Submission becomes her power because it places her at the helm of life with her partner securely in place, playing his role as God designed.

The concept of submission and all of its beauty continues through the life cycle. As someone who has studied developmental psychology, I am most amused by my inability to predict my own reactions to the wind and waves in my life. My own journey into ladyhood never fails to surprise me when I recollect it. Admittedly, the title *lady* sometimes feels a bit too fancy for someone who just wants to be on a boat with the wind at her back and the salt in her face. Still, it is the measure of a lady to know when she has arrived at ladyhood, so I sail on.

Having babies—giving birth—signals a monumental tack in the right direction of finding one's ladyhood, but that marks only the beginning of the journey. Perhaps ladyhood is perfected in the raising of children. The Bible says, "But women will be saved through childbearing—if they continue in faith, love and holiness with propriety" (2 Timothy 2:15). But this slice of woman's work has only just commenced on the day she gives birth. Raising children continues this justification.

Women who are childless are not left out of this refining process. I love the Psalms and Isaiah verses where God describes the "barren woman" as the "mother of many" children. I know many women who have never given birth, or adopted, but who have been blessed with many opportunities to be refined in maternal ways.

As her life rolls on past motherhood, every woman finds herself attempting the acrobatic practice of balancing marriage, friendship, motherhood, daughterhood, career, and even citizenship. Those who maintain a vision while trusting in God alone as a beacon find themselves feeling like and appearing to others to be a lady.

Ask a man about the beauty of his wife on the day she gave birth to his children. Ask a child about his mother who stayed strong and fought hard as life dealt her lemons. Ask a friend about Christ in the eyes of her friend as she held her hand when life's best escaped her. Ask God what is far more precious than rubies (Proverbs 31). These are all moments God designed specifically for women—exceptional moments where a woman has the privilege to be a lady.

## You-nique

For our female readers, what makes you—yes, *you*—a lady? The best part of being a true lady is that only you can know the answer to that, because you are God's unique design. Only you can identify what special gifts He has granted you, and only you can really submit fully so that He shines through in your life.

This process represents an intricate, intimate communication between a lady and her God. Certainly, He enlists others to guide, brainstorm, and verify, but danger lurks when others presume to inject themselves despite His Word or His instruction. The Father of the universe has an infinite capacity to communicate with his daughters clearly and specifically. And whether you know it or not, He has done so.

When people advise or direct you, and if you plan to make a decision based on their (even the most well-intentioned) counsel, it remains critical—critical—that you hold it up to Scripture. If an answer (or warning) is given to you by a person, no matter if it is your pastor, your friend, or the most holy person you know, you still must hold it up to Scripture. If the two don't "twain," then the person directing you, however pure their intentions, must be disregarded and their words replaced by the answer you can plainly perceive in the Word of God.

I remember when I first tried to define myself as a lady. I thought I needed to do so through the lens of God's provision of other women. My husband was the youngest senator in Missouri at the time, and we had legions of people lining up to tell us how I should behave as a lady. A host of feminine fingers pointed me to Old Testament verses about the meek, quiet, humble women of the Bible, explaining that they walked behind their husbands, served them, and did not wear jewelry. I wanted to be what God wanted me to be, even if it was the farthest thing from my design.

I began doubting my design as an outgoing, talkative, opinionated woman who loves all things artistic. I was different in this way from some women I thought were really strong Christians. I began to believe that if I wanted to be a strong Christian, I needed to abandon my individualism and my unique picture of femininity. I was afraid that my love of beautiful things was sinful, and I found plenty of contextual scripture that, in my mind, confirmed my worst fears. Now to be sure, plenty of sin resides in me, but I was succumbing to peer pressure. I was projecting another person's interpretation on to myself of what I thought God wanted me to be. In so doing, I ignored grace—His precious and personal gift to me. I became something of a legalist, failing to consider that my gifts and talents were exclusively my own because God deemed it so. I wanted to fit into the box that I saw other women constructing for me and the woman that men instructed me to be if I wanted to be a "good wife."

I chose to homeschool my children because my husband served in the Senate and I wanted to be in the Capitol with him when he was in session. The homeschool community was still finding its footing in being "in the world, and not of the world." Therefore, to delineate ourselves and define for ourselves how we were separate, we dressed, ate, talked, and churched—well, differently. Thus began the well-meaning voices that provided my slippery slope into legalism and away from ladyhood. I fell prey, as many women do, to comparing my walk to others'. I began to judge myself in light of others' talents and abilities. I didn't think my talents and abilities fit as well in the homeschool community, and my confidence plummeted.

Some women find a ready alliance with a society that bares no shoulders, maintains long hair, suffers no makeup or jewelry, and dons nothing but long skirts. Some women take solace in their very conformity to nonconformity. I wanted to. I desperately tried to tuck everything that was "me" inside so deeply that I eventually didn't know it was there. But like a long dormant volcano, my spirit finally burst, often in embarrassing statements, anger at my family, and a total resentment of myself as God had designed me. "Why didn't He make me like them?" I would ask. "Why am I not as excited about growing seeds or quietly knitting?" Even worse, "I want to be in the arena my husband is in, so why can't I be content to can fruit, clean, train and school my children, and simply submit to the life that they all say God intended for me?"

For all of my life, beauty and order mattered a great deal to me. I thought I needed to subscribe to a level of selflessness that meant that things like beauty and a sustainable order in my life should not matter if I were really "submitted to God." The simplification movement was well under way, and I started to trade my contemporary, artistic taste for a rustic, prairie style décor in my home. I tried to dress like most of the other homeschool moms dressed, and I tried to find "contentment" in the areas they seemed to find contentment.

And I was almost there! I was cooking constantly and cleaning more constantly, and if "simplifying" meant getting rid of my housekeeper so that I could find joy in cleaning up after my family, I would do that as well. I was determined to be the best at not being me that there ever was! I wanted so badly to please God in every way, and for my husband and family to know that I loved them so much that I was willing to become exactly what everyone said they needed. Abigail Adams would have been proud; Gloria Steinem would have been nauseous.

As I stood there on the Capitol steps in my prairie skirt, crushing all of my dreams into dust, crying out on the inside while planting a smile on my face as fake as my skirt was long, I knew I was lying. No matter how much I loved God and was willing to sacrifice to be the person everyone said He willed me to be, I could not forsake the special design He created in me.

I had twisted my heart into believing that I wanted the gifts of simplicity, meekness, quiet, and reverence. But I could not hide the fact that I was a complete failure in those areas! When I took an honest, hard look at my gifts, I had to admit they were completely embarrassing, and they were gifts I did not truly want. I finally admitted that God had gifted me in several diverse spheres such as politics, speaking, writing, teaching, encouraging, and theatre. I love the limelight and the stage; when I was really honest, I had to admit the worst—I

am driven. I am not content. I thrive on adventure, not chopping veg-
etables for that day's crock-pot meal. I cursed the fact that I am an
only child with this fierce sense of independence and confidence that
I can change the world, but then I came to the humbling realization
that I was rejecting God's design for me. I could blame my dissatis-
faction on being an only child or on my parents' decisions, but that
presumed to judge God's design for my life.

Reality hit me like a bolt of lightning when I came clean with the
thought that *how* He designed me with the gifts I had was irrelevant.
He designed me. I began to inventory my gifts without my prefer-
ences, others' biases, or my legalistic ideas of what would be better, if
only God could understand and change me. I began to see His perfect
design of the lady He wanted me to be. That vision was all I needed
to understand for the very first time in my life that the Creator of the
Universe uniquely designed me to be *His Own!*

## "And She Laughs at the Days to Come" (Proverbs 31, NKJV)

This reality meant a lot of changes had to take place, and change
can be painful and disorienting. I was haunted by words in the Bible
about meekness, quiet women, and head coverings, and I worried and
questioned my vision when I gave the enemy the smallest foothold.
Then one day an old verse—the oldest verse in my mind and one that
I knew by heart—answered so many questions for me. It was the
plain old Proverbs 31 woman:

> ### The Virtuous Wife (Proverbs 31:10–31, NKJV)
> Who can find a virtuous wife? For her worth *is* far above rubies.
> The heart of her husband safely trusts her;
> So he will have no lack of gain.
> She does him good and not evil
> All the days of her life.
> She seeks wool and flax,
> And willingly works with her hands.
> She is like the merchant ships,

She brings her food from afar.
She also rises while it is yet night,
And provides food for her household,
And a portion for her maidservants.
She considers a field and buys it;
From her profits she plants a vineyard.
She girds herself with strength,
And strengthens her arms.
She perceives that her merchandise *is* good,
And her lamp does not go out by night.
She stretches out her hands to the distaff,
And her hand holds the spindle.
She extends her hand to the poor,
Yes, she reaches out her hands to the needy.
She is not afraid of snow for her household,
For all her household *is* clothed with scarlet.
She makes tapestry for herself;
Her clothing *is* fine linen and purple.
Her husband is known in the gates,
When he sits among the elders of the land.
She makes linen garments and sells *them,*
And supplies sashes for the merchants.
Strength and honor *are* her clothing;
She shall rejoice in time to come.
She opens her mouth with wisdom,
And on her tongue *is* the law of kindness.
She watches over the ways of her household,
And does not eat the bread of idleness.
Her children rise up and call her blessed;
Her husband *also,* and he praises her:
"Many daughters have done well,
But you excel them all."
Charm *is* deceitful and beauty *is* passing,
But a woman *who* fears the LORD, she shall be praised.
Give her of the fruit of her hands,
And let her own works praise her in the gates.

I might have just seen what God wanted me to see that day when I read about the mother of King Lemuel in a way I never had before. I think the shock of what I didn't see was the most revealing to me—I did not see a definite meekness, quietness, or conformity to an image of a woman designed by other women. I did not see a woman who pleased everyone, and feared making enemies. I did not see a woman who tucked her gifts away as a silent sacrifice. I did not see a woman who held back for fear of doing something wrong. I saw something bold and declarative—a woman unafraid to live God's gifts to her in their fullest. I saw a lady!

The Proverbs 31 lady was (and continues to be) a business lady. She was the lady of her home. She was the lady of her man. She was a lady to her servants (she didn't live on a prairie somewhere to prove her worth). She loved order! She loved beauty! She even loved quality! She was driven—by her will to submit to God in exactly the way He designed her!

Once I honestly inventoried my gifts I was shocked to find them here in this passage, and, for the first time, I thought perhaps my gifts were not only acceptable to God but designed *by* God. If that were the case, I had repenting to do! I had to apologize for ignoring His words and listening to others. I had to accept His good and perfect will for my life, and I had to look hard at those gifts He gave me.

I had a lot to do now because my vision of the lady God designed looked and acted very different from what I had thought I needed to look like and act. She was intentional, authentic, honest, bold, and fearless. She was strong enough to be gentle, and she was full enough to be the empty vessel God could use. She was His own—and that was the most beautiful vision for my life I had ever seen.

I tried to imagine the modern-day Proverbs 31 woman. Would she wear a Brooks Brothers suit and bust onto the Wall Street scene? Would she teach, study law, or engage in politics? Might she be a doctor who took mission trips to save children in foreign lands? Would she be a stay-at-home mom who designed a beautiful den for her cubs to come home to, then made her nightly transformation into a delicious, enticing lover at night for her man?

I wondered if she would wear leather, or tight torn jeans, or simply whatever her husband's fantasy could conjure. I wondered if she would shop, chair charity events, or be CEO of her company. In the proverb, the ideal wife considered a field and bought it, so perhaps the modern-day version would be a real estate mogul. An investor. A banker.

I began to break it all down. "The heart of her husband trusts her." What way can a woman better prove to her husband that he can trust her? My mama taught me that men like two things—food and sex. I realized that my husband did not know, nor did he care, if I kneaded fresh bread dough to make his noodles for his pasta. In fact, it probably was not attractive to walk in at night to a sweaty, overwhelmed, exasperated, cranky wife who spent the day cooking and cleaning—and who hated every minute of it. I learned that a bag of frozen chicken wings thrown on a cookie sheet and a glass of red wine fit that bill and put a big smile on my husband's face. I learned that a nice, juicy steak with a simple salad meant more to him than canned apples that he had pretended to like. And instead of my clothes being handmade and covering enough skin to render sunscreen obsolete, I learned that he liked to see a little more of me, and that he even liked to be seen out with a wife who wasn't hiding from who God made her to be. Modesty can come in many forms, and man does not get to define it.

"She brings her food from afar." So does she travel? Or is she a carry-out kind of a girl (hey, I could really go for that). "She girds herself with strength." So does she work out or run for fitness? Maybe she does circuit training? Bottom line, she is fit. That is my goal, not an order, from God.

Most women would admit that their biggest struggle is their weight and/or body image. I fought to maintain my weight throughout every pregnancy, but do you know that when I began to find the daughter He designed in me, He showed me that I was covering up who I was. I am sure I was eating to hide all the pain it took to live the lie about who I was. Do you? He also showed me that when I welcomed the "me" He designed, and submitted to His will and not that of man or my fleshly, legalistic interpretation, He changed my body. Now not only could I wear the "fine linen and purple," as described in the Proverbs 31 passage, I could rock it. Nothing matches rocking the fine linen and purple!

Oh, and my home! I could leap for joy just knowing that God's description of a lady says nothing about her living without air conditioning on a chicken farm out in the middle of nowhere. I could clothe my home in scarlet! That is exactly what I did. I did one whole room in red leather furniture, with red-and-salmon-striped satin drapes with fringe fit for the tabernacle! So there! That was my statement on rustic and simple. I was finished with it. Finally, my home was a reflection of the temple He built inside of me.

I loved homeschooling and the heart that I saw from my children as they continued in their love for God, and our family! Just because I was finding the me God designed did not mean that I had to abandon every conclusion I had made during my attempt to find my true identity. I continued in homeschooling, pulling in tutors and online academies to simplify my life, free me to do more charity work and rediscover who I was in this world. I am happy to report that we still don't seem to encounter all the horrible traits that I was so afraid of when I thought I needed to run a one-woman military school for my children. Though imperfect, they are bright, ambitious, loving, creative, and they do not rebel against us or God. They were the biggest encouragement to me as I found my path to ladyhood. They were the most complimentary to me when I "arrived," and they have become my greatest inspiration. I am always shocked to discover again that just as I am their biggest fan, they are mine, everyday.

Inspiration cascades from the Proverbs 31 lady, but my favorite trait is sometimes translated, "She can laugh at the days to come." That is the faith I aspire to own. I aim to be so assured that God's plan for me is so special that I not only rest assured but can laugh at what my future holds because of *Who* holds that future in His hands. This is a work in progress to this day in my life, but at least I know the goal. I thank the Proverbs 31 lady for the example she gave and for the boldness with which she gave it.

There are other ladies in the Bible who give a clear definition of ladyhood. Deborah was a judge and a mother (Judges 5:7) whom God called to rise up and forge her own way when there must have been a thousand people there telling her she was wrong. She implodes the argument that claims if you are not tied to your home like a bug stuck in a rug that you cannot be a great mother, a great wife, a lady, and a warrior for the Lord. That is not to say you cannot be all of those things if the home is your calling. It is to say that the argument that homemaking is the only path to true ladyhood is at best, a misunderstanding. Just as modern feminism is a big lie, so, too, is the premodern patriarchal role of women.

And what about Jesus' mother, Mary? If Mary had been a legalist and tried to decide what her role was as a lady by the world's standards, would she have been open to listening to the angel who came to her and told her she would bear a child, unmarried (Matthew 1:18–25; Matthew 2:1–12; Luke 1:26–38; Luke 2:1–20)? Can you imagine the "churchy" scorn she must have endured? I can see all the church ladies with their pursed lips casting judging eyes and telling Mary she was making a horridly sinful mistake, can't you?

And there is Esther. Esther was the perfect levelheaded wise and worthy woman under pressure. With her life hanging in the balance (Esther 4:14), she kept a vigilant cool in ways that only a true lady can, and achieved her goal. Not once, but twice, Esther went unveiled (Esther 4: 1–2) before the king (a big no-no then). Due to her faithful, ladylike willingness to obey God rather than traditions imposed by man, she was richly rewarded and spared the lives of those she loved. Life is full of tight spots, and even life-threatening challenges like the one Esther faced. Had she not, the seed of Christ would have been abolished! She did not understand or comprehend the importance of her role in history; how could she?

You cannot fully comprehend your role either, but you have a place in God's narrative, and God the great Author deems it important. It could be as important as Esther's call. What if it were? What if you let it pass you by because you did not take the time to let God tell you about the lady He designed you to be—a lady of His design?

Esther is the quintessential example of a Lady who had humility, focus, determination, and grace under pressure.

There are numerous biblical and historic examples of true ladies, but the trick remains to avoid subscribing to anyone else's definition of *lady* for you. You may already be a lady, or you may have no idea where to begin. No matter where you are starting from, you can become God's version of the lady He designed you to be. As you read on, you will know that it is a fundamentally special calling in these times to be a lady. The need has never been greater for your important role in our culture, in the family, and in the world. You have been called.

If you have never paused to inventory the gifts He gave you, and the strengths He chose for your life, please do. Pray over them. Be honest. Grieve over those gifts that you wish you had but do not; the Lord's arms are strong and yet gentle enough to console you. His plan for you is perfect, but only He can help you find it. Though He will provide role models for you, he will not provide a perfect path for you through the life of another with different gifts. The joy in discovery consists of His relationship with you—and you don't want to miss the very best part. As you walk and talk with Him and listen for His Word in your life, wonderful surprises await you, because you are His own *lady*!

## A Guide to Finding the Lady in You, By God's Design.

If you are struggling to find the lady that God designed in you, enjoy the exercise below to help you find your way.

1. Without a lot of thought, name one thing you would do if it were okay with God and you knew for certain that you could not fail.
2. Name five times in your life when you felt God's approval.
3. Name three things others have told you about yourself that might be lies but you somehow believed and let that hinder you in your goals:
4. If you look at the skills that seem somewhat specific to you, what are your favorites?

5. What is the primary emotion that inhibits you from succeeding in areas where you would like to excel?

6. Looking back to question #2, take some time to find these qualities in women of the Bible, or heroic figures in history.

7. Taking your answers to questions #2 and #6, ask a trusted friend or relative to look over your answers (if you would like to share them) and tell you how they see those gifts in you, and why God may have placed them there.

8. Pray for God to help you see how those gifts fit together in His amazing plan for you as His own lady by design.

Once you can rest in God's design of you, you can move forward with confidence in that assurance. Take measures to avoid the questioning that comes when you submit to Him and not other people in your life who would control you. Remember to trust those whom He has placed around you for protection, security, love, and laughter. They are there for a reason—to guide you safely to your harbor of life—God's special place just for you.

One of my favorite prayers when I am at a loss and the storms of life are coming fast is very simple but helps me remember the crucial nature of my role as a lady. I say simply, "Lord, please, less of me, more of You." I imagine a ship on the horizon, and I know that if it is just me the people on land can see coming in from the ocean, my whole life will be missed, and I will be forever lost at sea. It is impossible to find one small person out on the horizon in a vast blue ocean. But it is a beautiful, stark, majestic sight when a ship comes in, bright, white sails bellowing in the wind, leading her to her safe harbor. Her dependence on the sails, her mate, her crew, and the strength it took for her to trust to that level—that defines her life and her legacy.

Unquestionably, this process is a long, sometimes arduous, journey, somewhat like an ocean passage. Sometimes we have to leave a comfortable cove, forego an attraction, or even re-navigate the voyage to be sure we are on God's path to His destination for our journey.

In my case, this meant leaving a church, a group of friends, and an entire wardrobe. It meant reclaiming a career and hiring a personal assistant. Those were enormous changes for me. I was surprised how quickly God moved in my life once I opened myself to His call for me as His lady. My children rallied and rose to the call, my career took off with a trajectory I could never have dreamed. He used my enemies as a footstool (Acts 2:32), and he turned my husband into my greatest admirer (despite the fact I wasn't a living *hausfrau* for him). He became my best advocate, and my very own gentle man of gentlemen. The biggest surprise came when those I thought might be most hurt by my decisions (my husband and children—I really thought that leaving **my** house for a few hours per day would hurt them somehow) actually thanked me, and confirmed all that God had whispered to me on that fateful day when I awoke from my guilty fog—"You are a lady of My own design!"

So what does that modern lady look like? I think that depends on what day of the week it is.

On Monday, she raises her sails, takes a deep breath, and gears up. She looks smart and sassy, as well as purposeful. Her suit is tailored and crisp, her hair is carelessly twirled behind her head, and the sparkle in her eyes matches a smile on her face as she enters the week with all of its possibilities ahead. Oh, I almost forgot—she has great shoes!

In the evening, she watches the colors dance off the water as she continues to sail through her week. She is efficient in her endeavors, watchful as the night falls, aware of what is on the horizon. She considers a stock option, and dials it in on her iPhone. She takes her place at the city gates, and grabs her children to come alongside her to learn as she works. By day, she thinks crisply, leads decisively, and accompanies her family confidently. By nightfall, she has transformed into her husband's empathic comforter, passionate lover, mysterious seductress, and watchful protector of all of those on board her vessel. She works tirelessly, lives intentionally, and submits wholly to her God. She sails on . . .

By Friday, she can look back at careful accomplishments and progress in the journey as she tacked, battened, and trusted in the One guiding her, and in her soul mate and trusty crew. She has kicked off her heels and sported her torn jeans and T-shirt, and bared her feet. Her hair is down now, a sign to all that the week has ended and it is time to loosen her sails. Her safe harbor ever in her heart, she presses on toward the goal as it becomes clearer and clearer in her line of vision.

She pauses to be adored by those who matter, and she kicks the debris out from under her as many try to distract her from her journey. She has a vision and a mission clearly defined. Her legacy established, she can choose to take the helm or stand at the side of her captain, ever vigilant. Her children wake with smiles and slumber with love. Her mate knows her worth and desires only more of her as each day passes. Her journey is underway. She is a lady of God's design . . . and she can *laugh* at the days to come. ★

*Chapter Twelve*

# My Forefathers' Virtues:
# Biological, Step, and Heavenly

*The True Gentleman is the man whose conduct proceeds from
    good will*
*and an acute sense of propriety and whose self-control is equal to
    all emergencies;*
*who does not make the poor man conscious of his poverty,*
*the obscure man of his obscurity,*
*or any man of his inferiority or deformity;*
*who is himself humbled if necessity compels him to humble
    another;*
*who does not flatter wealth,*
*cringe before power*
*or boast of his own possessions or achievements;*
*who speaks with frankness but always with sincerity and sympathy;*

*whose deed follows his word;*
*who thinks of the rights and feelings of others rather than his own;*
*and who appears well in any company;*
*a man with whom honor is sacred and virtue safe.*
— JOHN WALTER WAYLAND, *THE TRUE GENTLEMAN* (1899)

## Earthly Father #1

Like a large portion of my generation, I (Dr. Paterno) am a child of divorce. My parents married shortly after high school. My father, Robert, grew up in a working-class family just outside of Chicago. As his father before him was a Marine (having fought in the Battle of Iwo Jima), he enlisted into the Marines upon graduation.

My mother, Dyanne, was an Army brat, born in Chicago shortly after World War II. Her father had been orphaned during the Great Depression when he was twelve and had found refuge in a tree house for months. Authorities finally found him and forced him into foster care. As soon as he was able, he joined the Army, where he rose to the rank of Colonel. He was stationed, among other places, in Germany and Pakistan during my mother's middle-school years. Despite her expanded horizons, she had a contentious and cold relationship with her father; apparently her connection to her alcoholic mother wasn't much better. It seems that my parents' marriage was more about leaving than cleaving.

My father, by all accounts, was a jovial young man with plenty of friends. He played varsity baseball and was a decent student. He was shipped to Vietnam shortly after he and my mother became engaged. My father dutifully performed his tour, and then returned to civilian life. I never had a chance to speak with him about his service or his experience, but it seems to have marked a terrible shift in his personality.

Legend says that it was no coincidence that my birth on April 5, 1970 was remarkably close to nine months after Apollo 11 landed on the moon.[1] The math works out, although the same could not be said

---

[1] My father used to joke that I was "one giant *backward* leap for mankind."

194

for my father's introduction to parenthood. I have gathered over the years that when he returned from Vietnam, he was more interested in smoking pot and sitting on the couch watching baseball than in getting a job. My mother has told me that he adored me as a baby, but somehow it did not compel him to get off his duff to provide for his wife and child.

My mother was a fairly liberal woman, but not so much as to be comfortable playing both Mom and Dad. She decided to walk from the marriage shortly after I had learned to walk. Almost immediately, she began working her tail off in secretarial positions, while placing me with a girlfriend who also had a toddler boy. Over the following decades, one of the key mantras that stuck in my head was "A real man works and provides for his family." Message received.

My parents had a relatively tame divorce; my father didn't even attend the court proceedings, and there were no assets to distribute. However, I recall some nasty phone conversations during the following years, mostly because my father continued to be a bum—neglecting to get a regular job, failing to pay child support, and rarely showing up for his biweekly visitation.[2] From this, I learned another virtue from the "Don't grow up to be like your father" playbook: a gentleman fulfills his obligations.

By the time I was ten, my mother had had enough. She gave him two choices: pay child support and show up for every visit or remove himself from my life altogether. He chose the latter. I never saw my father again.[3]

## Earthly Father #2

In the meantime, my mother had married my first stepfather, Mr. Paterno, when I was about six. He was divorced and had five older children from his first marriage. He seemed like a nice enough guy at first. His family was of Sicilian descent; they were interesting and were phenomenal cooks, so I was relatively open to the change. They

---

[2] I also learned some creative cursing combinations.
[3] We reconnected via letters a few months before he died in 1999.

were also distantly related to Joe Paterno, which until recently was a source of pride. Finally, he was a good provider, which was likely one of the primary reasons for my mother's second round of matrimony. We moved to a house, had nice cars, nice furniture, and ate like kings.

The honeymoon didn't last long. He turned out to be a jerk. He was verbally, emotionally, and physically abusive to my mother and verbally and emotionally abusive to me. His older children were incredibly (and understandably) angry and hurt. Some of them took it out on me, taking every opportunity to say cruel things to both me and my mother. It was clear that we were not welcome in this new family. My younger half sisters received Christmas and birthday presents, while I did not. My mother urged him to confront his family and entreat them to treat me with equal respect. For whatever reason, he declined. Not exactly a knight of the Round Table.

At home, there were frequent, often violent, fights. I recall dishes breaking, highly creative strings of cuss words, threats, my mother locking herself in the bathroom, doors breaking, screaming, and late-night car rides to my grandparents' house.

One late night when I was six, there had been a long fight with several chapters. Between two such chapters, my mother tiptoed into my room. She had attempted to call the police, but my stepfather had ripped the phone out of the wall and destroyed the phone cord. She asked me to sneak out of the house, ring the neighbor's doorbell, and ask them to call the police. On another occasion, my stepfather was arrested after a particularly violent episode and spent some time in a psychiatric ward.

I have to give my mother credit; she was fiercely protective of me and my new sisters. She never had to explicitly tell me not to grow up to be like him. She knew I was smart enough to recognize that I shouldn't grow up to be like someone almost completely devoid of virtue.

This marriage didn't last either. When I was fourteen, there was a last-ditch effort to save the marriage. My stepfather offered to legally adopt me. He hoped this would placate my mother; she hoped it would induce him to behave like a decent human being.

A year after the adoption papers were signed, they announced their intention to divorce.[4]

## Introduction to My Heavenly Father

I attended the local Lutheran school, which had an excellent reputation for academics. The same twenty-five students matriculated from first through eighth grade. It was a very loving and challenging place of learning where we all knew each other quite well. The consistency was comforting, as was my introduction to organized Christianity. There was also a rare balance of male and female teachers.[5]

One of the most shameful episodes of my life occurred in fifth grade. We had a fantastic teacher, Mr. Tatone. He was funny, engaging, strict, and creative. Most of us liked him a great deal. I recall trying very hard to get his approval and make him proud.

In almost every classroom, there are a couple of overweight children. Every classroom also has a couple of students who are socially awkward or even bankrupt of charisma. Every classroom seems to have an emotionally fragile child as well. Some classrooms have one kid who inhabits all of those unfortunate traits. Karen was that kid.

We had recently begun a unit on poetry. Keen on writing, I eagerly learned about and practiced the different forms of verse. One of them struck my fancy. I thought it would be hilarious to take my gift for verse and invent a limerick for each classmate. If memory serves, the first few were fantastic; they were instant hits. Other students clamored to be the next recipient of my literary brilliance. Of course, I was all too willing to comply. Move over, Shel Silverstein.

When the demand waned, I didn't want to quit. I needed a fix. My ego was puffed, and I wasn't about to give that up. I couldn't find a willing participant, so I found a victim. I frantically searched the classroom for material; soon I recalled the phrase "How now, brown cow?" from an earlier grade. Eureka!

---

[4] One of the best days of my life.
[5] Something desperately lacking in today's elementary schools.

My brilliant poem wasn't even a poem. I bastardized and plagiarized it into a one-line dagger: "How now, brown Karen?" Not exactly Poet Laureate material, but I soon discovered that it had the desired effect of bringing back the giggles. For half a day, mini troubadours spread the one-liner from student to student. By lunchtime, we were choking on our Fritos with laughter from repeating the line *ad nauseum*.

That is, until Mr. Tatone heard it. The teachers all sat at a long table in the gymnasium, facing the series of tables of children. Only several feet away, he could clearly hear what we were reciting.

I had never seen Mr. Tatone so furious. He marched me into the hallway, his upper lip quivering with righteous anger. I remember him staring me in the eyes while he grilled me with questions, his wrath simmering, barely contained.

"Do you think your little poem is funny?"

"No."

"Don't lie. You wouldn't have laughed if you didn't think it was funny. I know you're not supposed to think it's funny now, but you sure did at first, didn't you?"

"Yes."

"Do you think Karen is so deaf that she won't hear it?"

"No."

"And do you think she will think it is as hilarious as you and your audience?"

"No."

"Do you think Karen's dad would think it's funny?"

Gulp. "No."

"Do you think Jesus thinks it is funny?"

"No. I'm sorry."

"I'm sorry too. You know, I think Karen has caught wind of your little joke. Do you think she is going to feel God's love in your poem?"

I burst out crying. "No!"

"What do you think it suggests about you that you feel free to use your creativity—something God gave you to use for good—to stab your neighbor in the heart?"

"I don't know." I was truly ashamed. Not just embarrassed and scared because I was in trouble. But I got it. I had done something I really didn't believe in.

Mr. Tatone taught me about integrity that day. As school let out, he called me to him while the other students shuffled out of the classroom. He suggested to me that he knew I didn't believe in hurting people's feelings, but that what was more important to me at that moment was attention, my own "fame," my likability, and enjoying the power of my words. He said that he forgave me and that he expected me to treat Karen and others with dignity and respect. I don't recall him ever using the term *gentleman*, but I knew exactly what he meant. I had violated core virtues that I believed in—strongly, in fact—but hadn't acted in accordance with them.[6]

It still makes me sick to my stomach to recall how black my heart must have been to have said that—to have trampled on a young girl's virtue for my own selfish gain. That episode taught me a valuable virtue: to care for those who are unfortunate and seemingly unlovable. If God loves them, then they are certainly worth my love too.

I never became Karen's best friend, but I never again teased her or took an opportunity to increase my ego by reducing hers. Mr. Tatone's forgiveness and his willingness to presume the best in me deeply embedded into my conscience. He taught me more about my heavenly Father and the virtues than my first two earthly fathers combined.

## Substitute Father #1

My best friend from the ages of six to fourteen was Paul Hannah. He was my classmate at St. Andrew's. Paul was an easygoing, active playmate; he was always up for any activity. We played tons of sports together, traded baseball cards, rode bikes, played video games and loads of board games, played pool, and enjoyed just about every kind

---

[6] Paul describes the sinner's lack of perfect integrity in this way: "For that which I do I allow not: for what I would, that do I not, but what I hate, I do. (Romans 7: 15, KJV)

of tag/adventure game you could imagine. We started listening to rock music together.

Paul and I didn't have many deep conversations. Whether it was because we were boys, were too active, or because he knew my family life was insane, we kept things superficial. In a way, he was my suppression partner; when we hung out, I forgot about everything for a while.

This apple didn't fall too far from the tree; Mr. Hannah was similarly reticent. I can't recall any serious conversations or episodes of discipline with him. What he did was take us everywhere and anywhere: trips to professional sporting events, movies, and all the other boy activities we did. He played pool, threw darts, and sometimes even shot baskets with us. I was invited to all of it. He wasn't my father, but his presence and active involvement became part of God's protective presence in my life. It also modeled masculine love, which is often more about doing than saying.

## Substitute Father #2

My fondest memory of high school is my youth group experience at the local church. Centered at South Park Church (no relation to the TV show) and started by Bill Hybels, the high school youth group was called Son City. It sounds a bit like either a retirement village or a cult, but it was actually a fantastic organization. Much of the leadership was peer led, with a focus on bringing in as many teens into the fun and innocent activities as possible.

The adult leader of Son City was Youth Pastor Doug Britton. He was a well-spoken, kind, humorous man who took a keen interest in the lives of the youth he served in that group. He wasn't only interested in sharing the gospel with us; he was interested in each person as a whole entity. That deep interest was evident.

Doug frequently invited me to play racquetball with him; I wasn't the most skilled player, but I played my heart out and gave him a good workout. Afterward, we got a bite to eat and talked about life and whatever was on my mind. I remember feeling as if a deep well were being filled when I spent time with him. He truly cared about me, my thoughts, my ideas, my aspirations, and my beliefs. He gently shepherded me in my fledgling faith, which had recently sprouted after a camping trip with some of my youth group peers.

Doug seemed to recognize that my family life was less than ideal. He didn't press me to talk about it or play psychoanalyst and try to fix my emotional wounds. He just loved me in a brotherly manner. My mother was pleased that I was involved in the youth group; it was something that I looked forward to with great excitement. I believe that there was a tacit understanding that I was getting some deep needs met with the group and its leader.

Here, too, I learned the virtue of putting others first by making time to be with them and listening to them. There is no doubt that God placed Doug Britton in my life for that and many other purposes.

## Earthly Father #3

Later, my mother married Dr. Michael Bresler, who was chief psychologist at the same hospital where she worked as a nurse. He was a very good man: kind, humorous, patient, generous, caring, intelligent, and devoted to my mother. Third time's the charm, they say.

Michael brought a great deal to the table that hadn't been part of our family. He was a solid provider, but without any of the overwhelming negatives of #2. He was an intellectual, which meant that my mother's keen mind finally had an equal partner who could connect with, challenge, and stretch her. He also had a fantastic sense of humor; it was good to see and hear them laugh.

I was twenty-five when they married, so my connection to Michael as a father figure had a somewhat minimized potential. Having been burned by #1 and #2, I was slow to warm to him in that regard. At the same time, I was doing my own cleaving. In some ways, I was fiercely protective of my new nuclear family, to the exclusion of any outside influences. Still, he was a good man with many virtues.

Michael possessed many of the virtues listed later in this chapter. Most importantly, he was faithful, humble, and gracious. A person could feel safe with him—likely one of the reasons he was such a successful psychologist.

Tragically, he became ill in 2005 and died two years later.

## Father-in-Law

My father-in-law has more virtue in his pinky than most men have in their entire being.[7] One of the most giving, selfless men I have ever met, he gives out of a genuine desire to love, not from any selfish gain. He is also remarkably honest and encouraging.

Diagnosed with a rare form of colon cancer in 2004, his courage steeled him during the wretched chemotherapy, helping him defeat it within two years. Today, he is a marvel of health, living a full life as a husband, father, and grandfather.

## Lifeboats of Virtue

God intimately knows the needs of His children. He does not offer sorry substitutes for Himself. He fills our cups so that they flow over. He has done just that for me throughout my life, providing men whose gifts taught me—either explicitly or by modeling—how to be a gentleman. I don't claim for a minute to be anything near perfect, but I have received a clear message from the multiple male role models in my life what it means to live out the virtues. I can only hope that God will bless me with the gifts and obedience sufficient to teach my son how to be a gentleman of complete virtue.

## The Gentlemanly Virtues

Now, we turn to the essential question of this chapter: What are the essential virtues to which modern men should aspire? We submit that the following are essential traits of a gentleman. An example or anecdote follows each.

*Graciousness*: A gentleman practices the wisdom of the parable of the unmerciful servant, found in Matthew 18:21–35. Because he has been forgiven so much, he is not only willing but eager to forgive others. Out of gratefulness, grace and mercy spring forth. He does not

---

[7] And I'm not just saying this so he will keep inviting me to his house to watch football games.

abandon justice, but tempers it with mercy. "Love," Paul reminds us, "keeps no record of wrongs" (1 Corinthians 13:5).

One day in Salt Lake City, a man was waiting for his bags at the baggage claim at the airport. A nearby woman was struggling to get her bags from the carousel when she noticed the towering, muscular man. She presumed he was an airport employee, so she asked him if he could carry her bags to the taxi station. Without skipping a beat, the man obliged. Appreciating his dutiful work, she offered him a tip. Only then did he gently inform her that he didn't work for the airport; he finally introduced himself as Karl Malone: NBA Hall of Fame forward.

*Manners/courtesy*: "Manners maketh man." Attributed to William Wykeham, founder of Winchester College and New College at Oxford, this refers to more than simply choosing the correct fork or refraining from burping at the table. It means all of the little daily behaviors a gentleman performs that reflect class, such as self-control, putting others first, and a recognition of propriety—all things that are sorely lacking in today's society.

My seven-year-old son and I performed an experiment last summer. At an upper-class department store, he held the door open whenever a woman approached. I stood by to observe, ready to validate for him how wonderful it felt to hear so many women thanking him for his excellent manners. Shockingly, only one woman said thank you during the ten-minute span. At one point, eight women in a row—old and young alike—completely ignored him.

What I had designed as a teaching tool for my son became a sorry exhibition of how many modern women have lost their manners.[8]

*Honesty*: A gentleman tells the truth, the whole truth, and nothing but the truth, no matter what the consequences and with very few exceptions.[9]

---

[8] Performing the same experiment at the local Starbucks a few weeks later, almost all the women said "thank you," many quite cheerfully. Perhaps caffeine maketh manners maketh man.

[9] Debatable exception: when a woman asks, "Does my butt look big in these jeans?"

An ethics professor once assigned his class to read chapter 18 of the primary textbook a week before spring break, reassuring the class that they would not be tested on the material. The next week, the professor asked for a show of hands: "OK, who read chapter 18?" About a dozen of the eighty students raised their hand, to which the professor responded, "OK, here's a quiz for those who read the chapter; it wouldn't be fair to quiz those who didn't." The students grumbled while the professor handed out the quiz. After a quick scan, they realized that they couldn't answer any of the obscure graduate-level questions. They quickly protested.

The professor then asked the rest of the class, "Can anyone tell me what ethic I am teaching by giving them this quiz and why?" One of the students raised her hand and replied, "Honesty; because the textbook only has sixteen chapters."

*Masculinity*: A gentleman is first and foremost a man. Not metrosexual, effeminate, or overly sensitive, he does not shy away from getting his hands dirty—or even bloody. He learns how to fix things. He knows how to throw a ball, light a campfire, and change the oil in his car. A man knows that "Righty tighty, lefty loosey" is not a book by Dr. Seuss. A man knows the difference between an uppercut and a hook, and he isn't afraid to give or receive either to protect himself or others.

I have only been in a handful of fights in my life. The last was in 2008, when my wife and I joined our good friends for a double date. After dinner, we decided to meet for a drink at a pub a block away from their house. While my friend went home to check on his children, the two women and I parked the car.

Across the street, we noticed a young couple embroiled in a nasty quarrel. As we approached, he became more belligerent to her, squeezing her in an aggressive bear-hug and berating her with foul names. My wife innocently suggested, "Hey, buddy, why don't you relax a bit?" He stepped toward us, menacingly. I got between him and my wife and her girlfriend and suggested that he take a break, adding that the woman seemed scared. I caught her mouthing to me with a terrified look on her face, "Help me!"

This guy would have none of it. After a few tasteless invectives, I turned to suggest to my wife's friend that she call the police. As I turned, the thug blindsided me with a punch, just missing my eye. It almost knocked me out and left a nasty, plum-sized hematoma. We scuffled for a bit, until the guy ran away.

I'm no prizefighter, but I am proud to have stood my ground and taken a punch.[10]

*Physical Appearance*: Not simply referring to a man's physical stature—after all, a short, fat man in jeans can be every bit the gentleman as a tall, lanky man in a tuxedo—we are referring to stewarding one's physical attributes. God has given each man a body. We can either misuse and abuse it and cover it with shabby clothes or take care of it to our best ability and adorn it with clean, appealing clothes.

A gentleman maintains excellent hygiene, seeks to remain fit, yet does not seek to make a spectacle of himself.

*Commitment to Family*: A gentleman prioritizes his time and resources:

- *God first*. He should be a gentleman's primary relationship and priority, getting the prime times and abilities. Everything else stems from the intimacy derived from this relationship.
- *Family and work tied for second* (since a gentleman's work serves his family). It may seem counterintuitive to quote *The Godfather*, but even Don Corleone reflected a modicum of virtue when he said, "A man who doesn't spend time with his family can never be a real man."
- *Church and friends are tied for third*. Church involvement and spending time with friends are both noble and necessary activities as long as they do not get in the way of family, work, or individual worship.
- *Community work* (such as political advocacy, volunteering, organizing) comes fourth. Although it is a dying practice these days, Christians of all stripes should be taking note of the Tea Party movement, which advocates all citizens involving themselves in the political scene.

---

[10] I conveniently went as Rocky for Halloween a few days later. No makeup necessary!

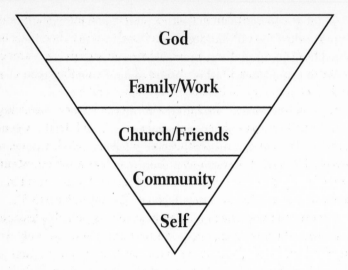

- *Self*-focused pursuits come last for the gentleman—although they certainly have their place. For example, there is nothing wrong with playing a round of golf with friends or as a reward for a long week at work, but regularly leaving one's family for a half day or more is a fairly selfish thing to do. A gentleman with children will "escape" more rarely than the days he stays home to work on the house, play with the children, help his brother clean his gutters, or call his parents.

*Humility*: Humility combines two essential elements: recognition of God's gifts and proper acknowledgement for those gifts. There is nothing wrong with observing and relishing one's strengths, gifts, or success. A man slips into sinful pride when he claims his gifts and success without giving credit to God.

A gentleman avoids false humility. If he has a gift, he should revel in it, enjoy it, and not shy away from using it in public. Of course, a gentleman protects himself from self-worship by constantly giving thanks for his gifts and success so that he does not forget who deserves the glory.[11]

---

[11] Hey, that sounds like Tebowing!

As we have argued, humility is one of the casualties of atheism. If God did not gift a man his strength, skill, and success, then there is no one to praise except self. A narcissistic view of success and strengths gives birth to statements like Muhammad Ali's "I am the greatest" and Terrell Owens's hymn to himself: "I love me some me."

*Self-control*: Catholic tradition refers to *temperance*, the ability to inhibit one's baser impulses (in thought, word, and deed). A gentleman practices and retains control over his body, mind, tongue, and passions. He does not succumb to the temptation for unrestrained desire of food, drink, sex, or any other pleasure. He controls himself when angry, as love "is not easily angered" (1 Corinthians 13:5).

A gentleman perceives moderation as the key to holy pleasure.

Barbara Bush once quipped, "I listen and give input only when somebody asks." Excellent advice. How difficult it is to restrain oneself from speaking one's mind! A gentleman understands the irony that remaining silent often induces others to ask for his thoughts quicker than when he offers them unsolicited.

*Faithfulness*: Not merely avoiding cheating on one's spouse, faithfulness encapsulates being true to all of one's alliances: work, church, family, friends, and politics. A gentleman takes all alliances with sincerity. *Semper Fidelis* (Latin for "always faithful") is the motto for a gentleman's compact with spouse, friend, family, military unit, country, God, and business partner.

The United States Declaration of Independence concludes with the founders' vow of faithfulness to each other and to their cause: "And for the support of this Declaration, with a firm reliance on the protection of divine Providence, we mutually pledge to each other our Lives, our Fortunes and our sacred Honor." The founders were remarkably faithful to this vow.

Ronald Regan's dictum, "Speak no ill of a fellow Republican," is an excellent modern example of the virtue of faithfulness. While not all Republicans display perfect virtue, and there are occasions for reprimand, Reagan realized that alliances are not only critical to success and difficult to establish but they are even more difficult to repair. Therefore, confronting and rebuking one's allies—whether they be fellow believers, fellow party affiliates, or fellow family members—should be done in private.

*Self-sacrifice*: We have no greater model of self-sacrifice than Christ Himself. A true gentleman models himself after the Lamb of God, willing to sacrifice for the people and causes he loves. He gives his time, money, gifts, ego, and sometimes his life.

In 1943, the US transport ship SS Dorchester was sailing near Greenland when it was torpedoed by a German U-boat. As the ship began to sink, all 902 people scrambled for life jackets, but there was a shortage. Four chaplains were aboard: a Catholic priest, a Methodist, a reformed pastor, and a rabbi. When they realized that four of the crew members were without lifejackets, the four chaplains relinquished their vests and perished along with the ship. Legend says that as the ship sank, they locked arms and began singing the Navy hymn *Eternal Father, Strong to Save*.

*Integrity*: This great virtue acts as a catalyst or *über*-virtue from which all other virtues flow. Integrity refers to the determination and ability to behave according to one's beliefs, values, and ethics. A gentleman with integrity behaves honestly, for example, because honesty is dear to him. Christ, of course, modeled perfect integrity, having always acted according to His Father's will. While a gentleman cannot hope to achieve this level of perfection in this world, he strives through love, self-discipline, and accountability to live out the virtues he holds dear.

Abraham Lincoln earned a reputation of solid integrity during his early years as an attorney in Illinois. One judge said of him, "Such was the transparent candor and integrity of his nature that he could not well or strongly argue a side or a cause he thought wrong." Lincoln simply was unable to do something he did not believe in.

Polonius's lecture in *Hamlet* to his son Laertes is essentially a call to integrity: "To thine own self be true, and it must follow, as the night the day, thou canst not then be false to any man."

*Courage*: C. S. Lewis wrote that "Courage is not simply one of the virtues, but the form of every virtue at the testing point." This makes courage a close cousin of integrity. Gentlemen aren't without fear; courage is not synonymous with fearlessness. They do their duty in spite of fear.

Dr. Gina and I are both humbled and awed by the men and women in uniform. The fact that young men and women hardly out of high school willingly enlist to serve our country, put themselves in the direst of circumstances, confronting evil and the most horrific devastation and violence imaginable humbles us. It also encourages us to speak out for political candidates who truly support those who serve and have served our national security. ★

*Chapter Thirteen*

# When God Calls a Rebel:
# The Digni-Tea Party

*If there must be trouble, let it be in my day, that my child may have peace.*

—THOMAS PAINE, 1776

*How dare they compare their low-rent, trashy movement to the Tea Party!*

—LLOYD MARCUS, AMERICAN THINKER

*The government's view of the economy could be summed up in a few short phrases: If it moves, tax it. If it keeps moving, regulate it. And if it stops moving, subsidize it.*

—RONALD REAGAN

*A general Dissolution of Principles & Manners will more surely overthrow the Liberties of America than the whole Force of the Common Enemy.*

—SAMUEL ADAMS, 1779

*Here, sir, the people govern.*

—ALEXANDER HAMILTON

## PART 1: EXCUSE ME, KIND SIR, WHILST I BEHEAD YOU . . .

*"He is a very shallow critic who cannot see an eternal rebel in the heart of a conservative."*

—G.K. CHESTERTON

## The Tide Turns

Conservatives have taken it on the chin for far too long. When the Left wasn't punching, the establishment GOP took their opportunistic swing at conservatives. Conservatives honored the "it's his turn to be president" rule of establishment power brokers through Bush, Dole, Re-Bush, McCain, and more. There was something that happened when Obama was elected. A tide deep inside the soul of the conservative simply turned. Something was organically different that day, and more than a movement was born. Boldness was seeded in the heart of the conservative that would change everything.

That day, we changed course. We knew we had listened, trusted, accommodated, submitted, and lost. We knew that something was wrong, and thought we should be heard, but we never want to be the pushy ones, or the bullies. But the day Obama was elected, visions of the end of our republic haunted our thoughts, and we cared less about being polite—even civil. We knew this was war, and that we had to put on our combat boots and get in the battle.

Gone were the days we could sit in the church pews and pray for good leaders to lead. Gone were the coveted days where good parenting—raising up an army—seemed our godly duty to this country. Gone, once and for all, were the days when our vote seemed to matter. This was going to be epic—we could feel it. When we didn't know what else to do, we dared to protest.

We made signs, organized events, tried our hand at the pen and our voices at the airwaves. We blogged and wrote and created e-mail threads. We held flags and hands. We jeered and we cried. We pledged and we recommitted ourselves to the country we believed God had given us, in His grace. We knew that the time had come to change everything. Even if we lost, we had to know we had given all. We were ready for a revolution.

"How do good people (with rules) battle bad people with no rules?" we wondered. As we watched a radical socialist agenda literally take over the country for which our forefathers died, we became enraged. We watched radical Islam and Sharia law with its principle of "all for Allah" take over our people, our politics, and our common sense. How could we, the religion of the Ten Commandments (namely, don't cheat, don't lie, don't steal, don't kill) battle a political system claiming religious status under our Constitution that believes it is okay to kill, cheat, steal, or lie if it is for Allah? How could we, as citizens, sit and watch foreign invasion happen and be called the aliens and criminals for wanting to put a stop to it? Where was civility?

We needed to fight. We needed to win or be owned, and know that our children would pay forever. How could we compete based upon a faith that said, "Be a lady; be a gentleman"? The liberals invaded our churches half a century ago with their "feminine Jesus" pictures, their "turn the other cheek" mantra, and their "Christians should always back down and be the nice guy" doctrine. Suddenly, we knew that we had been lied to. Even some good pastors had bought the liberal narrative and undermined our rugged, bold, mighty God.

Instead of "Amazing Grace" we were thinking "Onward Christian Soldier." Instead of a focus on "Lord, make me an instrument of Thy peace" we focused on the "Armor of God" and on righteous anger, and biblical war doctrine. Instead of the feminized, pale, thin longhaired

Jesus, we remembered that He was a rugged carpenter, a rebel of rebels against evil, who claimed his kingdom and boldly proclaimed the truth, regardless cost, circumstance, or implication. Instead of only praying for our leaders, we realized that God might have us act to throw the scoundrels out. We stood ready.

As we became more strategic, we realized that there is an art to war. We adopted the "starfish" model of a leader so they couldn't behead us. We read the playbook that liberals used to take over our churches, our schools, and our culture, and we rewrote Alinsky's *Rules for Radicals*, and added a touch of class, to claim it as our own. Instead of Calvin, Lewis, and Luther, we assigned our children Orwell, Rand, and Huxley. We loved the new liberty of expression. We were angry, and rightfully so. We enjoyed our First Amendment right to say so, in the streets, on television, over the airwaves, on the Internet. We felt like "We, the People" again, and it felt good.

Then we faced another crisis. We discovered that we could cling to our Constitution and protest, but we couldn't exact unprovoked violence to make our point stick. We could hold signs, but we wouldn't brandish pistols or pitchforks in the streets until we were sure there was no other option. We could talk tough, but Christians and other civil folks simply aren't comfortable crossing the line from protestor to revolutionary. We didn't know when to pull out the guns. "How much is too much?" we asked ourselves. "When does God authorize a revolution?"

Because the Evil One is truly evil, we can know that he will do all he can to confuse and convolute. We rose up and took elections in 2010, and felt emboldened. Then we tripped up a bit when we realized we had no real candidate for president, and the Occupy Wall Street movement swept the nation. They publicly fornicated, defecated on police cars, burned things, and emulated the Tea Party in devilish mockery. We couldn't do all of that because we don't play by their rules. They cuddled up with Islam, atheism, agnosticism, anarchists, and all the downcast in the country, then had the audacity to call themselves the "99%."

We stood by, confused and astonished, and not really knowing how to out-protest the protestors who had no bounds. We could never be that. So, what *were* we?

We weren't sure what to do, but we certainly knew God would not bless us acting like heathen savages to win the media war (at least most of us knew that). So some of us stood by, some became indistinguishable from the Occupiers, some opted to dance with the Devil (establishment GOP) in order to have something to show for all of their hard work, and some turned their guns on one another in a desperate attempt to understand where we had gone wrong—if we die, by God, we will make sure we chose to die.

> "To sin by silence when they should protest makes cowards of men."
>
> —ABRAHAM LINCOLN

# Pit Bull Politics

To ask the warrior to become the gentleman feels in some ways like asking John Wayne, with all of his raw bravado, to regress and reduce into the puny likes of Ashton Kutcher. That is not what we are asking. Nor would we. But to pretend that the rebel warrior had no honor is a socially liberal concoction of what history doesn't say. War is hell, but it is downright polite until the trigger blows. Chivalry is violent, but first, it is the business of ladies and gentlemen, and nights called "Sir."

## Gods and Dogs

Gentlemen of the jury: The best friend a man has in this world may turn against him and become his enemy. His son or daughter that he has reared with loving care may prove ungrateful. Those who are nearest and dearest to us, those whom we trust with our happiness and our good name, may become traitors to their faith. The money that a man has, he may lose. It flies away from him, perhaps when he needs it the most. A man's reputation may be sacrificed in a moment of ill-considered action. The people who are prone to fall on their knees to do us honor when success is with us may be the first to throw the stone of malice when failure settles its cloud upon our heads. The one absolutely unselfish friend that a man can have in this selfish world, the one that never deserts him and the one that never proves ungrateful or treacherous is his dog. Gentlemen of the jury: A man's dog stands by him in prosperity and in poverty, in health and in sickness. He will sleep on the cold ground, where the wintry winds blow and the snow drives fiercely, if only he may be near his master's side. He will kiss the hand that has no food to offer, he will lick the wounds and sores that come in encounters with the roughness of the world. He guards the sleep of his pauper master as if he were a prince. When all other friends desert, he remains. When riches take wings and reputation falls to pieces, he is as constant in his love as the sun in its journey through the heavens.

If fortune drives the master forth an outcast in the world, friendless and homeless, the faithful dog asks no higher privilege than that of accompanying him to guard against danger, to fight against his enemies, and when the last scene of all comes, and death takes the master in its embrace and his body is laid away in the cold ground, no matter if all other friends pursue their way, there by his graveside will the noble dog be found, his head between his paws, his eyes sad but open in alert watchfulness, faithful and true even to death. Senator George Graham Vest, praising his dog, Drum[1]

God models His perfect example of real strength in the warrior in the animal kingdom every day. My favorite example was a dog named Toblerone.

"Tobby" was a pit bull we rescued as a puppy from a shelter. Though I like most breeds of dog, I have long believed the pit bull to be a great metaphor to the conservative. The conservative is tough, hardy, grounded, loyal, and capable. The conservative only attacks for the most altruistic of causes. The conservative never attacks randomly, out of insecurity, or out of fear. The conservative knows his own strength, and rests confidently in that. The conservative knows who his master is, and is intensely loyal. Therefore, the conservative, like the pit bull, will only attack out of loyalty to his master. The bad

---

[1] *Senator Vest-Champion of the Dog* by Edwin M.C. French, 2007, Meador Publishing, Boston.

reputation comes in that when the pit bull does attack, the bite is deadly. The conservative is labeled "the hater" and the "monster of politics," while its animal counterpart carries the moniker "monster of the streets."

Tobby (named for the German chocolate, Toblerone) was my first dog, and I was altogether unworthy of his love and loyalty. He knew his own strength. While other dogs would bark and threaten in downtown St. Louis, where we lived, Tobby walked with a quiet, humble, friendly confidence. He greeted every day like it was the best day of his life. He gave love to all who crossed his path, and saved countless animal and human lives. He gave all and seemed happy to do it.

On the rare occasion that I needed him to act like the pit bull he was reputed to be, he did. I knew with full confidence that my warrior was there, at my beck and call, dutifully ready to fight at my simplest nod. I and others only needed him for that on one occasion, but the day he passed peacefully into heaven, I knew I needed to buy a gun. And I knew I wouldn't ever know the loyalty, the bravery, and the quiet confidence from a machine that I knew in my pit bull, Tobby.

It might sound odd, but Tobby is the one who taught me value of a warrior wrapped in the civility of a gentleman. He was polite, friendly, loyal, happy, and ready at any moment to use the strengths God gave him for battle. He knew he would win, and that confidence spared him the reactive combativeness we see in people every day.

## Partners and Politics

G. K. Chesterton is a titan of the conservative movement's history. He warned of the potential personality difficulties of the rebel—even the rebel who fights for a good cause:

> But the new rebel is a Skeptic, and will not entirely trust anything. He has no loyalty; therefore he can never be really a revolutionist. And the fact that he doubts everything really gets in his way when he wants to denounce anything. For all denunciation implies a moral doctrine of some kind; and the modern revolutionist doubts not only the institution he denounces, but the doctrine by which he denounces it.

I have seen the rise of the combative conservative and it concerns me. Of course, we want fighters out in front, and we want spine. We have tired of spineless, wimpy Christians who cower from their constitutional obligation to defend America (God and country) in the public arena. So when we first hear combative types speaking with strong language, even guttural or crass, we responded. This is dangerous. Both of our backgrounds are in psychology, and we can tell you that the combative personality is always born of a damaged soul. The damaged souls need healing and grace, but they are dangerous leaders. A healthy conservative movement cannot elevate them to leadership status or the unintended consequences will be dire.

We cannot be so hurried to save our nation that we settle for what feels new, simply so we don't make the same mistakes. God speaks to the necessity of tradition. We cannot throw tradition out with establishmentarianism. G. K. Chesterton warns, "In short, the modern revolutionist, being an infinite skeptic, is always engaged in undermining his own mines." In his political tome, Chesterton attacks men for trampling on morality. In contrast, his ethics book attacks morality for trampling on men: "Therefore the modern man in revolt has become practically useless for all purposes of revolt. By rebelling against everything he has lost his right to rebel against anything"

It is our call as conservatives to police our own. Those who are crass, ill mannered, shrill, destructive, hostile, selfish or belligerent in their approach to the battle need to be on the other side—they are already working for the Left. We are just as responsible for weeding in our own garden as we are for planting and harvesting. Check what you are calling *conservative*. What do you read? What talk radio do you listen to? What talking heads on TV? Who is compromised? Why are you supporting them by buying/watching/following/reading/listening? Patriots know how to discern false prophets, but all need to recheck themselves from time to time and avoid falling for those who emulate undisciplined radicals or loose cannons, and make our side indistinguishable from the Left.

Another example of this overreaction is to abandon party identities. The Republican Party is flawed. A brand-new clean-slate party can sound very appealing, like a brand-new sweetener that tastes just like sugar but has no calories. We wouldn't have to throw anyone out. We wouldn't need to make any enemies. We could simply build a brand-new party and make it right this time.

Already, you can see what is happening: we want change. If we lose, we don't want it to be because we didn't try something new. But this is why tradition is godly—because it is tempting to make radical change in the face of threat; it isn't always the path to victory. Sometimes the truth lies in the hard work that we just don't want to face—like reclaiming a party from the inside out, and reclaiming a nation with a frustrating two-party system. The reality is that nothing in life worth doing is easy. Well, almost nothing. War truly is hell, and yes, this is a war for the heart of our nation, and we do not battle merely flesh and blood.

That means it's going to hurt. It will be painful, and bloody, and exhausting. As any athlete can tell you, that means the victory will be all the sweeter, and the just reward for your work all the more meaningful and satisfying. That means we equip ourselves. That means we battle on.

# PART II: THE BATTLE BEGINS . . .

## Modern Warfare

*The battle, sir, is not to the strong alone; it is to the vigilant, the active, the brave.*

—Patrick Henry

Our war looks like this:

*Their bomb*: They tell the populous that we are bad people for imposing our morality on them, and that makes our God bad because we are bad and selfish to do so.

*Our strategy*: We *define the narrative*. Much of the battle that looms will be won or lost in the arena of words. Again, the liberals have an advantage here in that they can lie, because for us to say it is "wrong to lie" is for us to "impose our morality on them." Still, we are morally obligated to hold ourselves to that standard, so that battle is tough.

I believe the truth is self-evident, just as our Founding Fathers did. When provided the truth in love, most people will eventually come to understand it as such. But numbers are important here, and people are both fallen and fickle. Think of this as your battle cry, and don't let yourself be complacent in any arena. If it is church, or school, or work, or the grocery store, don't ever pass up the opportunity to speak the truth, boldly, and without fear.

If you are wrong, God's grace is sufficient. There is still gain in the civil discourse even if you are wrong. If you are right, you might plant the seed that saves a nation—and that's big stuff!

First, tolerate no less than your highest standards in your battle. Boycott the crass, cutting, belligerent, shrill, dark rantings of those who lack substance and therefore crutch on combativeness. If a leader in the movement uses their mouth more than their brain, you might question what a loose cannon on our side will look like to those trying to understand the difference between the two sides. It is important, as we heed the warnings from G. K. Chesterton, that we do not compromise who we really are as a movement by listening to or reading (or God forbid, monetizing) those who do not hold a higher standard! Review who you support and listen to in the movement, and count these as red flag warning signs:

*Circular fire*: Factions happen. It is a reality. I have never been a part of a political, professional, or religious organization that didn't have factions. But watch for the divisive people in politics. They criticize other conservatives without real cause; they rumor monger; they brag and self promote while cutting other conservatives down. They employ the most horrific of Alinsky's tactics on our own people. They are easily identifiable as destructive and while we don't need to reject them from the movement, we should not prop them up. When they fall, they always fall hard, and it can embarrass a whole church, business, or political organization.

*If it looks like a liberal, talks like a liberal, behaves like a liberal—it is probably a liberal (even if it is spouting conservative rhetoric)!* Just as the Bible warns of Pharisees in the Church, there will always be those who parade as conservatives for the purposes of intelligence gathering, making the right look reactionary, racist, or hysterical. A political and legal mentor of my husband's, Jerry Wamser, literally sat us down and named names, with evidence one time. I was shocked! I have seen evidence of liberals infiltrating conservative events, organizations, and races. Some are actually funded to do so. To be inside our camp is one thing, but to be elevated is another. So how do we know when there is an enemy in our camp? I have noticed that they often look and act like a liberal, but conservatives excuse that because they say all the right things. Once conservatives have given them a bully pulpit it is hard to take it away when they become embarrassing to the movement.

*"Johnny Come Lately . . ."* If they just came on the scene in time for the party (or when they got a job in the party, or the movement, or they became active in politics just in time to run for office), beware. If they were committed conservatives before that, it is one easy measure of authenticity and validation of their true leadership abilities. This is not to say that every leader who rose up in the Tea Party surge is bad, quite the contrary. This is simply to say that true conservative leaders are usually born of an ideology that is developed and underpinned over time, like Phyllis Schlafly, JC Watts, Pamela Geller, Wendy Wright, Penny Nance, Alan Keyes, Sarah Palin, etc. They have a trail of efforts and "street cred" long before limelight.

Pay attention to whom you listen, read, promote, and follow. Most of all, be prepared for God calling on you to lead in ways you hadn't thought of before. You will want to make sure you surround yourself with only the best quality of narrative. Just because someone is good at self-promotion or ambitious does not mean they have the substance, or even foundation to lead. Be discerning, and diligent in your judgment of those purporting to be leaders.

## Hear *Your* Call

I am in radio and television, so people will often say, "Doc, I am so glad you are out there to tell them . . ." I am honored to get to talk about politics for a living, but I don't want to replace anyone else's activism. The citizen journalist is every bit as essential to winning this war as the professional media personality. And the citizen journalist is you. Think of it as war, with the weapon of a pen (or a laptop).

There are many ways you can manifest your newfound status as citizen journalist. Tell your family, friends, neighbors, associates, coworkers, enemies, and uncomfortable others the truth about politics, all the time. When they say things like, "Well, personally, I feel sorry for the families split apart by the racist policies of conservatives who want to close our borders," simply reply with, "No, the reality is that the racism is on the left side of the political argument here. Families are split apart by lawlessness and social welfare. There is no other country in the world that would let us walk in and enjoy more rights than its citizenry. That is because societies can only function based upon the rule of law. Even though we are the most charitable nation in the entire world, we must operate based upon the rule of law, and illegal is illegal."

That is not always going to go over well at a cocktail party, but I promise you will have their attention. Ask yourself this question, citizen journalist: what are you going to tell your children if you don't use every venue to speak the truth for their futures right now?

Maybe you want to formalize your citizen journalism. That is actually a good way to force yourself to do the research necessary to speak intelligently on the issues, and to order your thoughts succinctly. I like to call it "triangulation" though I can often get even more than "three" miles out of the work I do, if I do it right.

When I get the call in the morning to do commentary on a national network, I sit down and begin to research the topic. Next, I compose a blog post with the information I gather. Then I often submit that blog post to a national outlet or local news source. I then go to the television station to complete my commentary. I always compose my monologue for my 3-hour radio show based upon my research/commentary, and often I send out an email to other radio shows or blogs looking for content or commentary and contribute to the narrative in that way, too. I cross-post on my own blog, use my research for any speeches I am giving that day, and at this very moment, I am even using my research and experience in a book. That way, I have maximized my time, outlets, and abilities, and you can, too!

**Blogs**: Blogs can be used as your own little editorial contribution to the issues that spark your passion. As you develop a following, you might inspire others to do the same. Eventually, when you look at the compilation of work you have completed, you might just see that there is a book in there somewhere! In the very least, it will be your place to formalize your research, organize your thoughts, and get feedback on what you write.

*Letters to the Editor*: Conservatives count the death of the mainstream media a major victory in the battle, and rightly so! The reality is that there are still newspapers out there, and you should not be afraid to submit opinions that run counter to their articles. A less formal, still effective means of injecting your own counterarguments is simply commenting on the thousands of blogs and online news items that invite your comments at the end of the post. As a talk show host, I can confide that I read the comments often to conclude popular opinion on a story before I present it to my audience. From time to time, I even read the comments on air that others have written regarding an article, even when they disagree with my perspective, if I deem it a compelling argument. For this reason, you can see how important your commentary can be. In certain instances, the commentators themselves develop their own following, and counter-commentary! In the court of public opinion, this can be a great way to define the narrative consistently, and even develop an audience of your own.

*Anonymity*: So you thought you could duck your civic duty at citizen journalism if you had a job that won't allow political engagement? Well, not so fast. I would ask again, what is more important than the future of your country and its children? If you are at a loss for an answer or cannot think of several things but are concerned about being known, then I have a suggestion for you—write anonymously. Create a Twitter username and a blog and commentary based upon a made up name. I have seen many do this and ultimately become so well known for their work that they have a "coming out party" where they let folks know who they really are! Many have even published their work and are paid to do it now. One never knows just how much God can bless you when you act based on obedience to a call, rather than self-preservation. Yes, that is your challenge, and I have just issued it.

*Start a movement:* Back in the early days of the patriot uprising, I would have said that "starting a movement" is something admirable to do—and it is, or at least it was. It might still be if you honestly have something to contribute to the patriot movement that isn't already out there in spades.

My first thought would be to find an established chapter of a national group that you like, and join. Work from within that group to establish your own movement. I like to recommend two that I have worked extensively with, but there are many more listed in Appendix C.

I work with Eagle Forum founded by Phyllis Schlafly, who was originally acclaimed for her book *A Choice, Not an Echo* and her defeat of the feminist movement and the so-called Equal Rights Amendment. Though Eagle Forum has been around for the better part of a century, it has stayed refreshingly independent of the establishment, laser-focused on its battles.

Another I recommend is Concerned Women for America, the largest national political women's organization in the country. Founded by Beverly LaHaye, she has handed off the mantle to good people like Wendy Wright and Penny Nance, who have led the organization successfully through changes that have wrought a strong, independent political group with many education outlets, and stories of success. I always say that these two organizations were the original Tea Parties or Patriot Movements. Working from within them will prove rewarding and effective, while avoiding the confines of an establishment political structure.

As I have watched seedling groups or movements rise up and fall flat, I encourage leadership within a framework of one of these truly independent organizations, and I recommend starting at the local level. If you love it, work your way up. But don't set out to reinvent the wheel or you will likely find yourself in a messy ditch along the side of the road.

*Run for Office*: I will never forget one night when I spoke at a Tea Party in a very liberal northern state. I was feeling horrible for this audience; they were bemoaning the fact that they have the worst, most corrupt elected officials in the entire country, and that I was so lucky to be from a more conservative state. Many were retired; with lots of time on their hands, they had started a movement. They were going to have the most rallies, the best rallies, and with all the best signs, because they wanted to send a message to their corrupt politicians that they weren't going to take it anymore! They cried out for leadership. They were begging me for answers.

During the question-and-answer period after my rabble-rousing speech, I could feel that they had brought me there that night to be their hero. They needed a leader, and maybe I would be it. They needed an answer, a fix to the problem of bad people holding office and acting corruptly. When I realized that that was indeed what they were asking of me, I felt my heart grow heavy and my knees begin to knock. Self-doubt rushed in. Didn't they know that I was just a little girl with an impressive sounding degree who was really from a divorced family from the Ozark Mountains who had run for office and lost and really had no business telling them their business? They did not seem to understand that. They implored me, "Doc, you have been in politics for a decade, you have run for office, you have degrees, you are inside the media, can't you please help us find a way out of this before our great state is gone?"

There were so many of them that honestly my first thought was hostile takeover. I had fantasy visions of all of us marching to some warehouse, grabbing our guns, and walking up to the next good ol' boys' club meeting and saying, "All right, get out your corrupt politicians, or we will . . . (oh gosh) . . . we will, uh, um, (knees knocking, heart pounding) . . . we will hold our signs up that say how bad you are!"

My face flushed as I thought of the audience reaction to such a bizarre declaration. I started that nervous church giggle as they sat trusting, waiting, believing I had answers for them that I simply did not have.

I gathered my scrawny little five foot one frame, cleared my throat, and groped for words, just anything, to say to these thousands of eyeballs turned artillery on me. Just then, that still, small voice led me to ask a question to the room full of hundreds of patriots grasping for answers to save their bankrupt, corrupt, quickly sinking state. I asked, "How many of you have considered running for office?"

It seemed an innocuous enough question, so I was taken aback when they sat, expressions unchanged, thousands of eyeballs fixed on me. I thought I might have lost my sound. They didn't hear me. So I repeated my stupid question: "How many of you have considered running for office?"

With thousands of people sitting before me, puffed up for "starting a movement," not *one* was thinking of running for office. Worse, when I asked which of the good guys' campaigns they were going to help with, one surly old guy off to the left side of the room peeked up over his green beans and said, "We can't help them; they are all establishment types. We need new guys. Maybe you could move here, Doc, and you could run for office."

I audibly gasped. Then I felt a terrible rumbling in my gut—the kind that begins just before I am either going to throw up or say something awful and not be able to stop.

"Don't you know? Don't you . . . ugh . . ." I was losing it and I knew it. "And you call yourselves *patriots*? Are you serious? I didn't work for the last decade taking on the establishment, helping found a movement, getting death threats, enduring sleepless nights, speaking to groups like this on the road without my children, screaming into a television camera or microphone for you to come here and have meetings and not even engage in the only process that can save your a—" Aw, geez. Now I had done it.

I tried to recover. "I have some quotes for you, 'Patriots'" I said sarcastically. Maybe you have heard them before. Maybe not. Truth is, I don't really care because if *you* are the movement, we are as good as dead," I told them.

"If good people don't lead, bad people will," I said. I waited for reaction. Eyeballs.

"Doing what is easy is not right, and doing what is right is not easy." Still nothing.

And my favorite, because it speaks to the complicity of the American voter, more specifically the evangelical Christian, who you all claim to be while you sit in your church pews and vote at the alarming rate of 20 percent . . . this one's for you, and you better listen, because I am probably the only one gutsy enough to ever tell you what you really need to hear."

I took a cleansing breath because I remembered that my high school drama coach told me that might help if I ever forgot my lines. "By Brooks Atkinson . . . he was talking about people just like you when he said this . . . 'People everywhere enjoy believing things that they know are not true. It spares them the ordeal of thinking for themselves and taking responsibility for what they know'—and acting on it," I added. You don't want to accept that having meetings and rallies and speakers in will not save America. But you can save America. You would just rather believe that it is not incumbent upon you to do so. Get on Facebook. Get on Twitter. Get a blog. Write an opinion piece. Be your own speakers. Be your own motivators. And yes, be your own candidates! Get up off your chairs and fix what's broken. Till then, don't bother me or anyone else who sees this crisis in our country for what it is, and plan to help those who are seriously helping themselves! We are the land of the *free* and the home of the *brave*, and we are only free because we are brave! So sprout a backbone and step up or step aside, because we have work to do!"

I turned on one heel and stormed off the stage. I paused at the door to apologize to the organizer, offering my speaker's fee back to her. "Did you see what they thought of you?"

"Oh no," I thought. In the roar of my head I could hear nothing, and I wasn't going to look for fear of the attack of the eyeballs, or something. I peered back and used my last ounce of strength to actually see hundreds of people standing in ovation. I waved, and mustered all the strength I could to smile, and got in my car confused and alone.

I had hours to reflect on what had happened. I arrived home to find an inbox full of e-mails thanking me for talking the hard truths to those patriots that day. I learned that sometimes the truth is best, and that if I really wanted to change things, I was going to have to do this again.

> *"The LORD said unto my Lord, Sit thou on my right hand, till I make thine enemies thy footstool."*
> —MATTHEW 22:44, KJV

## Fools and Footstools

There are many in media who do such an amazing job that watching them perform is like watching a ballerina wielding her body like a painter and brush. I would love to say they inspired me to get into media, and they have in many ways, but I have to be honest about my start in media. Many ask how I began in media, and the truth is that I did so based upon the realization that I saw people who did it, and realized some of them weren't all that smart or perfect (or even coherent in some cases). I saw through the stated motives of some of those in conservative media, and knew that I could trust no one more than me to be more honest, less corrupt, and less abrasive, so I began to build a media resume, and that set my course.

Even before that, when I began in politics, I did so because I saw the foolishness and failure of the only person looking at running for the Senate seat in my district.

The fools in the organization can be a frustration, but they are only as big as you let them be. If you don't like them, beat them. Or at least try.

When I ran for the Senate, I had no idea why God would let me run for office, and then lose. But that is exactly what He ordained. And now looking back, I thank him many times daily that I am not sitting in that Capitol building for another decade of my life (after spending more than a decade alongside my husband while he served in the Senate there). As a result of my obedience (however confused it was), God has geometrically multiplied my territory and my reach, and I can hardly believe that I get to do what I do every day. I am so thankful.

Not only will you encounter uncomfortable losses if you engage in the political process in any way but you will also encounter impossible people. But remember for a moment what God says about impossible people, and even enemies: "I humble your enemies, making them a footstool under your feet" (Psalm 110:1, NKJV). I believe Scripture. I believed that God would make my enemies a footstool, but I just didn't realize how clearly He would do that in *this* lifetime!

If you cannot find some really terrible, horrible, vile, raunchy, annoying, and loudmouthed enemies in your path, then you are not living well. The Bible clarifies in James 1:2 that we are to count our persecutions *pure joy*! Translate: trust and fear *only* God—that He will knit all things together for the good of those who love Him and live according to his precepts (Romans 8:28).

If you look back over your life, count your enemies a badge, based upon their illusion (or delusion) of power, and your own obedience to God in the situation against them. If you look back and those badges aren't so shiny, you need to get busy! The enemy, the *real* enemy, awaits you. No matter what your enemy claims, if you are obedient to God and living by His precepts (even if your enemy claims to be doing the same), if they choose to make you an enemy, they choose to make themselves an enemy of God. Vengeance is His! Your aggressive pursuit of righteousness through perseverance will lead to the use of your enemies as footstools in your efforts. No worries, Satan provides ample opportunities to earn your badges!

As the Irish blessing reads, "Here's to your enemy's enemies!" May you raise your glasses high! ★

*Chapter Fourteen*

# How to Raise a Lady or Gentleman

*Oh, what a tangled web do parents weave, when they think that their children are naïve.*

—OGDEN NASH

*In the final analysis it is not what you do for your children but what you have taught them to do for themselves that will make them successful human beings.*

—ANN LANDERS

## Reaping What We Sow

Natalie left my (Dr. Paterno's) office in a huff. Spotting her mother in the hallway, she curtly ordered her: "Let's get out of here." Since her mother was on her cell phone, she did not immediately respond, which only intensified Natalie's already snotty tone. *"Now,* Mom."

Natalie was a nightmare. During the initial consultation with her mother, I learned that, at fourteen, Natalie had already been introduced to a host of inappropriate behaviors. Her elder stepsister had introduced her to drugs and alcohol. Her grades had slipped from As and Bs to Ds and Fs. She was hanging out with a crowd of adolescents who definitely weren't pulling her in the right direction. Her verbal respect toward her mother had badly soured.

None of this change occurred out the blue or as a result of raging adolescent hormones. Her biological father hadn't bothered to speak to her for six years since her mother took him to court to pay his overdue child support. Natalie's mother admitted that her current husband—who chose not to attend the initial meeting—tended to have an explosive temper. For months, he ignored Natalie, until report cards came out. Then he led the chorus of screaming, threatening, and extreme punishments.[1] His primary mode of making amends: treating her to a shopping spree at Victoria's Secret.[2]

During my initial meeting with Natalie, I became the recipient of some of her venom. She was impressive; she could have taught a class on how to be a snotty teenager. Sitting on my couch, her entire demeanor—body posture, facial expression, and tone—screamed, "I don't want or need to be here, and you are the stupidest person who has ever walked the planet."

I doubt that I moved to the top of her Favorite Persons list when I told her that her mother was the one who needed to change, but that the change necessitated her mother taking more control of her daughter's life. I explained that despite Natalie's reasonable objections to her father's and stepfather's treatment of her, it gave her no right to behave in such an unladylike manner. I insisted that when her

---

[1] He was particularly fond of grounding Natalie for months, while expecting her mother to enforce the consequence. Of course she never did, which created even more conflict.

[2] Rule # 174 in parenting: a gentleman never takes his daughter to Victoria's Secret.

mom began protecting her while reestablishing her authority with her, she would be more willing to submit to that authority. Then she would have more peace in her life.

She was having none of it. She didn't trust that her mother could create the boundaries necessary to protect her and hold her accountable. She bet me that her mother would continue to reward her with plenty of privileges and freedoms, despite her wanton attitude and unhealthy behaviors.

## Nobody Wins the Blame Game

One of the most difficult challenges working with families involves convincing parents that they are the primary agents of change in their child's life. Many parents bring their child to a psychologist or therapist hoping that the clinician will be able to diagnose the problem and then fix it. They liken the therapist to an emergency room physician who can diagnosis a broken bone, wrap the limb in a cast, and write a prescription for pain medication. In this scenario, the physician is the primary agent of change; the parents support the child by giving consent, filling the prescription, and paying the bill.

Behavioral and emotional problems are fundamentally different. Many in our culture prefer to perceive these problems as originating in the child's brain: "Junior was born with his father's disrespectful gene!" Unfortunately, this represents the conventional wisdom of the medical community, which ignorantly supports the biochemical imbalance and genetic hypotheses. Of course, pharmaceutical companies are all too willing to advertise a medical explanation for abnormal behavior or feelings.

The mainstream medical community and pharmaceutical industry are dead wrong. Respect, obedience, and the skills necessary to perform basic and advanced tasks in school and at work (such as attention and organization) are not a result of good breeding. Children do not fail because of insufficient dopamine or any other neurotransmitter. Instead, they are all ladylike and gentlemanly behavior patterns. As such, they remain a function of training. It remains the parents' duty to raise a child into a lady or a gentleman.[3]

Of course, if a parent is the primary agent of change in a child's life, the corollary must also be true: the parent is almost always the primary cause of a child's patterns of misbehavior and lack of virtue and self-control. This is a hard sell. Parents don't want to believe that they have failed their child in some way. Inevitably, a parent concludes that if they have failed in one important sphere, that they are "bad" parents.

The truth is that *all* parents fail their children sometimes and in some ways. Just as there is no perfect president, child, or athlete, there is no perfect parent. The best parents recognize this fact and can accept imperfections, even those that have negative consequences. Their humility allows them to avoid defensiveness, which allows their passion for their children to motivate them to correct themselves and fix what they have broken.

Gratefully, Natalie's mother was humble and strong enough to admit her shortcomings and failures—a very ladylike virtue. Over time (and with great struggle), she reclaimed the mantle of authority in her home, and with moderate success recaptured her daughter's heart. Some damage remained, but by behaving like a lady herself, she created better boundaries with both her current husband and Natalie. This was the first step in training her daughter to be the lady they both truly wanted her to be.

## Solemn Duty

Scripture implores parents to perform their most important duty:

> Now this is the commandment, and these are the statutes and judgments which the Lord your God has commanded to teach you, that you may observe them in the land which you are

---

[3] It is the extremely rare child who cannot be trained by sufficient, consistent parenting to learn and maintain ladylike or gentlemanly habits. Some legitimate examples are children with severe autism, mental retardation, and other true disabilities—children who lack the cognitive skills to learn advanced concepts like virtues.

crossing over to possess, that you may fear the Lord your God, to keep all His statutes and His commandments which I command you, you and your son and your grandson, all the days of your life, and that your days may be prolonged. Therefore hear, O Israel, and be careful to observe it, that it may be well with you, and that you may multiply greatly as the Lord God of your fathers has promised you—'a land flowing with milk and honey.' Hear, O Israel: The Lord our God, the Lord is one! You shall love the Lord your God with all your heart, with all your soul, and with all your strength. (Deuteronomy 6:1–5)

The Proverbs contain many passages that speak to the need and urgency of parental correction, training, and discipline of children. Proverbs 23 says, "Do not withhold correction from a child" and "What parent then, that trembles for his child's eternal destiny, can withhold correction?"

Parents are a child's primary role models, trainers, providers, teachers, gurus, protectors, and priests. R.J. Rushdoony writes in *The Politics of Guilt and Pity*: "The family is man's first state, church, and school. It is the institution which provides the basic structure of his existence and most governs his activities. Man is reared in a family and then establishes a family, passing from the governed to the governing in a framework which extensively and profoundly shapes his concept of himself and of life in general."

Parents who fail in their duty more often err on the side of permissive parenting. Wimpy parenting almost always produces narcissism, which is mutually exclusive from gentlemanly and ladylike behavior. Solid parenting requires firm, loving, sometimes tough resolve. Wimps need not apply.

## Teach the Virtues

The "Four Expectations" provided later in this chapter encapsulate the basic virtues that we should teach our children: *safety, respect, obedience,* and *work.* It is a good starting point from which to build the greater arsenal of virtues. The author of Deuteronomy instructs parents to directly teach them God's commands:

"And these words which I command you today shall be in your heart. *You shall teach them diligently to your children*, and shall talk of them when you sit in your house, when you walk by the way, when you lie down, and when you rise up. You shall bind them as a sign on your hand, and they shall be as frontlets between your eyes. You shall write them on the doorposts of your house and on your gates." (Deuteronomy 6: 6-9, emphasis added)

Parents are to proactively teach their children God's commands, beginning with the Ten Commandments and summed up by Jesus's explanation of the greatest commandments: " Love the Lord your God with all your heart and with all your soul and with all your mind' . . . and the second is like it: 'Love your neighbor as yourself.' All the Law and Prophets hang on these two commandments." (Matthew 22: 37–40). The rest of the virtues, values, ethics, and manners will naturally follow.

## Live the Virtues

The most crucial training mechanism parents own is their own behavior. Virtues are not only taught, they are *caught*. A parent who attempts to enact a "Do as a say, not as I do" philosophy will soon find that this does not work.[4]

Ensure your child's safety by modeling safe behavior: in your car, in the kitchen, in living out the Second Amendment, in your use of alcohol, how you do fireworks on Independence Day. Do you want a respectful child? Show respect to your spouse, your neighbor, and your children. Follow Paul's exhortation to parents: "Do not exasperate your children; instead, bring them up in the training and instruction of the Lord" (Ephesians 6:18).

---

[4] How many parents don't understand that if you curse in your child's presence, a "no cursing" rule will have very little effect? Children sniff out hypocrisy like bloodhounds and will make you pay for it.

If you wish to train an obedient child, you must yourself exhibit obedience. Obey the rules of the road, pay your taxes on time, leave handicapped parking spaces free for the handicapped, and tithe. Finally, in order to instill a strong, independent work ethic in your child, you must evidence one yourself.

Fathers, work hard; strive to provide for your wife and children. When you are home, take care of what you and your spouse have agreed to: the lawn, home repairs, chores, helping one or more of your children with homework, or other tasks. Mothers, perform whatever work you and your spouse have agreed on to the utmost of your abilities, whether in or out of the home.

We are not advocating that all women stay in the home; nor do we advocate all women should be employed outside the home. We advocate that a man and wife prayerfully discern God's will for them: for their marriage and their individual needs and gifts. Understanding that this will likely be done imperfectly, walk out in faith, pursuing whatever work you determine God has in store for you.

## Demand the Virtues

We both strongly perceive a marked tendency toward entitlement in our culture, reflected in the political arena, the public sphere, and in many homes. Children are provided many privileges that they have not earned. Over time, these privileges—from video games to sleepovers, dessert to cell phones—have become to be perceived as rights. This puts the child in an unfortunate position of entitlement and reduces the parent's power and authority in the child's life.

This hierarchy must be reversed. Other than a handful of rights, children should have to earn all the privileges they enjoy. The following chart delineates rights and privileges. Remember, just as adults must work in order to receive pay, children should perform in order to earn their reward. Call it pay, reinforcement, reward, or whatever you like. Just insist that children earn their goodies; this template will foster the virtue of hard work!

## Rights versus Privileges

|  | Rights | Privileges |
|---|---|---|
| **Definition:** | Things children may have or do simply because they are human and are part of this family | Things they are allowed to do that must be earned by being safe, respectful, obedient, and doing their work |
| **Result when not given:** | Rebellion<br>Righteous anger | Disappointment<br>Often working harder to earn |
| **Examples:** | Love<br>Valid, fair discipline<br>Knowledge of rules, expectations<br>Freedom of religion<br>Freedom of speech (respectful)<br>Food, clothing, shelter<br>Freedom of thought<br>Freedom to feel<br>Treated with fairness<br>Be informed about medical treatments<br>Some privacy<br>Sexual integrity<br>Not be physically misused/abused<br>Not be emotionally abused, bullied | Driver's license, use of the car<br>iPod<br>Video Games<br>T.V.<br>Computer/Internet<br>Cell phone (and use of it)<br>Sleepovers<br>Having friends over<br>Choice of music<br>Concerts<br>Going out<br>Dating<br>Attention<br>Money<br>Use of own money<br>Speaking to parents like adults<br>Choosing schedule (e.g., when homework and chores are done) |
| **What happens when granted in spite of misbehavior** | Feel respected, cared for<br>Sometimes grateful-ness results in behavior/attitude change | Do not learn the ethic of work<br>Sense of entitlement<br>Child confuses privilege with right<br>Unmotivated to respect or obey<br>Confusion/indignation when parent makes demands |

## Reward the Virtues

Behaving safely, offering others respect, obeying proper authorities, and performing adequate work are all intrinsically rewarding. All of those should be self-reinforcing and normally become more so as the child develops. However, we are a deeply imperfect people; as such, we do much better and learn much quicker when rewarded by an external source. Children learn new behaviors and their correspond- ing virtues much quicker and more solidly when externally reinforced. In other words, they learn better when you reward them. Parents play a crucial role in establishing this pattern.

## The Four Rewards

Rewards take four different forms: *trust*, *respect*, *freedom*, and *privi- leges*. Obviously, they are all connected and are not completely dis- tinct. But in our experience, these are the four most powerful rewards that children and adolescents desire:

1.  *Trust*. Examples: allowing younger children to do things themselves (like cook, take care of a pet), older children to drive or use the internet, choose their friends.
2.  *Respect*. Examples: your attention, affection, speaking to them with equal respect, age-appropriate privacy.
3.  *Freedom*. Examples: going to age-appropriate places indepen- dently (walking, bike, or car), speaking to adults in an adult manner, choice of clothes, deciding how to structure free time, decorating room how they wish, deciding when to go to sleep, having a part-time job.
4.  *Privileges*. Examples: money, play time, dessert, sleepovers,[5] driver's license, driving hours toward earning one's license, use of electronics (TV, movies, video games, cell phone, com- puter, iPad).

---

[5] Although we continue to be far from excited about the "Stay-up-all-night- and-be-crabby-for-the-next-two-days-over," it seems to be a standard reward in many households.

Your child should have none of these if he or she has not earned them by meeting your expectations. At the same time, if Junior does meet your expectations, this array of reinforcers will give your child plenty of external incentive. As your child grows and matures, the most potent reinforcers become the trust and respect you offer. By young adulthood, hearing that you are proud of them will replace cell phones and cookies as the primary rewards in their life. Well, maybe not cookies.

## Codifying Your Family's Expectations and Virtues

Most legitimate systems of government have a constitution. The *American Heritage Dictionary* defines a constitution as "the system of fundamental laws and principles that prescribes the nature, functions, and limits of a government or another institution." It also refers to the document that describes the system. Just as our nation's Constitution sets forth the separation of powers and the Bill of Rights, The Family Constitution[6] is designed to help parents organize their family structure, ensure that parents are aware of and communicate a proper family hierarchy, and communicate to the children their expectations and the consequences—positive and negative—that will result from meeting or not meeting those expectations.

If you want to live out the virtues in your family, it might help to formalize the values and virtues your family by creating your own Family Constitution.

Your Family Constitution does not need to be as formal sounding as the following. You can create it any way you like, but for now, a formal sounding document can support the serious tone you need to take.

## The Family Constitution

*Preamble:* Here you will spell out the purpose of your Family Constitution. You will establish the design and significance of your family. You will also list the vision and overarching goals that you have set for

---

[6] If you would like a full copy of *The Family Constitution Worksheet*, e-mail Dr. Paterno and he will send you one: drpaterno@prpsych.com.

your family. Go ahead and sound formal and lofty; remember, you are founding a great institution that will achieve great things.

*Example:*

We the Smith Family, in order to form a more perfect Union, establish justice, insure peace in our home, provide for all our needs, promote the development of all family members, and to teach godly principles, virtues, and knowledge, do ordain and establish this Constitution for our family.

## Section One: The Structure of Your Family

First, you must establish who is in charge. Explain why you are in charge. Feel free to refer to God, the government, and common sense. Inform your children of their position in the family. Why are they not equal partners? What is the relationship between Mom and Dad? What role does Grandma have? Who holds the mantel of authority when Mom and Dad are not around? Establish the hierarchy.

*Example:*

Mom and Dad are the leaders and originators of this family. Their authority stems from several sources, including God and common sense, as well as their superior knowledge and wisdom in caring for this family. The governments of our city and state also support Mom and Dad's authority.

Both Mom and Dad are equal authorities in this family. Dad maintains final say in most matters because there are times when one person will need to make a final decision about difficult things. However, Mom's say is equal to Dad's; when Dad is not present, all rules and expectations must be followed as if Dad were there. The same applies when Mom is not present. Furthermore, all respect owed to one parent is also owed to the other; any disrespect shown toward one parent will be perceived as disrespect toward both parents. Grandma and Grandpa possess authority in all matters when Mom and Dad are not present. The family rules fully apply; they have authority to enforce the rules.

When Jenna, Alex, and Susan are by themselves—either downstairs or outside—none of them is in charge of the others. For example,

Jenna does not have authority over Alex and Susan. However, because of her older age, she has more responsibility and can remind either sibling of the rules and possible consequences. It is not her job to discipline the others; in fact, she may not discipline her siblings.

## Section Two: Rights and Privileges

Your children need to be aware of your commitment to provide for their needs. At the same time, they need to comprehend your policy regarding privileges: that they will reap the full complement of privileges by earning the desired rewards. At the same time, they must recognize that you will unconditionally care for their basic needs. Remember, you *love* your children unconditionally but you do not *express* your love unconditionally!

*Example:*

Because Mom and Dad love their children unconditionally, there are certain rights that all children will have in this family:

- Love
- Protection
- Valid, fair discipline
- Rules and expectations will be clear and fully explained
- Freedom of speech
- Food, clothing, shelter
- Freedom of thought: about rules, religion, politics, etc.
- Freedom to feel
- Be informed about medical issues and treatments
- Privacy
- Sexual integrity
- No physical abuse or misuse
- No emotional abuse or bullying

Mom and Dad are committed to respecting all of these rights. All other privileges must be earned. These privileges are described in Section Four of this Constitution.

Parents also have rights! It makes sense to clarify these with your children.

*Example:*
Mom and Dad also have rights. Mom and Dad have the right to:

- Verbal and physical respect
- Have their possessions respected
- Consult with other parents and professionals about parenting challenges
- Establish their authority in the family and household
- Decide meals
- Privacy (purses, wallets, dresser drawers, do not enter parents' room without first knocking, etc.)
- Downtime (not to be bothered after 9 PM, except in case of emergency)
- Choose the music in the car when they drive or the house

Respecting these rights is nonnegotiable.

## Section Three: The Four Major Expectations

The four major expectations in a household are safety, respect, obedience, and work. Establish what each of these means in your house. Be specific—very specific. Do not hesitate to explain the importance of each. Explain that meeting expectations will result in rewards—and are designed to teach you the virtues that God and your family wish for you to develop into a lady or gentleman.

*Example:*
The children must adhere to four major expectations; almost all rules fall under these four categories. If they follow these expectations, they will earn not only Mom and Dad's respect but will also earn appropriate freedoms and privileges. They will also develop into fine young ladies and gentlemen.

The first and most important expectation is to *be safe*. This means your safety, the safety of your family, and the safety of the home. Specifically, this means that drug use or possession will not be tolerated. Drug paraphernalia will also not be allowed. This includes cigarettes. There will be no compromise on this expectation. Drinking alcohol will be allowed on special occasions only with parental permission, supervision, and limits.

All family members are expected to take reasonable care of their bodies, as they are each temples of God. This means that you will not engage in unreasonably high-risk behaviors. Whitewater rafting, paintball, roller coasters, and parasailing are not included (Mom and Dad might even drag you along with us when we do them!). Music concerts that are likely to involve drug use, "mosh pits," or otherwise questionable activities will be deemed unsafe.[7]

The second expectation is to *be respectful*. Jesus said, "Love your neighbor as yourself." All family members are expected to respect all other family members, including parents, siblings, grandparents, aunts, uncles, and cousins, just as they wish to be respected. More specifically, respect means the following:

*Verbal respect*: Speaking kindly in word and tone both to and about family members.

Verbal respect includes appropriate manners:

- Responding when spoken to
- Maintaining eye contact during conversation
- Validating another's perspective or feelings
- Saying "please" and "thank you" and other niceties
- Offering genuine compliments
- Constructive criticism
- Saying "Yes, Mom" or "OK, Dad" in response to a command
- Maintaining self-controlled voice during debate/argument
- Taking responsibility for one's mistakes and apologizing

Some examples of disrespect are:

- Rolling eyes when spoken to
- Saying loudly, "I know!"
- Defying (saying "No!" to a command)
- Lying

---

[7] Some of the items in a Constitution would be overkill for younger children. You don't need to tell your five-year-old to say no to drugs. You shouldn't need to tell them not to be serial murderers either.

- Correcting adults in a challenging, unloving way
- Not looking at adults when spoken to
- "Storming" out of the room: huffing and puffing sighs, stomping
- Destructive criticism

*Physical respect*: Respecting the personal space of others
Some examples of disrespect are:

- Excessive, unwelcome affection (bear hugs, tickling, kissing)
- Uninvited wrestling, boxing, and other forms of aggressive play
- Spitting

*Respect of property*: Maintaining the safety and privacy of others' things and room
Some examples are:

- Not going in siblings' room without permission (for older children/teens)
- Not touching "special" belongings (e.g., iPad, diary) without permission
- Stealing
- Not defacing or otherwise damaging others' things
- Respecting the cars by not messing them

*Respect of your body*: Taking reasonable care of yourself

- Maintaining sound hygiene
- Going to sleep at a reasonable hour
- Following physicians' orders, such as medication and other treatments

The third and related expectation demands that children *obey the rules*. While there are many rules in our home and some specific rules may change from time to time, most of the general rules always apply. Primarily, we expect you to do what you are told/requested/commanded to do immediately and without argument, complaint, or dawdling. We do not expect you to immediately stop something you are doing if it requires finishing steps (for example, if you have to save a computer game or finish writing a sentence); in this case, you may say, "OK, Mom, I'm just finishing this sentence/saving the game; I'll do it right away." If you abuse this by consistently dragging out the completion of activities in order to avoid doing what was requested, we will then begin to expect you to drop everything immediately.

Mom and Dad agree to avoid asking you to do things when you are in the middle of a task or fun activity. Sometimes our requests can wait. However, sometimes they cannot and we will make it clear that we expect you to comply immediately with our command. For example, if Mom is in the bathroom and you are in the middle of a television program and the phone rings, you might be told to answer the phone. This cannot wait and we expect you to leave the television and answer the phone.

One important rule is keeping your room clean. All bedrooms must have beds made and clothes picked up off the floor before school.

Another important rule involves curfew. You are expected to be home on time, according to the kitchen clock. For every minute that you are late, you will have to be home ten minutes earlier the next time you go out. In extraordinary circumstances when you cannot get home on time, you must contact Mom or Dad immediately to let us know and collaborate on a plan for getting you home as soon as possible.

The fourth expectation is to *do your work*. This includes both schoolwork and chores. God expects us to use the talents and gifts He has bestowed upon us. All children go to school to prepare for their career and to learn the fundamentals of life. We expect you to work hard in this endeavor. To this end, we have the following expectations:

- You must attend school every day. The only exceptions will be when you are significantly ill. Sniffles don't count.
- You must complete all homework satisfactorily (neatly and according to your teachers' expectations). You must hand it in on time.
- You must complete your homework independently and in your room. Mom and Dad will be available as much as possible to help with any questions you may have, but we will not

complete work for you under any circumstances. If we are not available, you remain responsible to get the help you need. You may contact other students or go to school early. It is not Mom and Dad's job to rescue you from any mistakes you make, including forgetting books, assignments, or any other materials you might need. If the school places unrealistic expectations on you, we will intervene on your behalf.

- You may listen to music while you do homework, as long as you earn that freedom by performing your work satisfactorily. However, you may not have the TV or computer on while doing homework, unless you are using the computer to complete the assignment.
- You are all intelligent and able enough to achieve Cs or better on all tests and quizzes. We expect you to achieve As or Bs, but understand that some subjects or classes might be particularly challenging.
- We expect you to behave like good citizens in the classroom, giving your teachers and other students respect and following all appropriate school rules. If there are any rules you feel are not appropriate, you must first discuss this with Mom and Dad and get permission from them to break the rule.[8]

Mom and Dad work hard to take care of this family, both financially and in the upkeep of our home. Because we expect you to help with these, we have developed daily and weekly chores for you to perform. These are your home jobs. We expect you to complete your chores daily in order to earn the privileges you enjoy. Similarly, you are expected to complete your weekend chore(s) before you go anywhere or enjoy any of your privileges. We are committed to being flexible with your busy schedule and not giving you chores when you are not home for long enough to be expected to complete them.

---

[8] While parents in charge generally defer to school authority and encourage respect and obedience, some school rules/expectations are so foolish that they invite civil disobedience (example: being expected to participate in a mock worship service for a different religion).

## Section Four: The Four Rewards

Describe what your response will be to your children following the Four Expectations—what will they get out of it and how you will feel about it:

We are confident that all of our children will be able to maintain their safety, respect one another, obey Mom and Dad, and perform their work adequately. You will naturally feel God's peace and joy when you obey His Commandments and learn his virtues. Additionally, we are committed to making these expectations as rewarding as possible. When you are adequately meeting the Four Expectations, you will earn the following:

1. Our respect
   - We will be more likely to be pleasant and affectionate with you.
   - We will pay attention to you.
   - It will be far easier to consider your requests.
   - We will also give you as much privacy as is safe.

2. Trust
   - We will trust you to walk to the next block by yourself (with friends).[9]
   - You may keep a private diary that Mom and Dad will not look at except in case of emergencies.
   - We will not doubt your word.

3. Freedom
   - (For girls) You may wear makeup for special occasions.
   - You may choose your own clothes (subject to parental approval, of course)
   - You may ride your bike or walk to school on your own or with friends.
   - You may have access to your own bank account.
   - You may spend your money as you choose (within reason, of course).

---

[9] For older teenagers, this area of trust will pertain to driving or using public transportation.

4. Privileges
- We will give you an allowance of $10 per week, half of which will be placed in a savings account for your college education. One dollar will be given to church as an offering.[10] You may spend the remaining $4 on anything you wish.
- We will allow you to have friends over on weekends.
- You will be able to buy and use a cell phone (when you are fourteen).
- You may play video games for a half hour per day after your chores and homework are both done satisfactorily.
- You may watch TV for a half hour per day, after your chores and homework are complete.
- You may use your iPod during homework[11] or when you are out.

Describe what your response will be if they do not follow these expectations. You don't need to be specific here; sometimes the unknown can keep them on their toes.

*Example:*

Mistakes are part of the learning and growing process; we expect you to make plenty of them. Our job as parents will be to respond to these mistakes in a way that trains you to learn from your mistakes and to make better choices in the future. Just as it would be foolish to pay an employee who does not complete his work, we will not pay you (offer you the Four Rewards) when you do not do your job (meet the Four Expectations). However, we will be ready and eager to reestablish those rewards as you meet the Four Expectations.

The primary method of training will be to withhold your "paycheck." You will earn less Trust, Respect, Freedom, and Privileges.

---

[10] Or whatever amount you decide for each child. If your family does not go to church, they can give the dollar to a local charity. The point is instilling the idea of tithing, regular giving, and service.

[11] For older children who have already proven their ability to complete work with music playing.

Of course, minor mistakes will result in smaller consequences or fines. Major mistakes, such as gross disrespect, unsafe behavior, or defiance, will result in an automatic, near-complete withdrawal of rewards. Mom and Dad will specify the rewards and consequences with each of you separately.

## Conclusion

If you want to create a culture change, start with how you parent your own children, or assist in raising your grandchildren or relatives, friends, or neighbors with children. Building ladies and gentlemen is primarily the parents' charge, but it also requires the quantity and quality of the other sources of influence on the Hierarchy of Cultural Change pyramid chart (see page 151 Parents can and should enlist the help of teachers, pastors, neighbors, friends, and relatives in not only supporting their efforts to train their children but using common language of virtue.

Ask your family, friends, and teachers to use the terms *lady* and *gentleman*. Let them know what you mean when you use those terms with your children and what expectations you have for them. That way, when a child's teacher corrects a student, she can use the same terminology as the parents, which deepens the sense that these virtues and values are universal. After all, how can girls aspire to be ladies when Lady Gaga is their introduction to the term?

# APPENDIX A:
## THE TOP TEN TRAITS
## OF THE MODERN GENTLEMAN

1. A gentleman cultivates his masculine traits: strength and power. Rather than shying from them, he revels in them and thanks God for them. He harnesses his masculinity to create, build, and protect.
2. A gentleman learns and maintains good manners, not because manners make him a gentleman but because they evidence respect for himself and his neighbors.
3. A gentleman always seeks to build up others by showing genuine interest in others' lives, thoughts, and opinions more than his own.
4. A gentleman avoids neither disagreement nor judgment but tempers his boldness, passion, and forceful intellect with respect and a genuine desire to understand, rather than a desire to quibble or puff himself up by dominating others.
5. A gentleman's word should be so true that his friends, colleagues, and family take it at face value.
6. A gentleman admits wrongs, failings, and weaknesses. Because he knows that his value and worth come from God and not from his personal traits, he maintains his confidence despite recognizing his shortcomings.

7. A gentleman is as eager to forgive as he is to seek justice.

8. A gentleman does not shy from contests or shun success or victory. Regardless of the outcome, he is generous and complimentary to his coaches, teammates, and opponents.

9. A gentleman elevates and sacrifices for women, family, children, peers, friends, and colleagues—for their good and to communicate their value, not because they are weak or unable.

10. A gentleman holds the door for a woman. He also holds the door for an elder, child, another man who has his hands full, or anyone who could use it. Similarly, he offers his seat to another person on a bus or train. He does not perceive the recipient of his gesture as weak or unable; he simply does it out of a spirit of good will and helpfulness.

# APPENDIX B
## THE TOP TEN TRAITS OF THE MODERN LADY

1.  A lady cultivates her feminine traits: gentleness, grace, nurturing, helpfulness, respect, supportiveness, submission to Godly authority, and strength. Rather than asserting traits she doesn't have, she builds on what she does have and thanks God for the protected role that God gave her in His perfect Order. She harnesses her femininity to nurture, encourage, support, protect, and love.

2.  A lady learns and maintains good manners, not because manners make her a lady, but because they evidence respect for herself and those she loves, and they reflect God's order in her life.

3.  A lady always seeks to build up others, by showing genuine interest in others' lives, thoughts, and opinions more than her own. An encouraging word, a gentle touch, a swift hand of discipline, a tear in empathy…these are the jewels in a lady's crown.

4.  A lady doesn't rebel against the protections offered her, but tempers her gentle supportiveness with a genuine desire to be strong when appropriate, and even aggressive when she or her values are threatened, or when her family needs her.

5. A lady's devotion to the blessings in her life should be so true that she is beyond reproof by those entrusted to her. Those who love her should have full confidence in her. A lady can listen well and love greatly. She doesn't need to prove her strength unless called to do so, because it is evident to all. She can admit when she is wrong, comfort when there is need, console a hurting heart, lead when faith awaits, and defend when those she loves are threatened.

6. A lady loves life and laughter, and uses both in full glory! Avoiding folly, she knows how to lighten a moment or bring a smile to the face of a wounded soldier. Her gift of love may take her to the bedside of a dying elder, the scene of a scraped knee on concrete to gently dab the tears and blood, or the blood-soaked battlefields of heroes to be the gentle, nurturing strength God designed her to be in those moments.

7. A lady can use more than one weapon, and she understands and is willing to fight for her right to have them for her protection and for those around her.

8. A lady carefully examines her own opinions against that of someone she deems wiser on a regular basis. She recognizes the beauty and power of other women in her life, and chooses mentors wisely. She becomes a mentor to younger women.

9. A lady elevates and sacrifices for men, family, children, peers, friends, colleagues and other women—for their good and to communicate their value. This is born of her internal strength and power.

10. A lady graciously accepts gentleman's efforts to attend her. When he opens a door for her, offers a seat to her, uses his strength for her, fights for her, or simply holds her in silence, her feminine response welcomes and validates his masculinity. She recognizes this as one of the central beauties of femininity.

# APPENDIX C:
## YOUR ACTION PLAN

## Heroes

Take a moment and use the space below to write down some of the people you admire. They do not have to be political powerhouses or world changers, although they certainly can be. You can admire them for simple things like great hair or legs, or you can admire them for leading a revolution. They can be modern or historic, personal or public. Let your thoughts go as you give yourself the freedom to admit whom you really admire, and why you admire them.

_____

_____

_____

_____

_____

_____

_____

_____

_____

_____

Now take a hard look at this list and their predominant admirable traits. Which of those traits do you most admire in yourself?

_____

_____

_____

_____

Which do you wish you had and/or are willing to work for?

_____

_____

_____

Going back to the first question asked in Chapter 10: If you really could not fail, what would you do with the rest of your life?

_____

_____

_____

_____

_____

_____

Describe the person above as someone *else* would describe you. Remember, this is you, *minus* fear.

_____

_____

_____

_____

The amazing thing is that this is how God sees you. He designed you exactly as described above. The goal is coming to know yourself as God sees you: His perfect creation, fallen and sinful, yes, but being transformed and renewed at this very moment for His purpose.

Now, I want you to write your legacy. Looking forward, imagine when all of your work on this earth is complete. What did your life mean? What will it mean to others? We will talk about this more later, but for now, write what they will say about you when you are gone.

Those who knew me will say:

_____

_____

_____

_____

_____

My friends will say:

_____

_____

_____

_____

_____

My enemies will say (Remember, the content of your character is best measured by the power of your enemies). Make good enemies!

_____

_____

_____

_____

_____

_____

My family will say:

_____

_____

_____

_____

_____

My spouse will say:

_____

_____

_____

_____


I will say:

_____

_____

_____

_____

_____


My God will say:

_____

_____

_____

_____

_____

Each of the above groups is important, because each will play a role in what you do with the rest of your life, and help you develop your focus. Each can be employed in your personal mission, and each can contribute, detract, distract, or complete your legacy. These are tools in your arsenal for you to think about, pray about, and visualize using. You will find them useful in amazing ways as we proceed to find your place in politics.

This is what motivates me:

_____

_____

_____

_____

_____

_____

This is what I like about what motivates me:

_____

_____

_____

_____

_____

This is what I don't like/trust/feel good about what motivates me:

_____

_____

_____

_____

_____

Looking at the above, this might be the way I could use my motivations:

_____

_____

_____

_____

_____

We all know amazing people who have exhibited amazing grace in playing the hand that God has dealt them. Take a moment to identify your biggest temptation:

_____

_____

_____

_____

_____

Now create a fictitious but real "trial" for that temptation. Who or what tempts you the most? Where exactly are you the most vulnerable to jealousy, envy, strife, gossip, selfishness, arrogance, slander, gluttony, impurity, or other vices? Envision a scenario where your greatest temptations are all around.

_____

_____

_____

_____

_____

Write your victory plan. How do you overcome it and handle the temptation with honor, civility, and sincerity?

_____

_____

_____

_____

_____

_____

_____

_____

_____

Look back on the hero who escaped the natural temptation to fall into the fray, and talk about the courageous victory! Describe how your hero looked, smiled, triumphed, and overcame his or her weakest place, to know true victory. Who admired them? Who learned from the grace demonstrated? Were any souls saved that day? Were any seeds planted? Describe the future of relationships gained, work accomplished, and grace demonstrated by the victory.

_____

_____

_____

_____

_____

_____

_____

_____

_____

# ABOUT THE AUTHORS

DR. GINA LOUDON IS a syndicated national talk show host of *The Dr. Gina Show* and also Politichicks.TV. She is a commentator who has appeared on local and national media outlets including *FOX News*, *Jon Stewart Daily Show*, FOX Business, *The BBC*, *Radio Ireland*, *AFR*, *Greta Van Susteren*, *Neil Cavuto* and others. She is a national speaker, having spoken to hundreds of thousands over the last 3 years. She is a columnist for Townhall, and also writes for FOXNews, Breitbart, World Net Daily, and others.

She originated the BUYcott concept, as well as the field of *policology*—the nexus of politics and psychology. She is credited as one of the one hundred founding members of the Tea Party movement. Andrew Breitbart called her his "official troublemaker," and Michael Reagan called her "a TRUE conservative." Neil Cavuto calls her "The Tea Party Titan" and Bill Federer defines her as "The conservatives' secret weapon—a double-edged sword. She is adorably disarming, and masterfully brilliant—a rising star in America's renewal."

The wife of State Senator John Loudon (R-MO, ret.), she educates their children at home. They have five children, including one by the blessing of adoption who has Down syndrome.

After doing her part to destroy the socialist agenda and restore the republic, she plans to sail around the world with her family.

DR. DATHAN PATERNO IS a fully licensed clinical psychologist, serving as owner and Clinical Director for Park Ridge Psychological Services, a private group practice. He has twenty years' experience in the mental health field, having worked in inpatient psychiatric hospitals, therapeutic day schools, residential treatment centers, and two private practices. He has also been an Adjunct Professor of Psychology.

Dr. Paterno is on the board of directors of the International Society for Ethical Psychiatry and Psychology, a think tank and advocacy group of mental health professionals committed to holistic and humane treatment of emotional disorders. The author of the powerful and well-received parenting book, *Desperately Seeking Parents*, Dr. Paterno has enjoyed a steady stream of invitations to speak publicly on his conservative, parent-first parenting philosophy; his ability to communicate controversial ideas with a gentle but common sense approach has endeared him to his readers and listeners. He is an expert commentator on The Dr. Gina Show. He also maintains a parenting and psychology blog at www.desperatelyseekingparents.com.

Dr. Paterno has been interviewed on many radio programs and Chicago news programs, commenting on psychology, politics and parenting.

Dr. Loudon is on Facebook at Dr. Gina and Twitter at @DrGinaLoudon. Dr. Paterno is on Twitter at @DrDathanPaterno.